# BASEBALL IN SAVANNAH

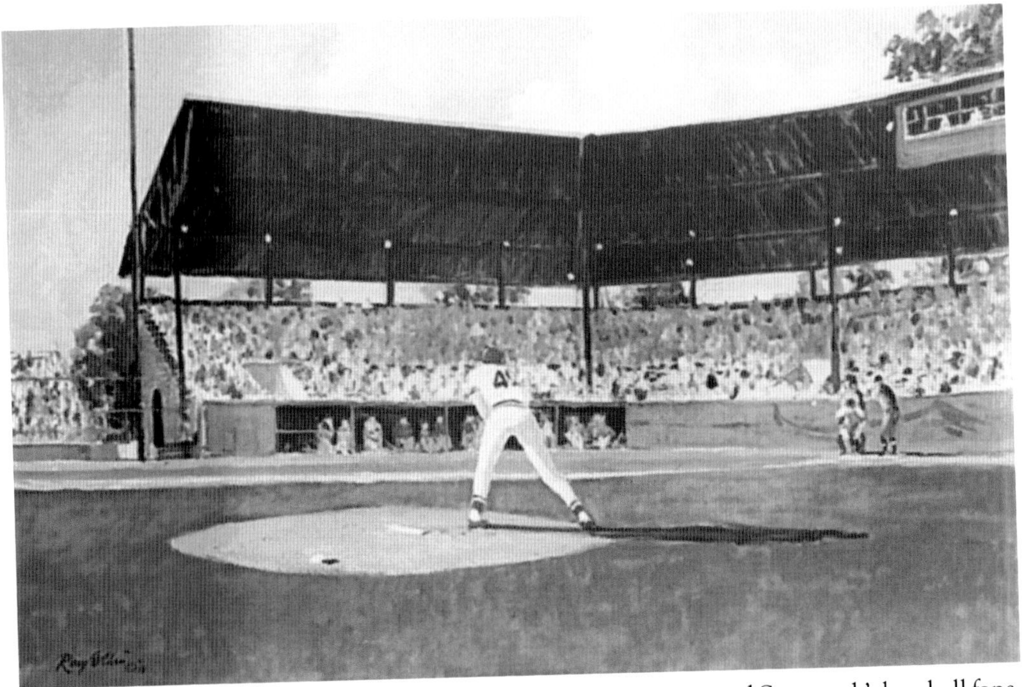

For over 90 years, players in the field have had this view looking toward Savannah's baseball fans. Legendary names such as Lou Gherig, Jackie Robinson, Hank Aaron, and Bob Gibson have looked back at the old grandstand that has become one of Savannah's many cultural icons. Players today look into the heart of the oldest operating minor league ballpark in use. Although generations of players and fans have come and gone, Grayson Stadium has anchored the northeast corner of Daffin Park, always ready for a ball game. Although considered an outdated relic and past its prime by some, many others consider Grayson Stadium to represent the true essence of what baseball stands for. Simple, classic, and intimate, Grayson offers fans a close view of the action on the field while its antique atmosphere reminds one of the golden age of baseball, when the action on the diamond truly was America's pastime. (The Ray Ellis Gallery, Compass Prints, Inc.)

FRONT COVER: Managed by Hubert Kittle, the 1969 Senators featured 19 players with major league talent. This talent, combined with Kittle's 21 years of experience in professional baseball, should have provided a recipe for success for the Senators.

COVER BACKGROUND: The 1957 Savannah Redlegs finished the season in third place. Led by future major leaguers Curtis Flood, Chico Cardenas, and Buddy Gilbert, the Redlegs' bats were on display throughout the season as the team led the Sally League in home runs, runs per game, hits, and RBIs.

BACK COVER: When Albert Isreal and Junior Reedy started for the Savannah Indians on opening day, they became the first African American players to play in the Sally League. Isreal and Reedy's Indians played in front of a record Grayson Stadium crowd on May 7, as over 15,000 fans packed into the park for Merchant Appreciation night. The 1953 Indians finished the season in fourth place, winning 68 games.

# BASEBALL IN SAVANNAH

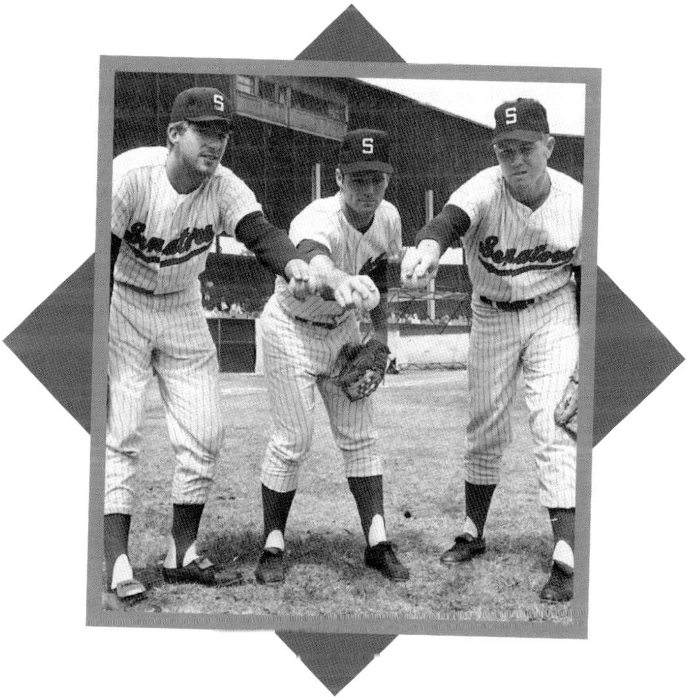

Brian Harold Lee
Foreword by Skip Jennings

ARCADIA PUBLISHING

ISBN 978-0-7385-9126-1

Published by Arcadia Publishing
Charleston, South Carolina

Printed in the United States of America

Library of Congress Control Number: 2011937372

For all general information, please contact Arcadia Publishing:
Telephone 843-853-2070
Fax 843-853-0044
E-mail sales@arcadiapublishing.com
For customer service and orders:
Toll-Free 1-888-313-2665

Visit us on the Internet at www.arcadiapublishing.com

*This book is dedicated to all of the baseball players who have chased their dreams in Savannah.*

# CONTENTS

# FOREWORD

Brian Lee has done what I have wanted to do for many years.

I moved to Savannah in the fall of 1970. I was 14 years old. Prior to that, I had never been to a minor league game. We lived in New York City, where going to a baseball game meant going to Yankee Stadium or Shea Stadium.

Then, my father got a job in Savannah. Going to see major league games was no longer an option. In the spring of 1971, I attended my first minor league game at Grayson Stadium. From the moment I stepped in the stadium I could see that I was in someplace special, a place that harkened back to the glory days of baseball, when it truly was the national pastime. It just oozed with the history of the game. Surely there had been many great moments on this field!

But unlike major league teams such as the Yankees, Dodgers, and others, there were no written histories of Savannah baseball. Your only options were to talk with old-timers who had seen some of that history or go to the Bull Street Library and look at microfilm of old editions of the *Savannah Morning News.*

In the early 1990s, I cobbled together the information that I had collected into a brief history of Savannah baseball. The then–Savannah Cardinals included it in their program for a season or two. I also turned it into a presentation that I gave at several local civic group luncheons and at a meeting of the Atlanta Chapter of SABR (Society for American Baseball Research). It was always my intent to eventually expand it into a full-fledged history, but family, work, and other civic activities never allowed the needed time.

Now, Brian Lee has done it! He has brought the history of baseball in Savannah alive, in a way that I had never dreamed possible. Who knew that so many great images of Savannah baseball existed? Savannah baseball fans owe Brian a deep debt of gratitude for finding these wonderful images and gathering them in one place. Now, the next time some baseball crazy 14-year-old kid moves to Savannah from a major league town, he won't have to wonder about the rich history of baseball in Savannah. It will be right there for him to see and from which he will be able to build his own memories of baseball in Savannah.

—Skip Jennings

# ACKNOWLEDGMENTS

The images, stories, and history within this book belong to the people of Savannah. Without the support of the Savannah community and others throughout the country associated with Savannah's baseball history, this book would not have been possible.

I would like to thank in no particular order Skip Jennings, Tom Autry, Miles Wolff, Ray Ellis, Lynn Wright, Clarence Watkins, Buddy Gibson, Dight Olliff, Ken Boyd, Luciana Spracher, Benjamin Baughman, Chip Grayson, John Tomat, Tom Coffey, Lou Brissie, Jerry Rogers, Frank Sulkowski, Alice Massimi, Jody Chapin, Thomas Hagerty, Patrick Rodgers, Joel Cadoff, Mike Nola, and Eugene Beals.

I would also like to thank everyone who has supported the project and offered help that led to stories and images. There are far too many names to list, but their help is greatly appreciated.

Finally, I need to thank all of my friends, family, and wonderful wife Nora. Without their patience and support, this project would not have happened.

Unless otherwise noted, all images appear courtesy of the author.

# INTRODUCTION

Long considered the national pastime, the game of baseball has entertained communities and cities for over a century and a half. For nearly the same amount of time, baseball has been Savannah's pastime as well. A city that has played a part in nearly every major topic in United States history, Savannah's place in baseball's history is equally rich. While much of the city's history is well documented, Savannah's role in baseball has not been given much attention, until now.

When most think of the early days of baseball, places like Cooperstown, New York City, and Boston quickly come to mind. Savannah should be included in that list of early cities where baseball was played. Arriving in 1862 with the 48th New York Infantry when they occupied Fort Pulaski during the Civil War, baseball would be here to stay. Baseball pioneer Edward Saltzman brought organized baseball to Savannah in the late 1860s and ever since then, Savannah has had either amateur or professional teams playing throughout her parks.

Through the rest of the 19th century, Savannah fielded teams in a variety of amateur leagues and negro leagues. The Pioneers, Electrics, and Modocs were among the early teams that Savannah fans would follow, while Savannah's African American community cheered on the Broads and Lafayettes in the negro leagues.

In 1904, professional baseball arrived in Savannah when the South Atlantic League was organized at the Hotel Desoto. Playing their first game on Memorial Day in 1904, the Savannah Pathfinders took the field after sights of parades and sounds of marching bands filled the city. Despite having the capable Joe Welch on the mound for Savannah and an abundance of confidence, Savannah lost to the Charleston Sea Gulls by a score of 3 to 0. The Savannah Pathfinders joined seven other teams from around the Southeast in the new league, and two years later changed their name to the Savannah Indians. Winning three league championships before giving up their spot in the league in 1915, the Indians proved that Savannah was indeed a baseball town.

Professional baseball arrived back in Savannah in 1926 and the team had a new park to play in. The Indians called Municipal Stadium in Daffin Park home through the 1940 season. Although professional baseball left again in 1928, it resumed in 1936 following the Great Depression. Throughout the 1920s and 1930s, nationally-known major league teams would continue to stop by Savannah as they played their way north, ending their spring training. Savannah fans were thrilled to watch the big leaguers in Savannah and ecstatic that their hometown franchise won another Sally League pennant in 1937.

When a hurricane destroyed most of the grandstand and bleachers of Municipal Stadium in 1940, civic leaders stepped up to help raise funds for the construction of a new and modern stadium. Heading the fundraising effort was Spanish American War general William L. Grayson. Through the efforts of Grayson and others, $150,000 was raised for the new park, with about half of the money coming from the Works Progress Administration. The design called for the option to include football games as well, since Municipal Stadium was often used for both sports. After the death of General Grayson, Savannah's City Council passed a resolution naming the new stadium in his honor. The outbreak of World War II halted construction on the stadium. Except for the South Atlantic League suspending operations during World War II, baseball would return every spring and summer in Savannah through the 1960 season.

This stretch saw several name changes for the franchise: the A's, Redlegs, and Pirates at times replaced the Indians moniker. This period of baseball saw Savannah win two more league championships and one of the best teams ever assembled in town, the Lou Brissie–led 1947 Savannah Indians. After suffering severe leg injuries in Europe during World War II, Brissie overcame multiple surgeries and ended up playing for the Savannah Indians after the Philadelphia A's owner extended a contract to him. Brissie headlined a team that many Savannah fans still remember to this day. Putting together impressive stats, Brissie and the Indians won 85 games that year, yet finished in second place. Making the playoffs though, the Indians advanced to play the Augusta Tigers and won the Sally League title in five games.

Six years later, the Sally League and Savannah team was changed forever when Al Isreal and Junior Reedy started for the Indians. Isreal and the Savannah-born Reedy were the first African American players to play in the South Atlantic League. Despite their welcome to the league, Isreal, Reedy, and other African American players throughout the Sally League had a difficult time throughout cities in the south. Segregated restaurants, restrooms, and water fountains welcomed them wherever they went and in their own ballparks, their families had to sit in segregated bleachers. In addition to the isolation, insults and threats were a constant companion for these players. Because of integration, however, Savannah baseball fans got to see even more talented players, such as future major league all stars Hank Aaron, Frank Robinson, and Bob Gibson.

As minor league segregation ended in the early 1950s, so did a much more popular tradition in Savannah in the late 1950s, that of major league clubs stopping by Savannah to play exhibition games near the end of spring training. Since the 1880s, Savannah baseball fans got to see some of the best players in the country play in Savannah's ballparks. Early major league stars, such as Christy Mathewson and Hugh Duffy, created excitement when they came to town near the turn of the 20th century, as did Babe Ruth and Lou Gherig in the 1920s. In fact, children skipped school and adults left work when Babe Ruth came to town in 1935 to play the local Georgia Teachers College. The 1950s saw a Hall of Fame roster play at Grayson Stadium as Ted Williams, Stan Musial, Mickey Mantle, and Whitey Ford, among others, all came to Savannah.

For a variety of reasons, Savannah only fielded four teams in the 1960s. Racial tensions in 1962 caused the Savannah franchise to be moved to Lynchburg; even with only eight games remaining in the season and the team on their way to a first place finish. Concerns over the stability of Savannah as a professional baseball city remained until 1968, when the Washington Senators placed a team here for two years. The Cleveland Indians gave Savannah a try for the 1970 season, the last year Savannah was known as the Indians. In 1971, however, baseball returned to stay when the local favorite Atlanta Braves placed one of their franchises in Savannah.

With the Braves franchise recently relocating to Atlanta, fans in Savannah were quickly becoming fans of the nearby big league club. The addition of one of their minor league clubs to Savannah helped strengthen the local fanbase. Although yearly attendance numbers do not necessarily reflect it, Savannahians loved watching the future Atlanta Braves stars play in their own backyard. Many people to this day have fond memories of watching Dale Murphy, Steve Bedrosian, and Rafael Ramirez play at Grayson Stadium. Savannahians also loved that as Hank

Aaron was catching Babe Ruth's home run record and subsequently adding to his own record, his brother Tommy Aaron was managing the Savannah Braves.

The Braves played at Grayson Stadium until 1984 when the St. Louis Cardinals began their affiliation with the Savannah franchise. In 1986, new Cardinals owners James Hutchinson and Thomas Lewis became the first African American owners of a professional baseball group. Bouncing around the standings through the 1992 season, the Savannah Cardinals of 1993 won the city's eighth championship and then won the ninth pennant the following year.

When the Savannah Sand Gnats replaced the Cardinals in 1996, Savannah fans welcomed a new big league affiliation, the Los Angeles Dodgers. The Sand Gnats quickly created a buzz in Savannah as they won the ninth Sally League championship in their first year of existence. Following the Dodgers as the parent club of the Savannah squad were the Texas Rangers, Montreal Expos, Washington Nationals, and the New York Mets.

The purpose of this book is to collect the stories, images, and history that bring to life baseball in Savannah since its arrival 150 years ago. Many of these images reside in scrapbooks and attics, and a lot of these stories remain with fans who have been coming to games for years in Savannah. As time goes by, these photographs and memories are disappearing. Hopefully, this book will keep a few of these memories for future generations. This is by no means meant to be a complete history of the subject. Many players and stories have been left out, not intentionally, but due to space constraints. I hope you enjoy the history of baseball in Savannah as much as I have.

1

# THE EARLY YEARS

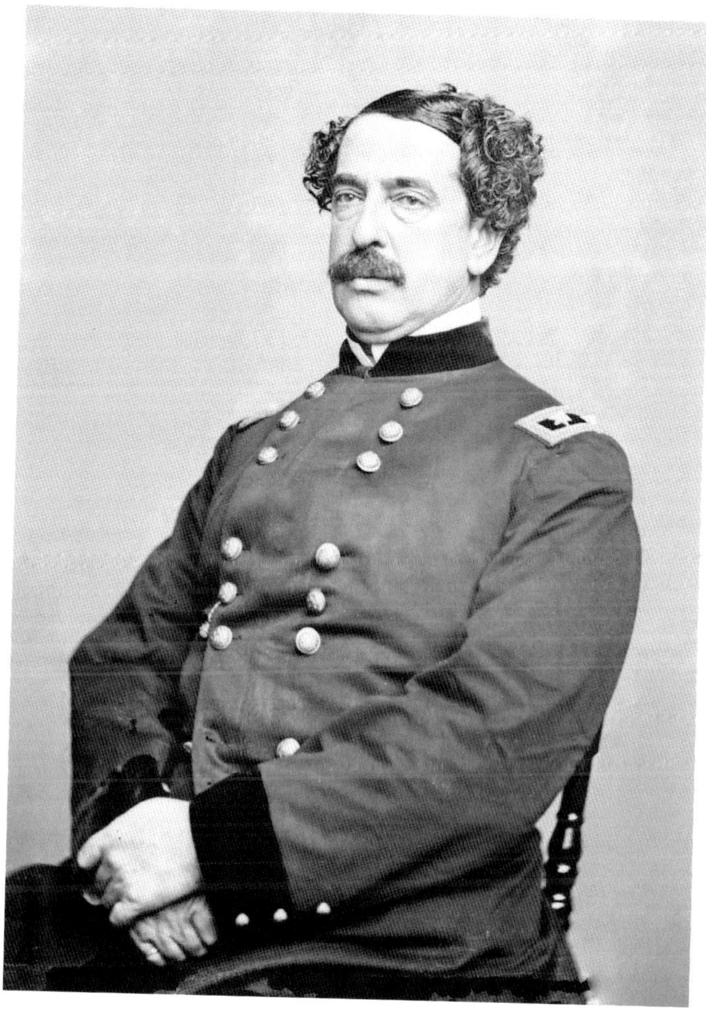

Abner Doubleday, who for years was thought to have invented baseball, served as a Union general during the Civil War. Although it was proved that he was not the founder of America's pastime, he is credited with firing the first shots for the Union during the attack on Fort Sumter in Charleston Harbor on April 12, 1861. (Courtesy of Library of Congress.)

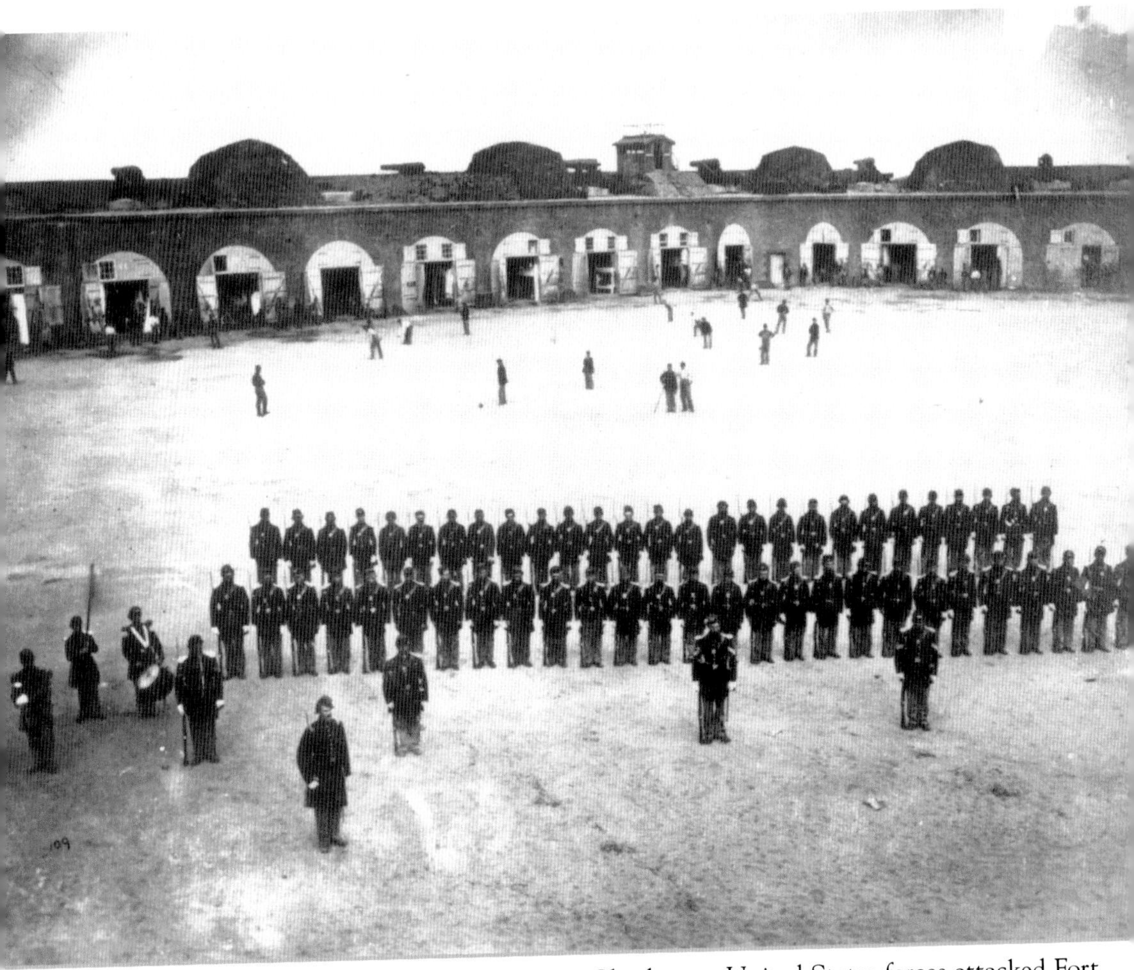

One year after the assault on Fort Sumter in Charleston, United States forces attacked Fort Pulaski guarding the entrance to the Savannah River. Despite its reputation as impregnable, Fort Pulaski fell to the Union army after a 30-hour bombardment. Following the Confederate surrender, United States troops reoccupied the fortification. Among the troops to retake Fort Pulaski, the 48th New York Infantry often performed guard duty and drilled on the parade ground of Pulaski, as shown in the foreground of the image above. When not on duty, soldiers found ways to entertain themselves during down time as seen in the rear of the image. More importantly than showing garrison life at Fort Pulaski, this image and the two that follow are some of the first known photographs of an organized game of baseball being played. (Courtesy of the National Park Service, Fort Pulaski National Monument.)

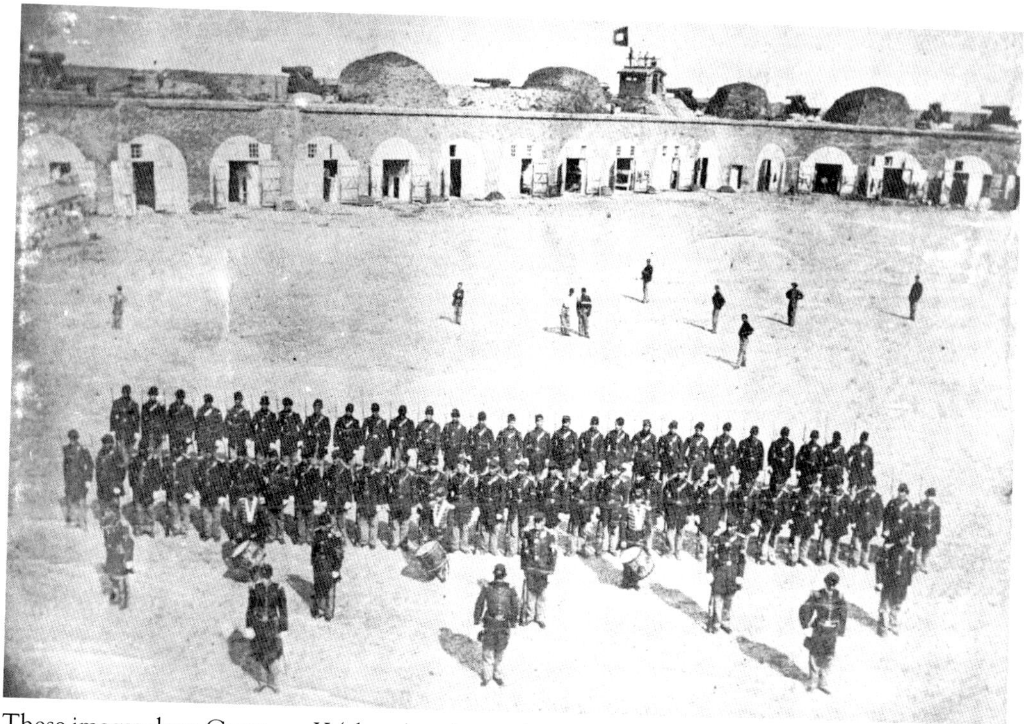

These images show Company K (above) and an unknown company (below) of the 48th New York Infantry at drill, while others are off duty playing baseball at Fort Pulaski. Still in its infancy as a sport, the rules were quite different than today's game. For instance, balls and strikes were not counted unless a hurler (pitcher) felt the batter was wasting time or a striker (batter) felt the hurler was not throwing quality pitches. Any ball caught on the first bounce after hitting the ground was considered an out. Also, overhand pitching was illegal; hurlers had to throw the ball underhand. (Both, courtesy of the National Park Service, Fort Pulaski National Monument.)

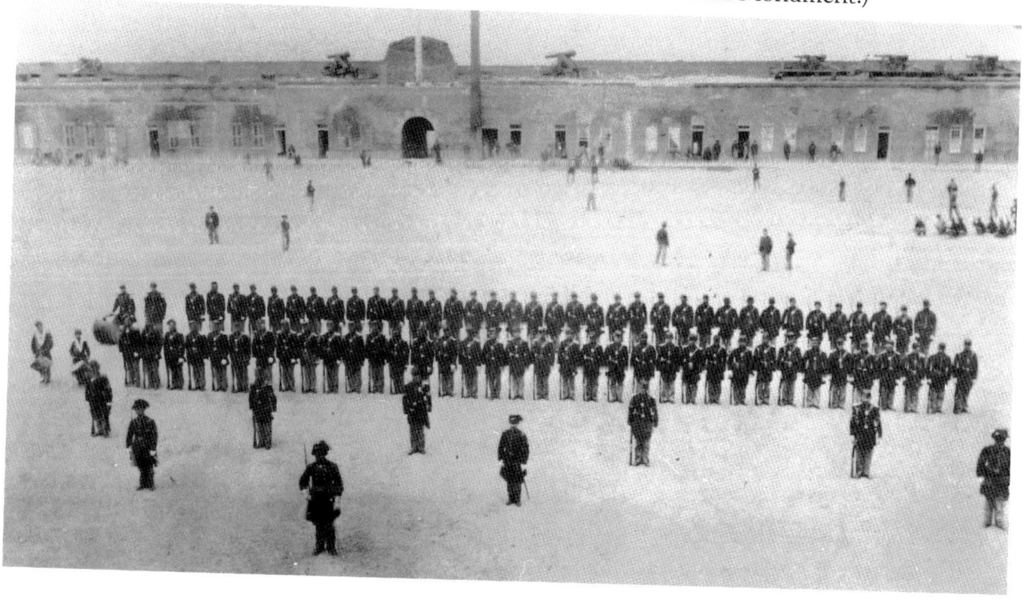

☞ A SPECIAL MEETING OF THE Pioneer Base Ball Club will be held THIS (Thursday) EVENING at 8 o'clock at the corner of York and Whitaker streets. A punctual attendance is earnestly requested.

EDW'D. G. SALTZMAN,
President.

feb14-1t*

Following the Civil War, the popularity of baseball exploded throughout the nation. This 1867 advertisement announces a meeting of what is believed to be the first amateur baseball team in Savannah. The Pioneer Baseball Club was formed by Edward Saltzman, who played for one of the first baseball teams, the New York Gothams. In addition to bringing organized baseball to Savannah, Saltzman is associated with introducing the sport in New York and Massachusetts.

**Base Ball in Georgia.**

[From the Savannah Republican.]

We had the pleasure of witnessing a very interesting game of base ball last Friday afternoon, played in rear of Forsyth Place, by the "Pioneer Base Ball Club," of this city, which afforded a lively time and much amusement to those engaged, as also to a number of visitors, who seemed to take much interest in the game. The game was well played (considering it was the first lesson of this young club) according to the rules of the National Association of Base Ball Players. The "Pioneer" is a new organization, under the management of E. C. Saultzman, member of the Gotham Club, New York, of the Tri-Mountain Club, of Boston, and founder of this game in the State of Massachusetts, and Mr. James E. Wilson, of the Eckford Club, of Brooklyn. The members, not wishing to be behind other cities in the cultivation of this manly sport, have set apart Tuesday and Friday afternoon of each week, at 3 o'clock, to exercise in this game, and they hope to receive the encouragement of the citizens of Savannah, and that they may

The *Boston Daily Advertiser* reprinted this 1867 article from the *Savannah Republican*, describing a game played by Saltzman's Pioneer club in Forsyth Park. Although few details are given about the game and team, the article provides a lot of hints about the growing popularity of the sport.

**OPENING THE BASEBALL SEASON.**
**SAVANNAH, Ga., March 20.—The Detroit League nine opened the season here to-day, defeating the Savannahs 4 to 2.**

By 1886, baseball had established itself throughout the nation. Professional leagues were organized and teams would travel great distances to play each other. Many teams would travel south to train in the spring. Savannah became a popular location for many of these teams. The article above mentions the opening of the 1886 season and how the Detroit Wolverines of the National League beat the unnamed Savannah team of the Southern Association in an exhibition game. The image below shows the 1886 Detroit Wolverines. This Detroit squad went on to win 87 games that year, yet finished in second place. (Above, courtesy of *The New York Times*.)

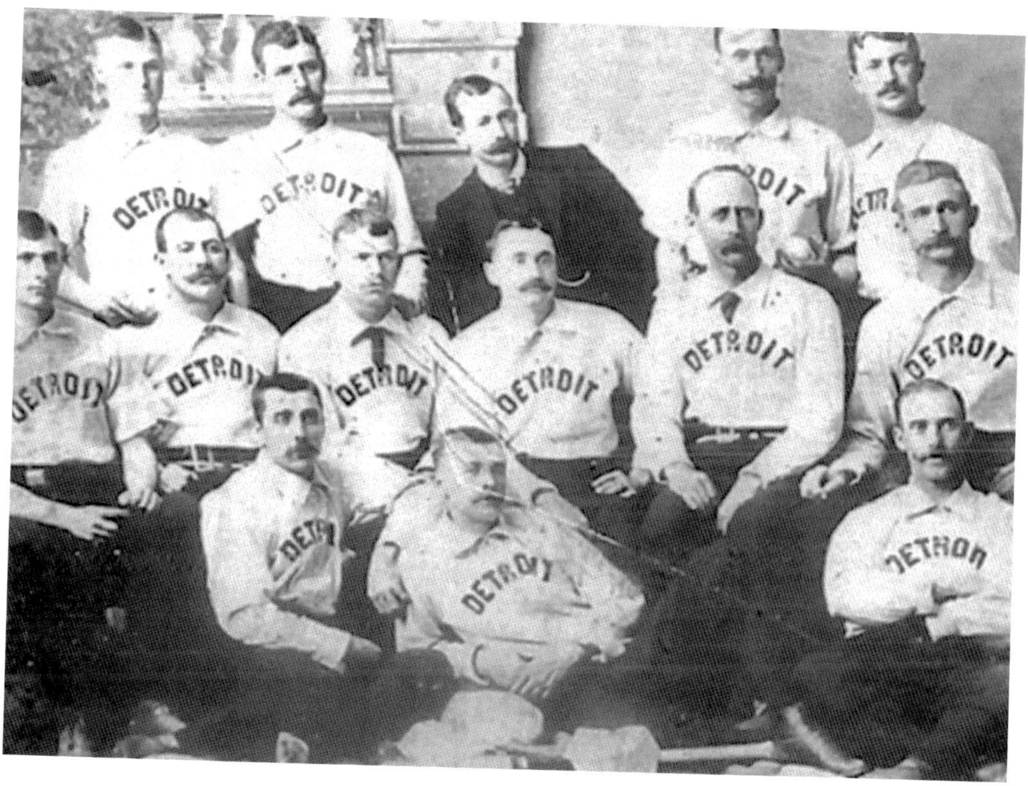

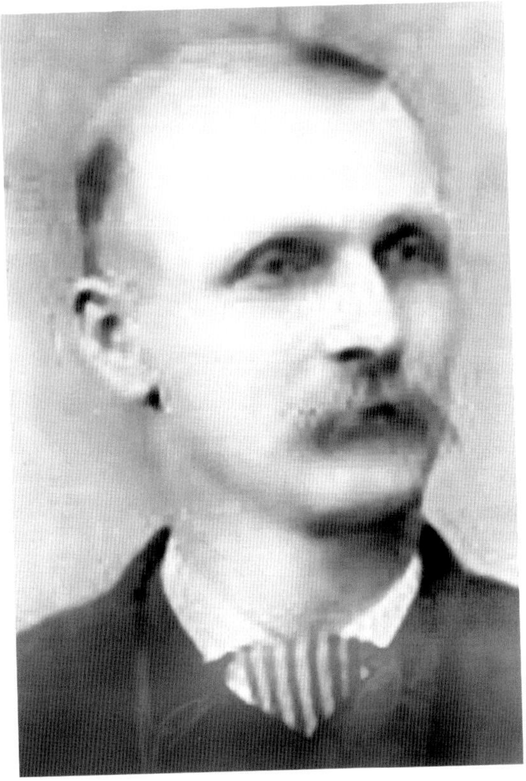

The 1886 Wolverines were without one of their managers and utility players from the previous year when they arrived in Savannah. Charlie Morton, who played third base and shortstop for Detroit, now managed the local Savannah squad. Morton had a decent baseball career, playing three years in the majors and managing both major and minor league teams for 10 years.

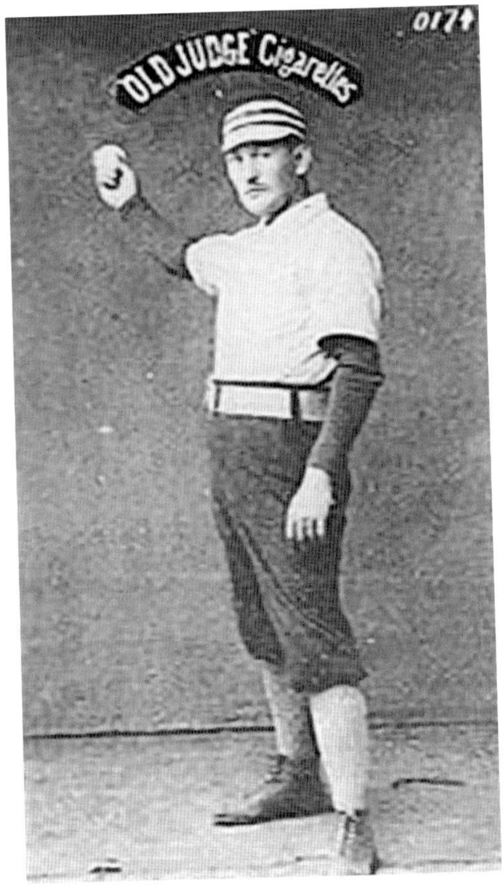


Henry O'Day was Savannah's star pitcher in 1886. He was tops in the Southern Association, with a record of 26 wins and 11 losses. Considering his 1.03 ERA and 224 strikeouts, O'Day was destined to pitch in the major leagues, which he did for seven seasons. O'Day also spent two years managing in the majors, leading the 1912 Cincinnati Reds and the 1914 Chicago Cubs.

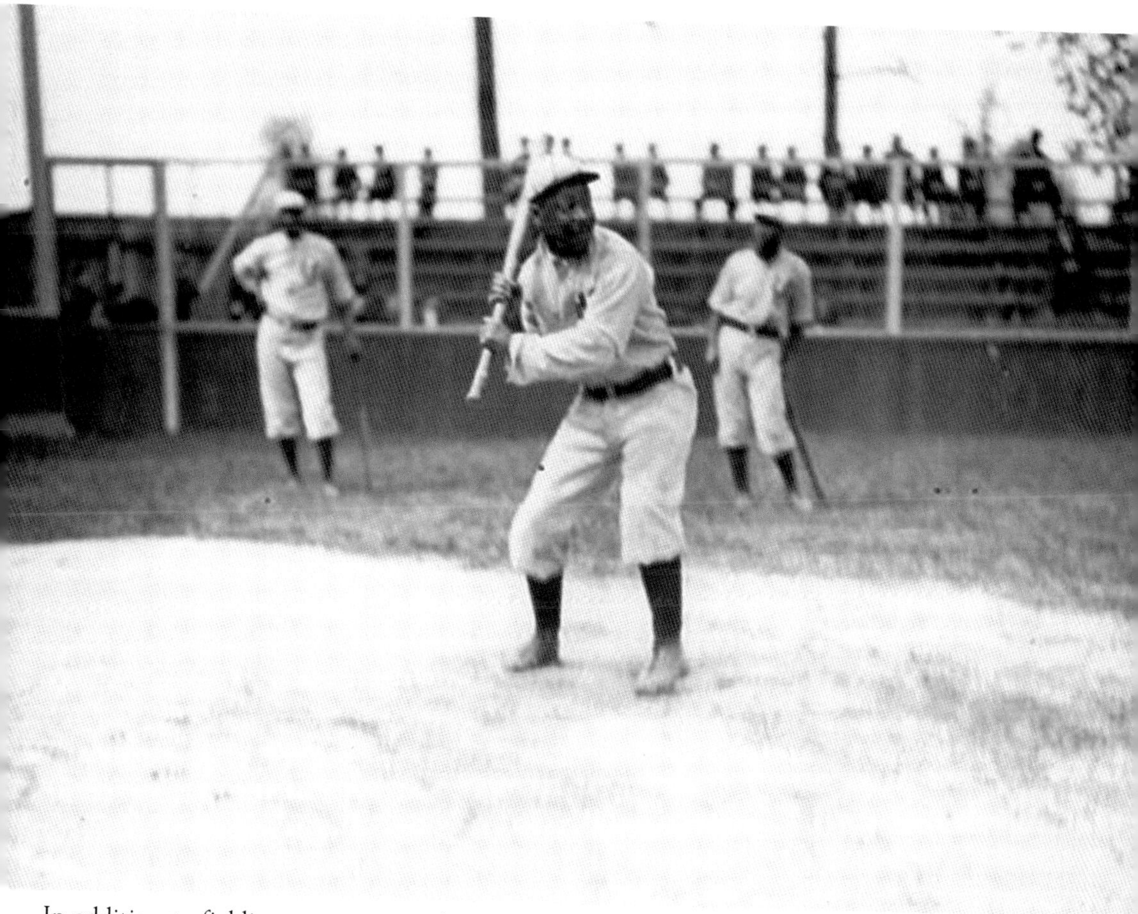

In addition to fielding one team in the Southern Association in 1886, Savannah hosted two teams in another professional league, the Southern League of Colored Base Ballists. The first attempt to organize African American baseball, the SLCBB quickly faced mounting debt and only lasted one year. Despite its brevity, the league generated a lot of interest from its players, with Savannah and Memphis forming two teams while Jacksonville fielded three teams. Savannah contributed the Broads and LaFayettes to the league. Coverage of the league and its players is difficult to locate in the various newspapers of the league's cities. The coverage that does exist mentions teams and cities that were not in existence at the beginning of the season, implying that the league was unstable during its only season. It is unclear where the teams in Savannah would have played. (Courtesy of Library of Congress.)

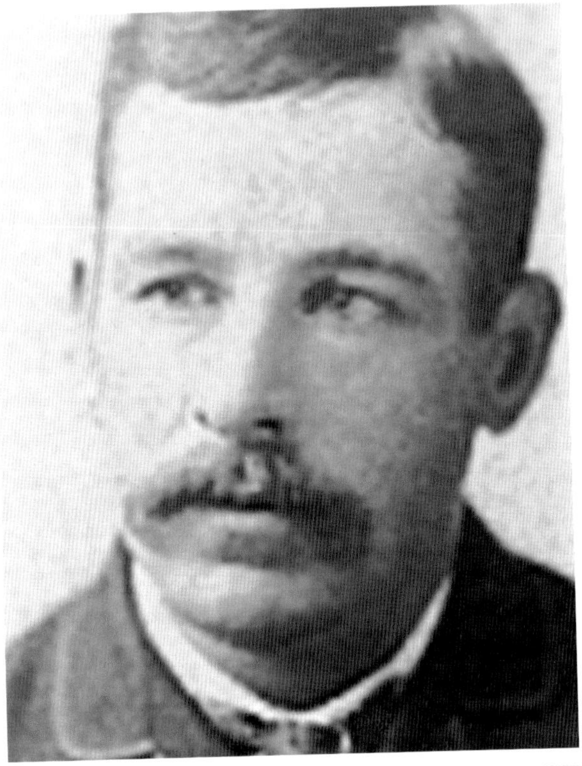

The 1887 Savannah club playing in the Southern League apparently once again did not field a nickname. They did, however, have nine players who played in the major leagues. One of them was a pitcher and outfielder named Frederick "Tricky" Nichols. Nichols only played a handful of games in Savannah, yet played six seasons of major league ball. Following 1887, Savannah was without a team until 1893.

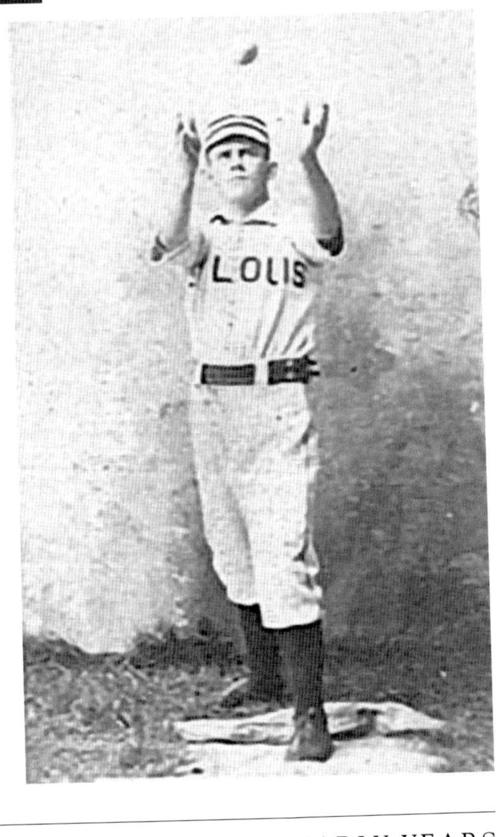


Considering the last team Savannah hosted went without a nickname, the 1893 squad was quite remarkable since they were known by two names, the Savannah Electrics and Savannah Rabbits. Twelve of Savannah's Electrics/Rabbits played in the majors at some point. One of these players, James McGarr, also known as "Chippy," played five seasons of minor league ball and 10 years in the big leagues.

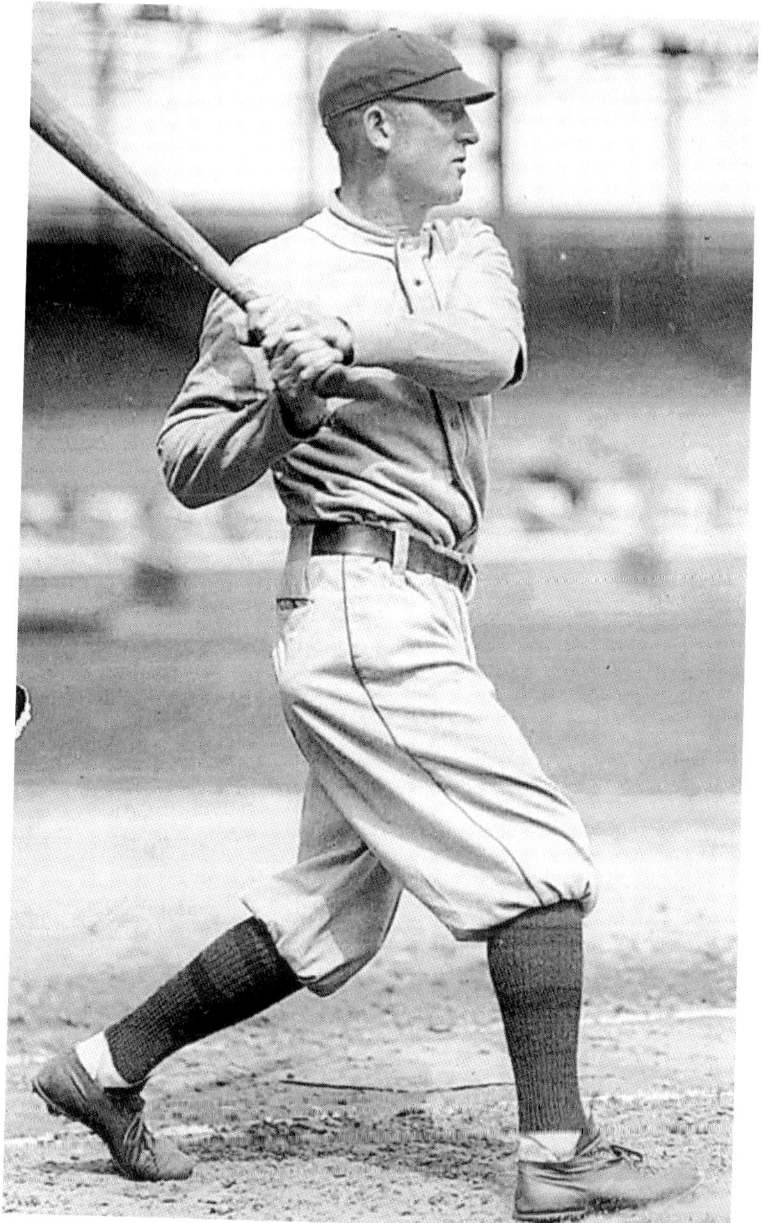

Known in 1894 as the Savannah Modocs, the local team featured 12 players with major league talent. One of those 12, Fred Clarke, possessed Hall of Fame skills. In his second year of professional baseball, Clarke played in Savannah, batting .311 in 54 games. Later that year, he was added to the Louisville Colonels, the first of his 21 seasons in the majors. Clarke spent six years with the Colonels and in 1900, began his tenure with the Pittsburgh Pirates. He spent the next 16 seasons as a player and manager for the Pirates and helped them win three straight National League pennants from 1901 through 1903. A fourth pennant and World Series victory over Ty Cobb and the Detroit Tigers followed in 1909. After his much decorated 19-year career, Clarke was elected into the Baseball Hall of Fame in 1945.

SAVANNAH, Ga., March 30.—The Boston baseball players suffered defeat at the hands of the Savannah team to-day by a score of 4 to 3. Until the seventh inning Savannah had nothing but goose eggs to its credit. In that inning, it piled up three runs and got another in the eighth. Lewis pitched the first seven innings for Boston, and Hopkins the two last. Savannah's pitchers were Nichols, Klobedanze, and Stivetts.

In 1897, Savannah welcomed the Boston Beaneaters to town for spring training. Featuring five future Hall of Famers, the Beaneaters were looking to improve their fourth place finish the previous year. Despite their discouraging beginning to the 1897 season, losing to the Savannah team by a score of 4-3, the Beaneaters won the National League pennant with a record of 93 wins and 39 losses. The Boston Beaneaters finished two games ahead of the Baltimore Orioles and are widely regarded as one of the best teams assembled during the 19th century. This Boston franchise later evolved into the Boston Braves, Milwaukee Braves, and the modern Atlanta Braves. (Above, courtesy of *The New York Times*.)

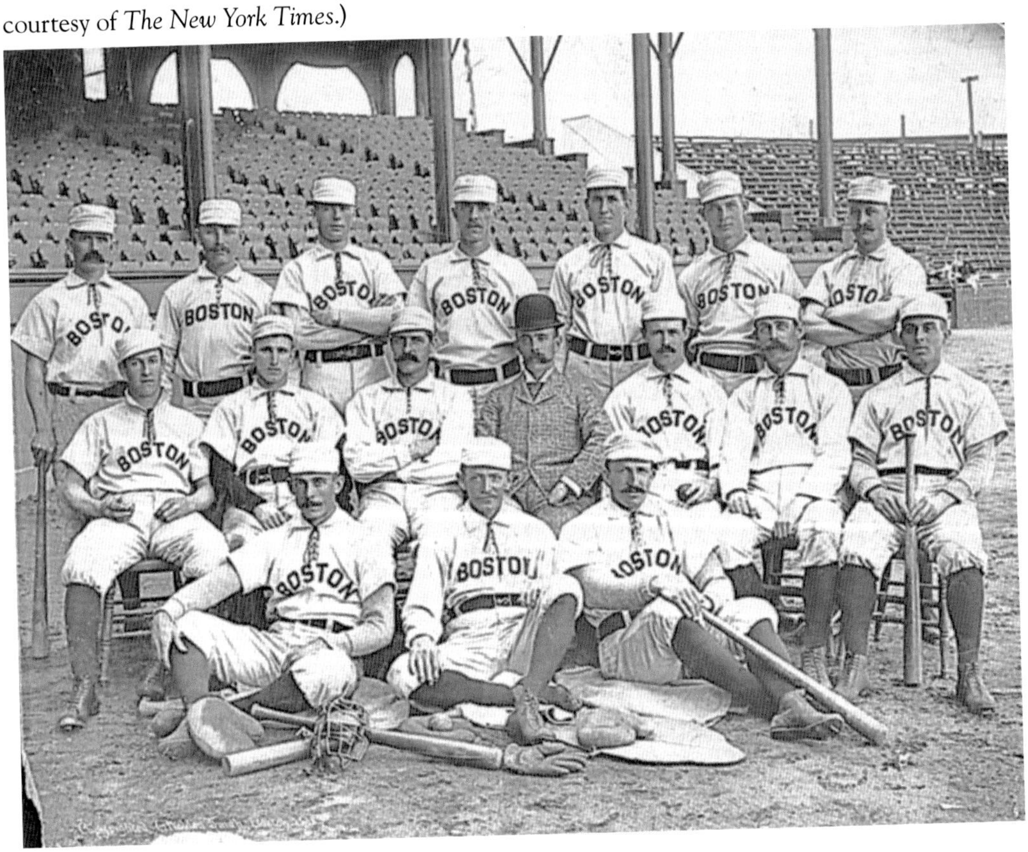

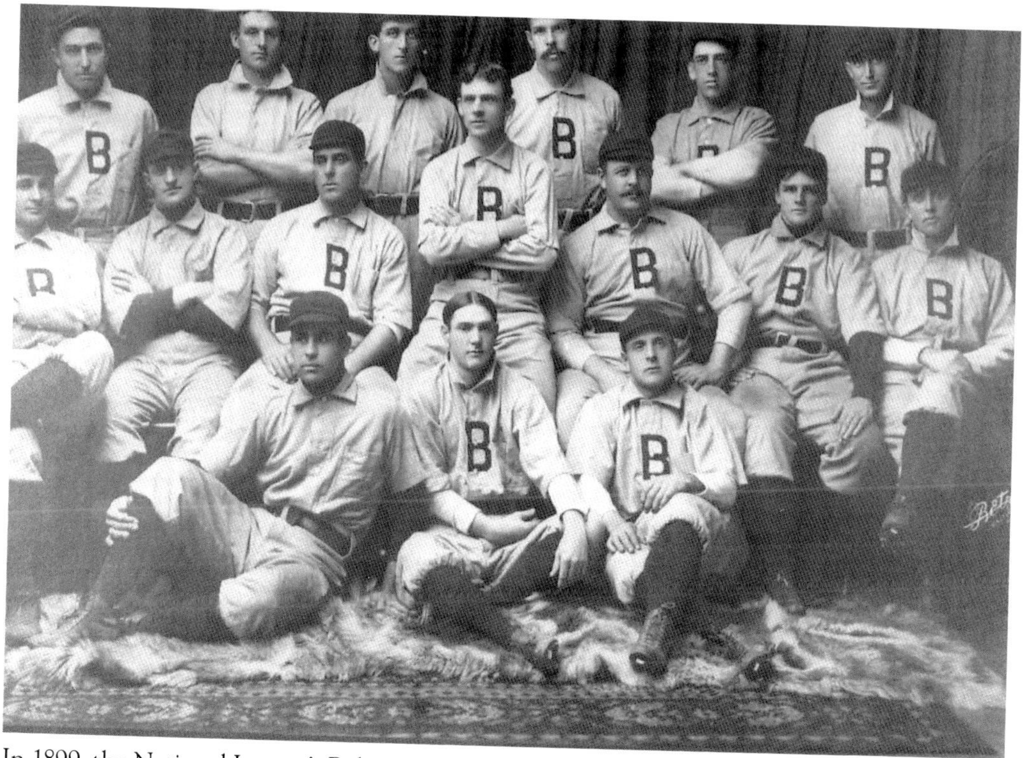

In 1899, the National League's Baltimore Orioles came to Savannah to train in the spring. Led by manager John McGraw, the Orioles looked to improve on their second place finish from the year before. Unfortunately, their departure from Savannah would see them drop to fourth place and see the Baltimore franchise fold.

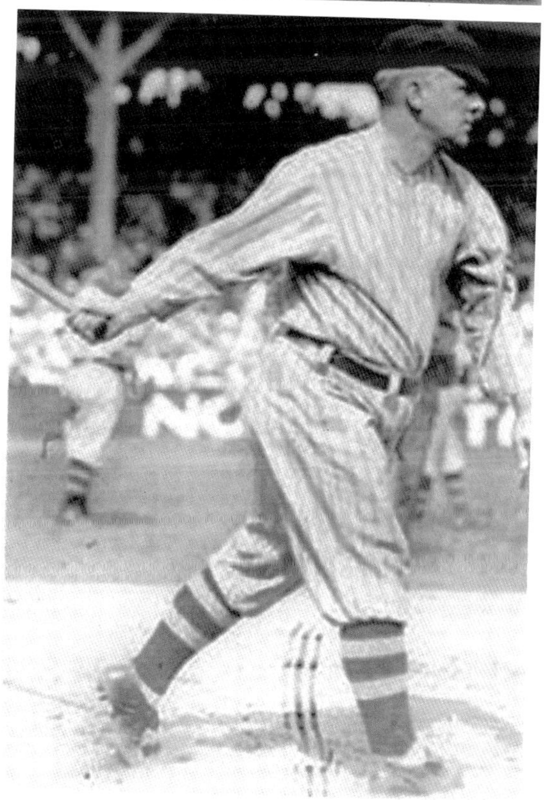

Known by the nicknames of "Mugsy" or "Little Napoleon," John McGraw was also known as a stellar ball player and one of the best managers that professional baseball has ever seen. He had 2,763 wins as a manager, 10 National League pennants, three World Series titles, and was elected to the Baseball Hall of Fame in 1937. Throughout his years as skipper of the Orioles and New York Giants, a lot of his success began in Savannah, where his teams came to train.

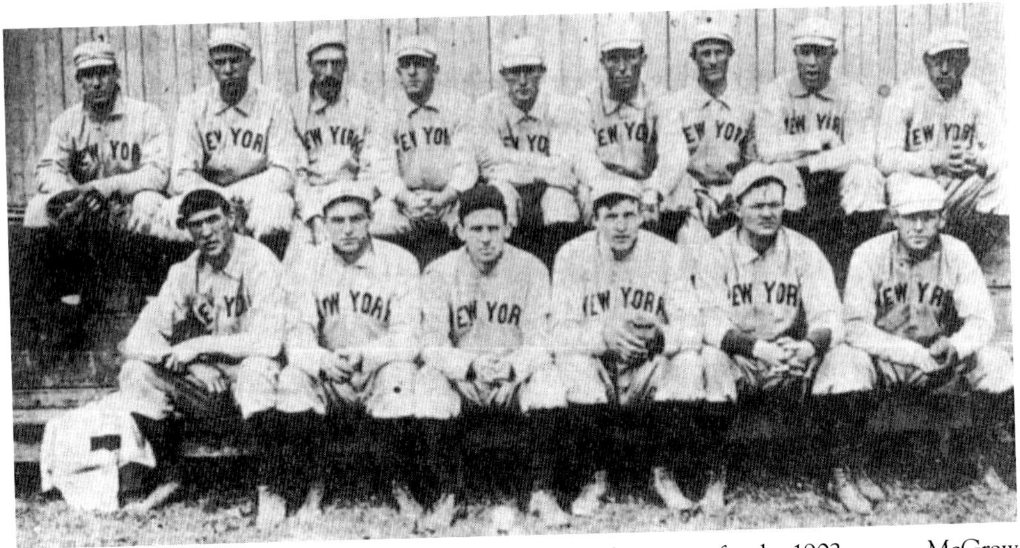

After signing on with the New York Giants as a player and manager for the 1902 season, McGraw led the Giants to Savannah in 1903 to begin their season. Finishing in last place the previous year, the Giants had nowhere to go but up upon their arrival in Savannah for training. Their training paid off, as the Giants made a remarkable turnaround and finished in second place in the National League. (Bill Burgess Collection.)

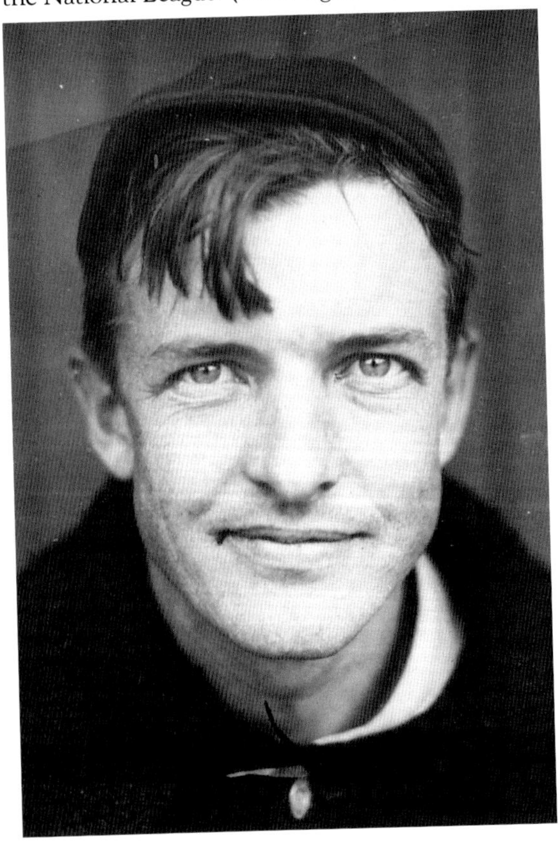

Savannah fans watching the 1903 New York Giants train saw a young right-handed pitcher by the name of Christopher Mathewson. On March 21, the Giants faced the local Fort Screven team with Mathewson pitching the fourth and fifth innings. Few Savannah fans could have known that Mathewson would become one of the greatest pitchers the game has ever seen. Mathewson ended up winning 373 games during his career and was one of the five initial inductees in the Baseball Hall of Fame.

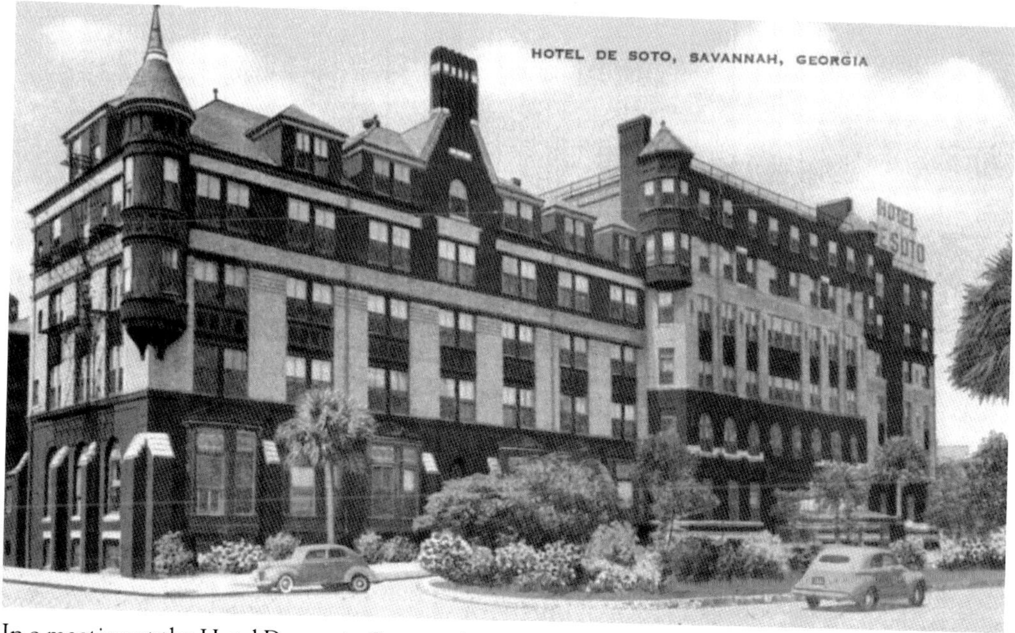


In a meeting at the Hotel Desoto in Savannah on November 23, 1903, the original South Atlantic League was formed. Through the correspondence between Jacksonville businessman J.B. Lucy and C.B. Boyer, secretary of the Atlanta Baseball Club, the class C league was organized with six charter teams: the Macon Highlanders, Charleston Sea Gulls, Columbia Skyscrapers, Jacksonville Jays, Augusta Tourists, and Savannah Pathfinders.

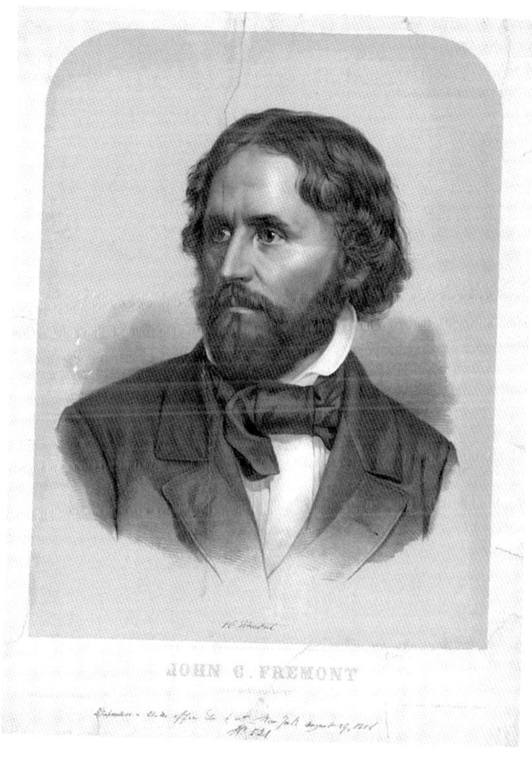


The first professional team in Savannah took its name from Savannah native John C. Fremont. Also known as "The Great Pathfinder," Fremont was a celebrated explorer of the west, a skilled yet controversial military officer during the Mexican and Civil Wars, and the first Republican Party candidate for the office of US president.

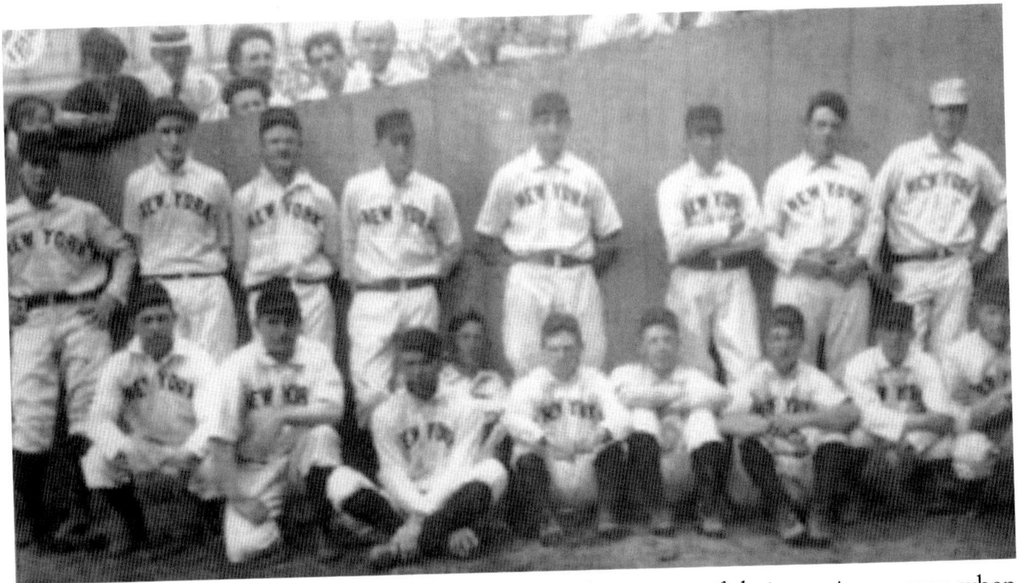

The 1904 New York Giants were looking to build on the success of their previous season when they arrived in Savannah to begin the year. Despite winning 84 games in 1904, the Giants, led again by John McGraw, were looking for more success. In their March 12 warm up game against the Savannah YMCA, the Giants collected 20 hits against the local amateurs, something the New York Polo Grounds fans would have talked about for days. The Giants' good hitting carried over to the regular season as the New York club finished first in runs scored in the National League and won the pennant with 106 wins. They would have played in the second ever World Series, except their owner, John T. Bush, refused to play the American League champions. (Above, courtesy of Kevin Graham; below, courtesy of *The New York Times*.)

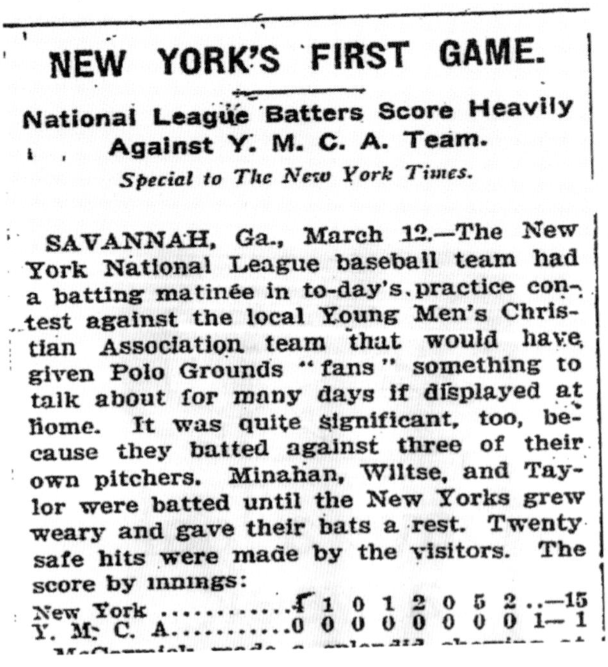

**NEW YORK'S FIRST GAME.**

**National League Batters Score Heavily Against Y. M. C. A. Team.**

*Special to The New York Times.*

SAVANNAH, Ga., March 12.—The New York National League baseball team had a batting matinée in to-day's practice contest against the local Young Men's Christian Association team that would have given Polo Grounds "fans" something to talk about for many days if displayed at home. It was quite significant, too, because they batted against three of their own pitchers. Minahan, Wiltse, and Taylor were batted until the New Yorks grew weary and gave their bats a rest. Twenty safe hits were made by the visitors. The score by innings:

New York ............4 1 0 1 2 0 5 2 . .—15
Y. M. C. A...........0 0 0 0 0 0 0 0 1—1

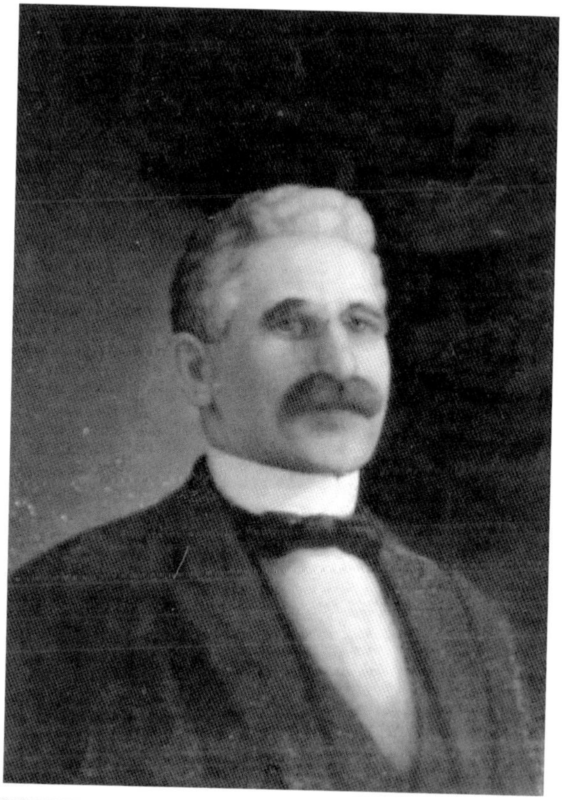

On April 26, 1904, as flags flew proudly, parades passed by, and bands played, Savannah mayor Herman Myers threw out the first pitch to begin the inaugural game of the South Atlantic League and the Savannah Pathfinders. Despite the pomp and ceremony in front of a crowd of 3,200 on this Memorial Day, Savannah lost to the visiting Charleston club by a score of 3-0. (Courtesy of the City of Savannah, Research Library, and Municipal Archives.)

Led by the hitting of William Oyler, who led the league with a .302 batting average, and Joe Welch with his 28 wins, the 1904 Pathfinders won 63 games and finished in second place. Despite their success, the financial backing for the team fell through and Sally League president Charles Boyer operated the Savannah club.

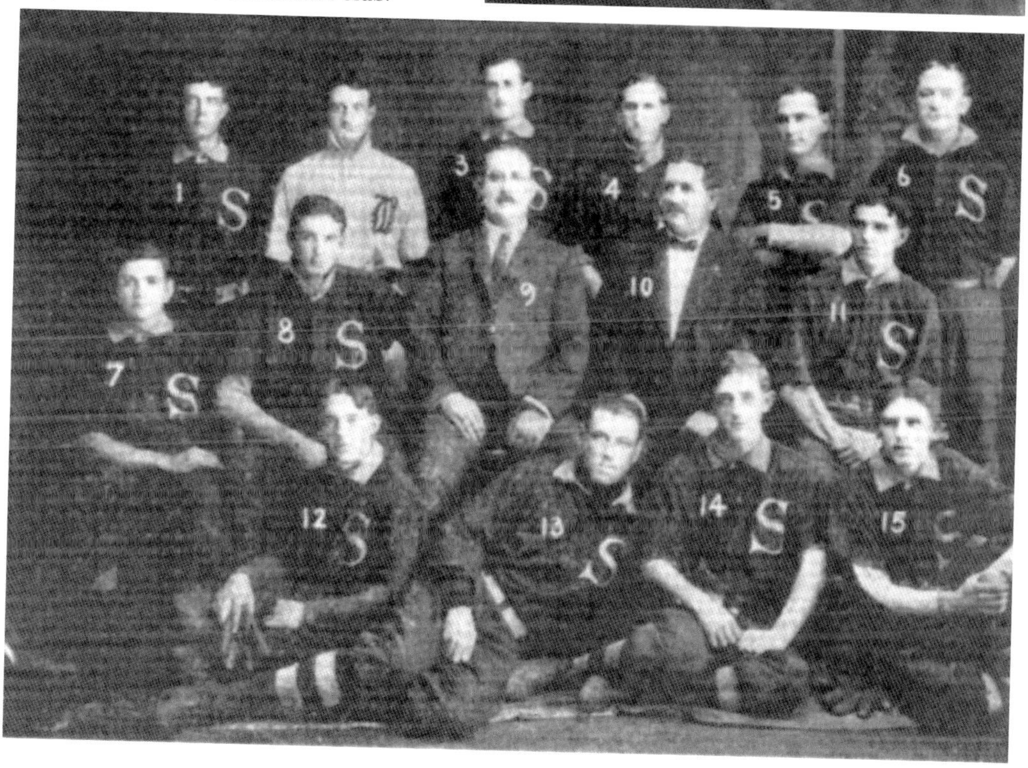

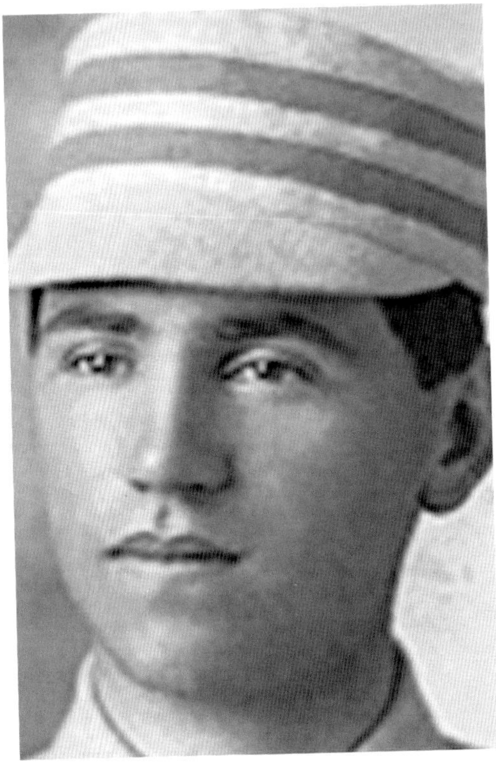

Although Theodore O'Hara Sechrist, better known as "Doc," only played 10 games with the 1904 Pathfinders, he exemplifies the type of player that Savannah would host for many years to come. A journeyman pitcher, Sechrist played seven seasons of minor league ball from 1896 through 1904. In 1899, however, he got his shot at the big time, appearing in one game for the major league New York Giants.

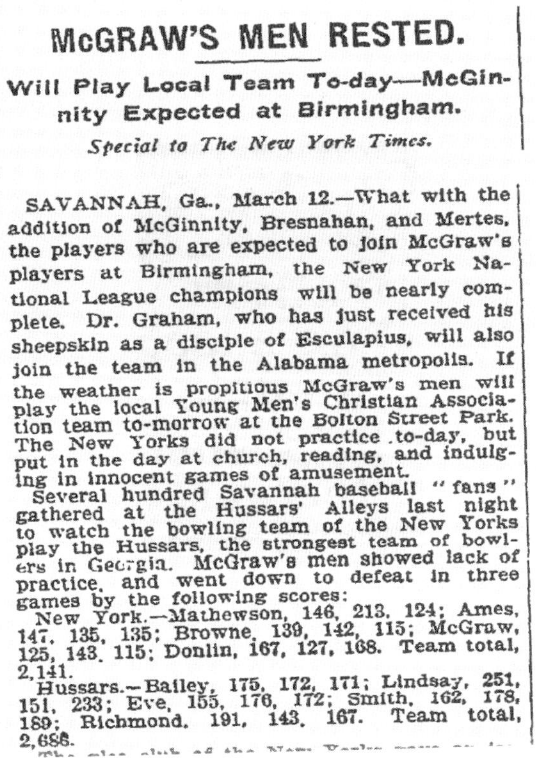

## McGRAW'S MEN RESTED.

**Will Play Local Team To-day—McGinnity Expected at Birmingham.**

*Special to The New York Times.*

SAVANNAH, Ga., March 12.—What with the addition of McGinnity, Bresnahan, and Mertes, the players who are expected to join McGraw's players at Birmingham, the New York National League champions will be nearly complete. Dr. Graham, who has just received his sheepskin as a disciple of Esculapius, will also join the team in the Alabama metropolis. If the weather is propitious McGraw's men will play the local Young Men's Christian Association team to-morrow at the Bolton Street Park. The New Yorks did not practice to-day, but put in the day at church, reading, and indulging in innocent games of amusement.

Several hundred Savannah baseball "fans" gathered at the Hussars' Alleys last night to watch the bowling team of the New Yorks play the Hussars, the strongest team of bowlers in Georgia. McGraw's men showed lack of practice, and went down to defeat in three games by the following scores:

New York.—Mathewson, 146, 213, 124; Ames, 147, 135, 135; Browne, 139, 142, 115; McGraw, 125, 143, 115; Donlin, 167, 127, 168. Team total, 2,141.

Hussars.—Bailey, 175, 172, 171; Lindsay, 251, 151, 233; Eve, 155, 176, 172; Smith, 162, 178, 189; Richmond, 191, 143, 167. Team total, 2,686.

The return of spring in early 1905 meant the return of the New York Giants. Coming again to Savannah to train for the upcoming season, the Giants scrimmaged with the local YMCA team once again and spent some down time bowling. While Savannah fans were happy to have their own professional team to cheer on, the annual return of the players from the majors thrilled the local crowds. (Courtesy of *The New York Times*.)

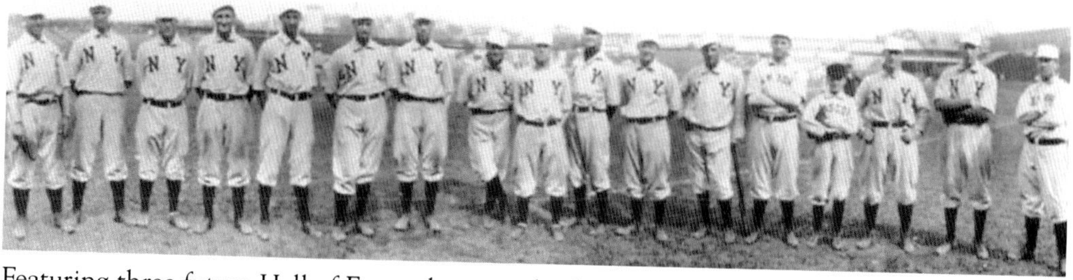

Featuring three future Hall of Fame players and a future Hall of Fame manager, the 1905 New York Giants returned to Savannah once again, looking to continue their championship play. Their training in Savannah enabled them to repeat once again as National League champs, and this year they participated in the World Series, beating the Philadelphia Athletics in five games.

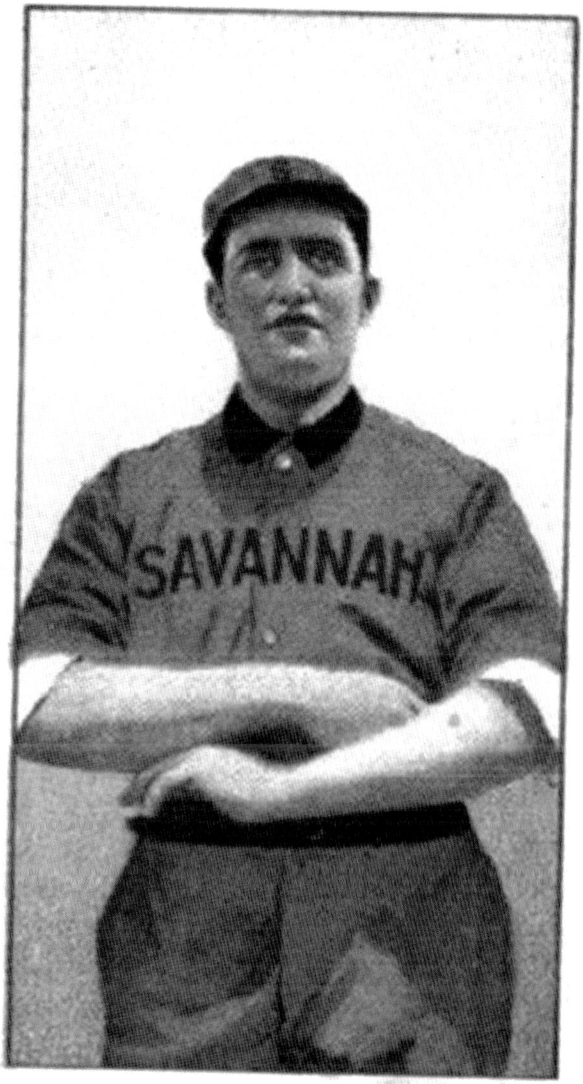


HOWARD, SAVANNAH

Ernie Howard has perhaps the longest tenure as a player of anyone in Savannah's history. Arriving from the Baton Rouge team after the 1904 season, Howard spent the next six years as a part-time player and manager for the Pathfinders. This team featured 10 players with big league talent, but unfortunately, Howard was not one of them. He retired in 1915 after playing 11 years of minor league baseball.

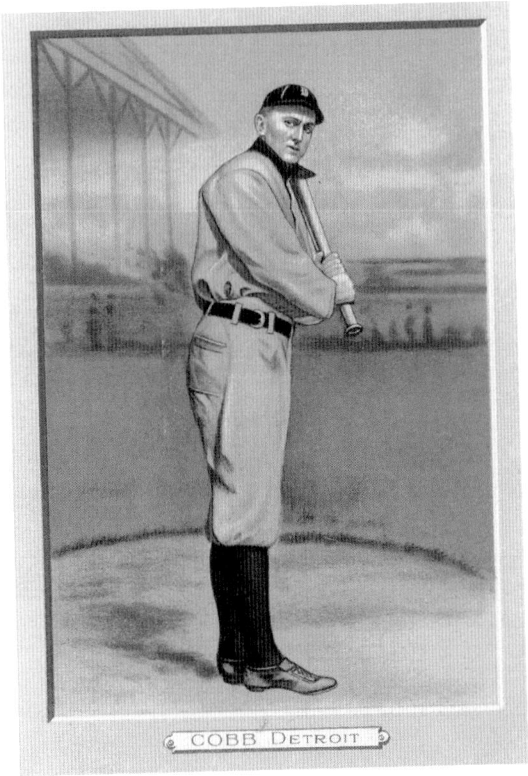


Tyrus Raymond Cobb roamed the outfield for the 1905 Tourists and while playing against the Pathfinders in Savannah, his questionable antics were already on display. Legend has it that while in the outfield during one particular game in Savannah, Cobb was eating a bag of popcorn. When a fly ball was hit in his direction, he let the ball drop to the ground instead of dropping his popcorn. When confronted by the manager from the Tourists about this poor decision, Cobb proceeded to get in a fist fight with his skipper.

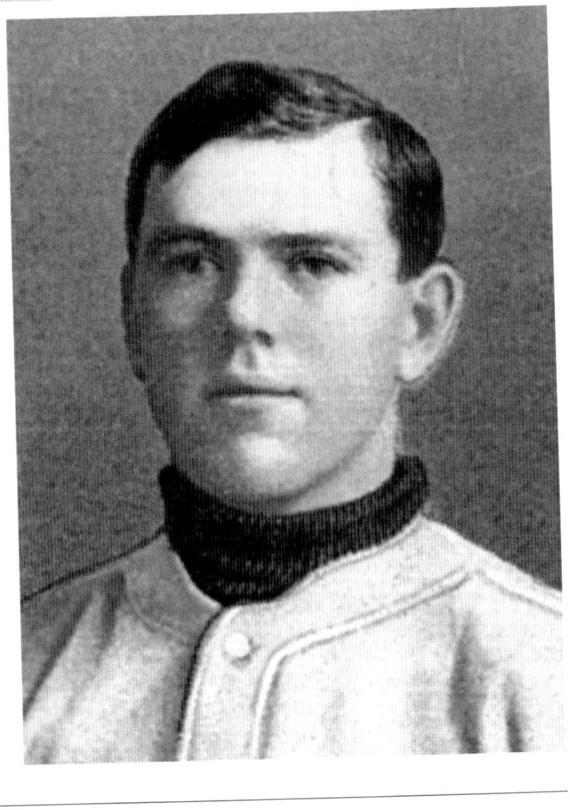

In 1906, another Augusta Tourist thrilled the crowds at the Bolton St. Park when they came to play the newly named Savannah Indians. George "Nap" Rucker dominated that year for the Tourists, winning 27 games. Rucker went on to the majors that following year, pitching 10 seasons for the Brooklyn Superbas and Dodgers.

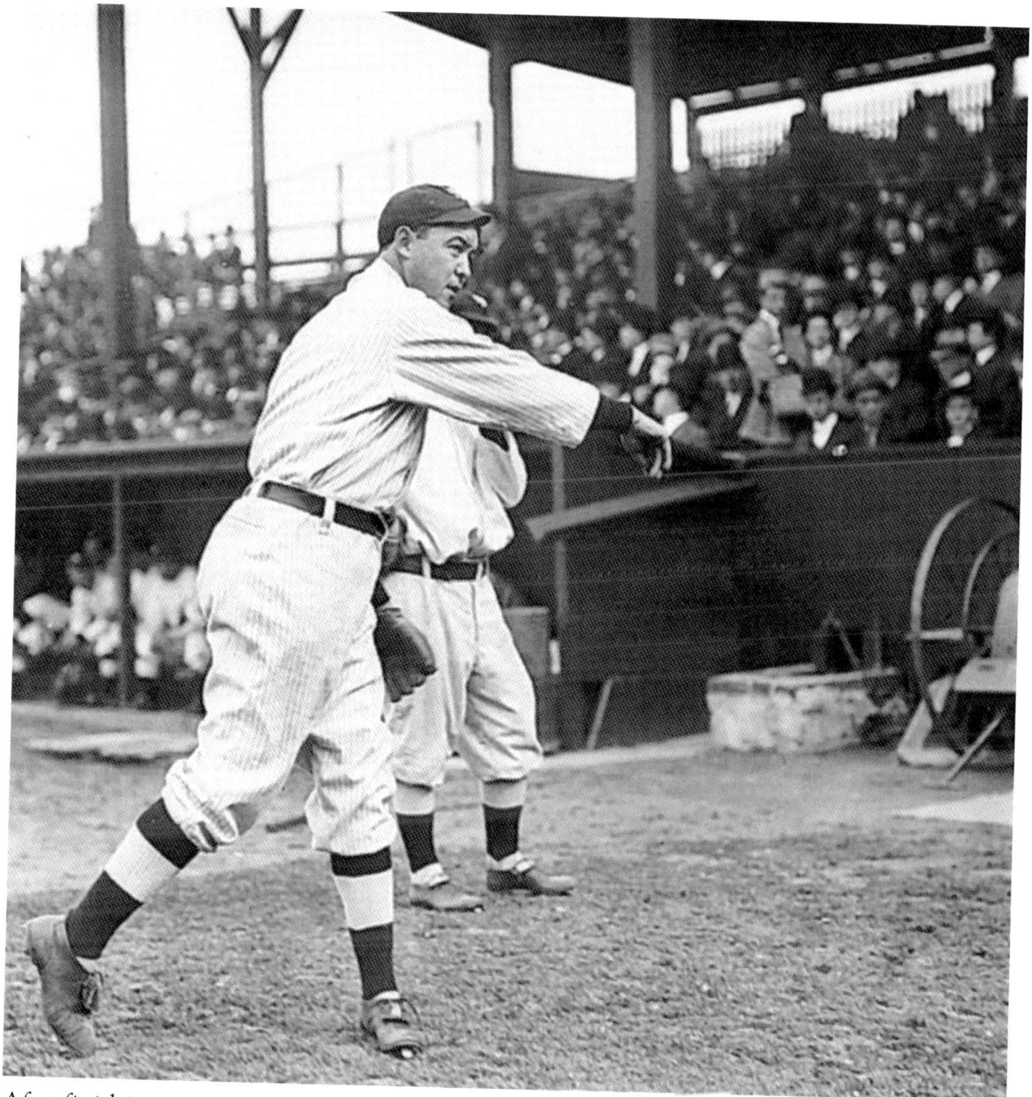

After finishing in second place for the first two years of the Sally League, the Savannah club was finally able to capture its first championship in 1906. Arthur Lawrence "Bugs" Raymond led the way for the newly christened Savannah Indians with 18 wins. While his talent was abundant, winning 35 games in 1907 for Charleston, so were his personal demons. Raymond struggled with alcoholism throughout most of his adult life. Many stories circulated about his erratic, alcohol induced behavior. One such tale involves Bugs pitching the first game of a doubleheader and then going to a bar in between games. After drinking six beers, Raymond returned to the ball field and pitched the second game. Another story has Raymond showing up late to a game and beating the Cubs, despite the fact that he was drunk and did not even warm up before taking the mound. Raymond was found dead in a hotel room in 1912.

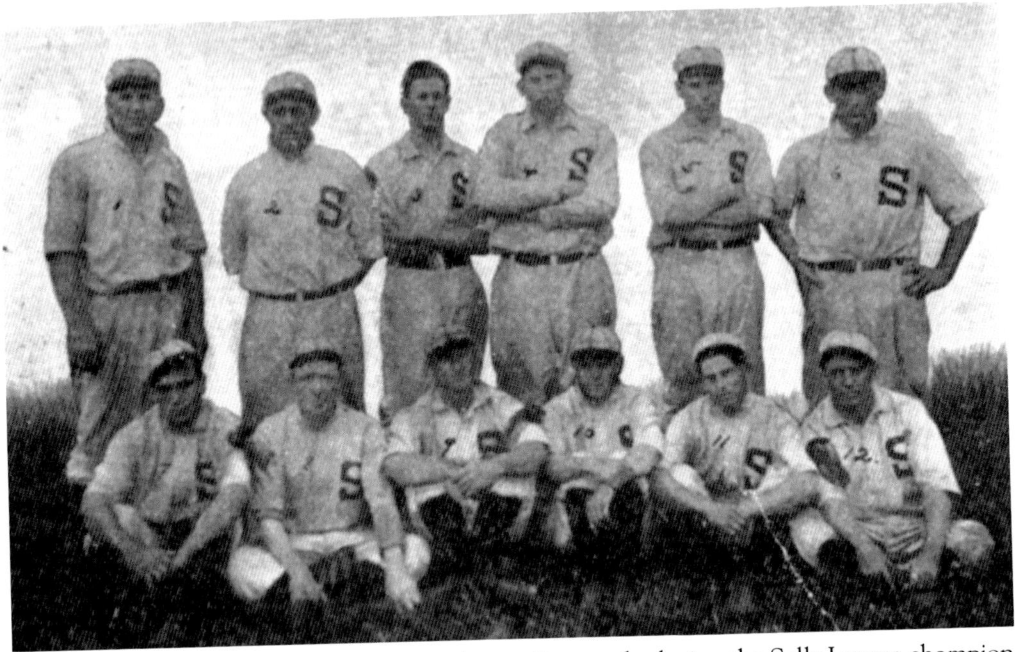

The spring of 1907 saw the Brooklyn Superbas in Savannah playing the Sally League champion Savannah Indians in an exhibition. Despite losing the game 10-3, the Indians were looking to repeat as champions. The Savannah team unfortunately took a step back, finishing in fifth place with a record of 56 wins and 63 losses. (Courtesy of Skip Jennings.)

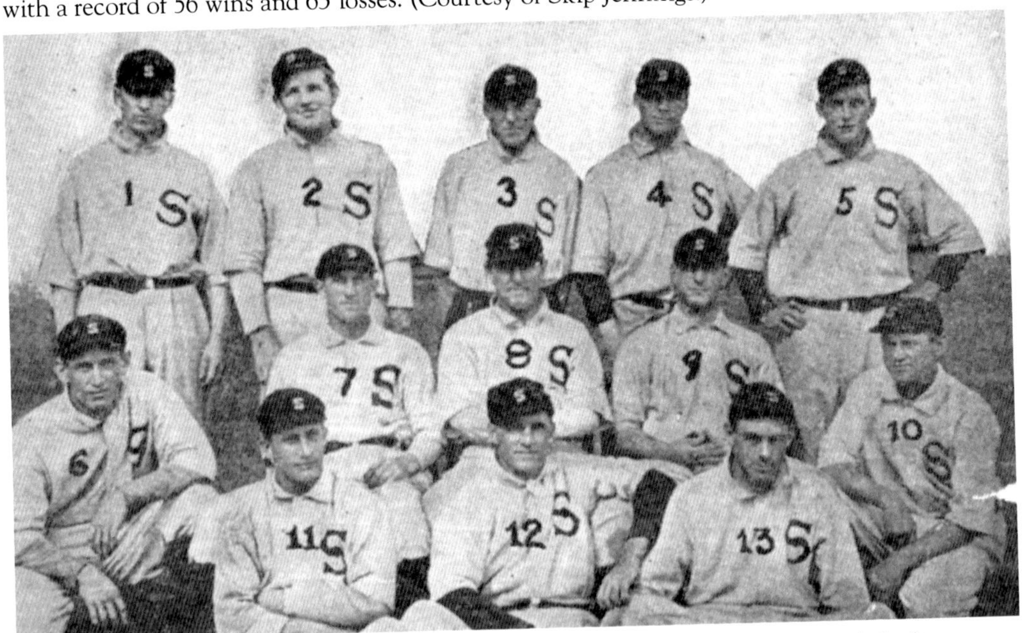

With the Philadelphia Phillies in Savannah for the spring, the 1908 Savannah Indians were anxious to get back to their championship form. The previous year's disappointment with fifth place was somewhat forgotten as the Indians of 1908 won 64 games, improving in the standings to a second place finish. (Courtesy of Skip Jennings.)

Louis Pelkey provided little help for the Savannah Indians as they moved toward second place. In his first of four years in Savannah, Pelkey played in the outfield while batting a weak .152 in 120 games. Only his first year in professional baseball, Pelkey's average climbed, but never above the low mark of .238 in 1910. (Courtesy of the Richard B. Russell Library for Political Research and Studies.)

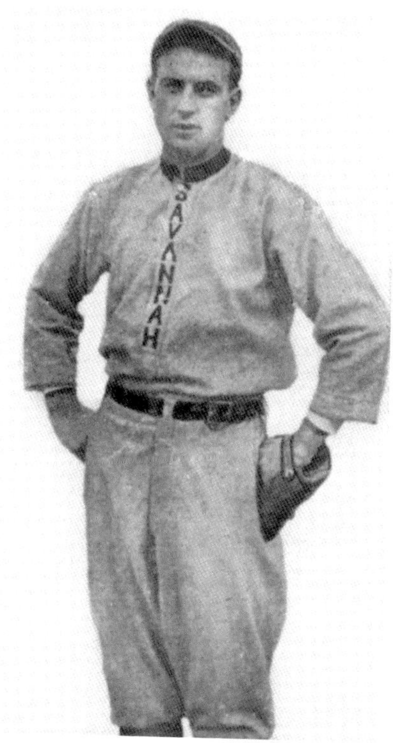


This image shows another team photograph from the 1908 Savannah Indians. Most importantly, it also provides a unique view of Bolton St. Park, where the Savannah professional teams played for a number of years. Located just east of the Atlantic Coast Line Railroad tracks between Bolton Street and Park Avenue, few images of Savannah's first real ballpark exist today.

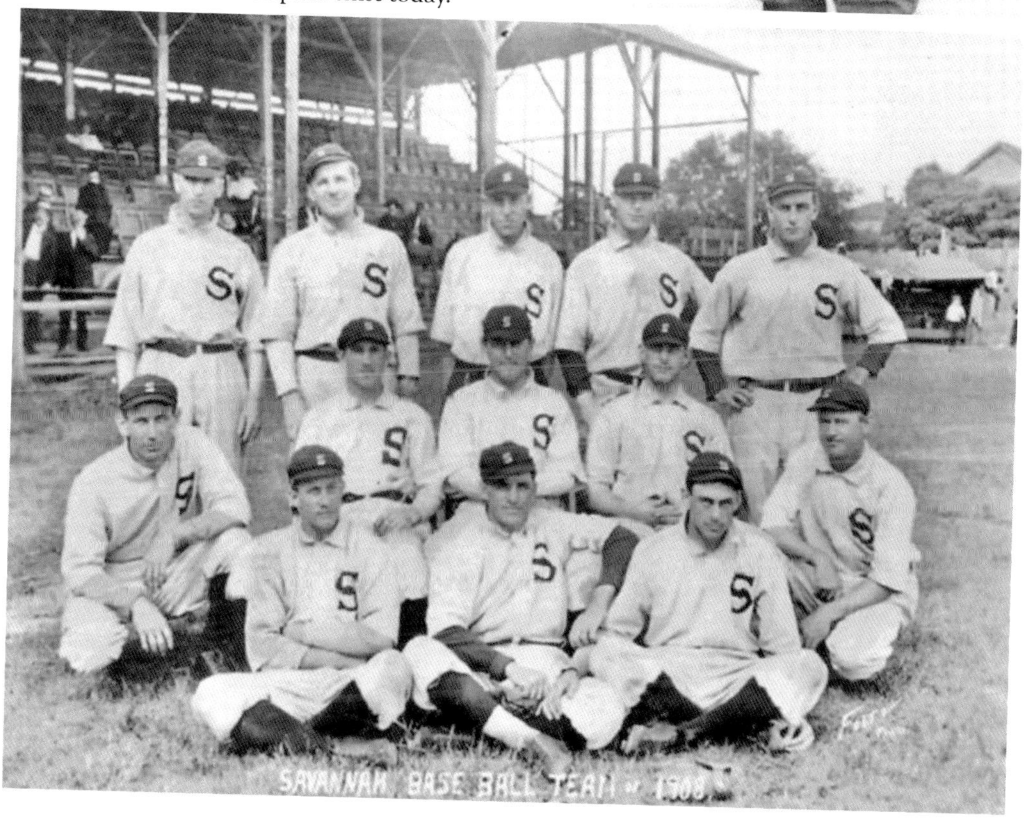

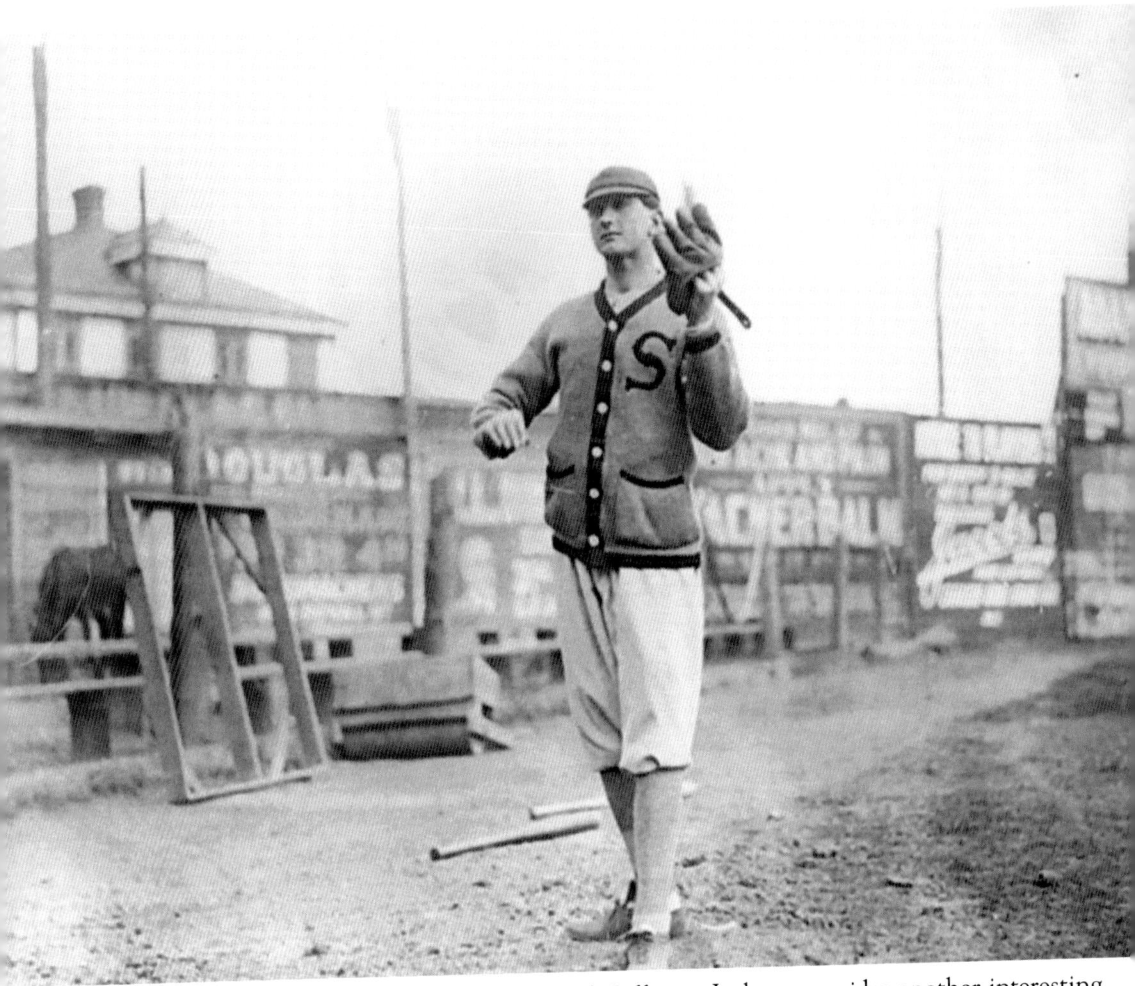

This image of a young outfielder named Joseph Jefferson Jackson provides another interesting look at the old Bolton St. Park. Joe Jackson began his career playing for local textile mill teams throughout his home state of South Carolina. After playing semiprofessional ball in 1905, Jackson eventually signed with Philadelphia A's owner Connie Mack. Playing his second year of professional baseball with the 1909 Savannah Indians, Jackson made quite a name for himself, leading the league with a .358 average. Despite his skills at the plate, his nickname "Shoeless" was almost as famous as his game. According to a legend, Jackson received his nickname when a pair of cleats created blisters on his feet during his days playing with the local mill teams. A spectator saw him running the bases in his stockings and called him a "shoeless son of a gun." The nickname stuck. (Courtesy of Mike Nola.)

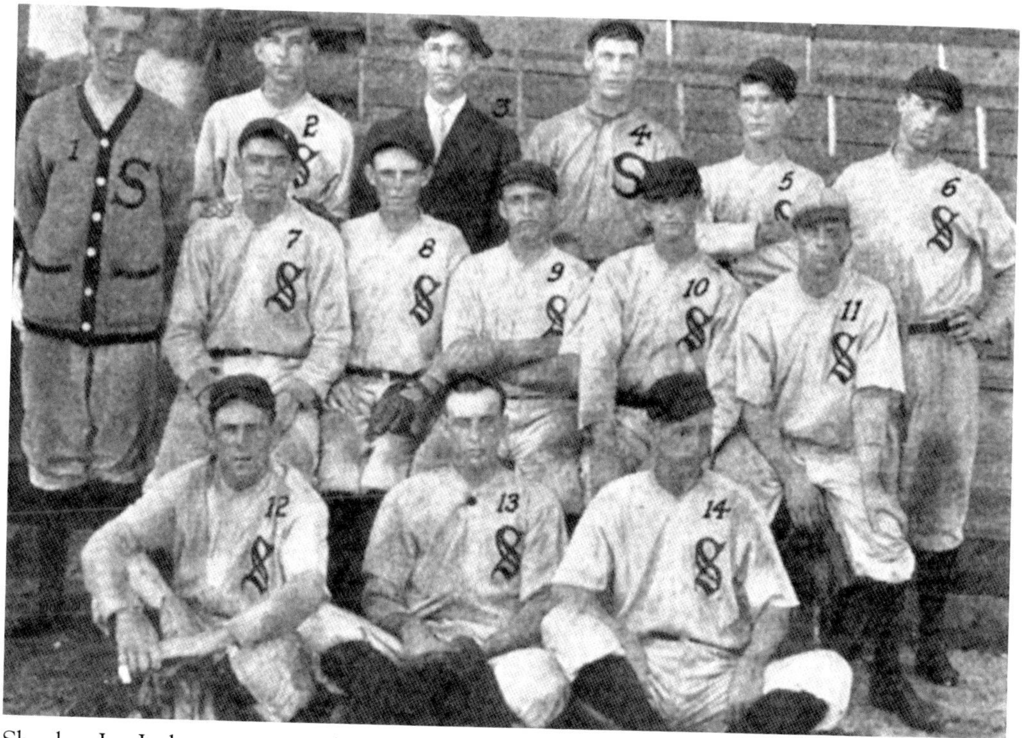


Shoeless Joe Jackson was considered by most to be the most talented player on the 1909 Savannah Indians, but he was not the only player who had major league experience. Six others played in the big leagues. Even with such a skilled group of men, the 1909 Indians could only muster a fourth place finish with a record of 60-61.

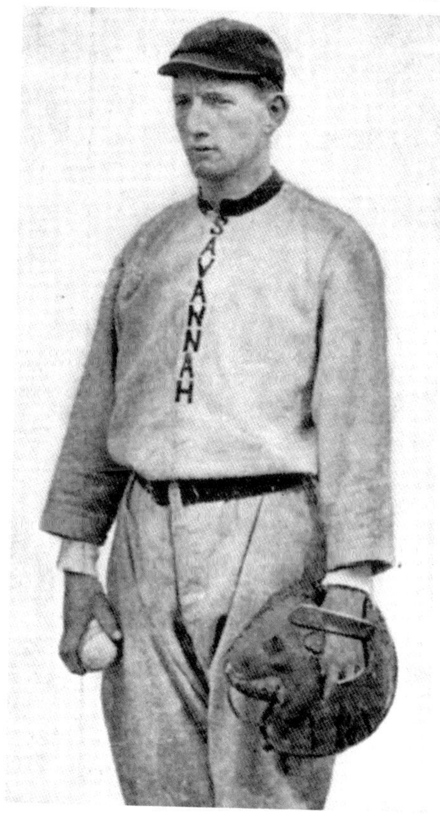


Andrew Petit spent seven seasons playing catcher throughout the minor leagues, two of them in Savannah. Playing alongside such talented guys as Jackson, Al Demaree, and Harry Kane, all future major leaguers, Pettit may have felt a little overwhelmed. A career .213 hitter, Pettit's best year came in 1908 at Shreveport, when he hit .271. (Courtesy of the Richard B. Russell Library for Political Research and Studies.)

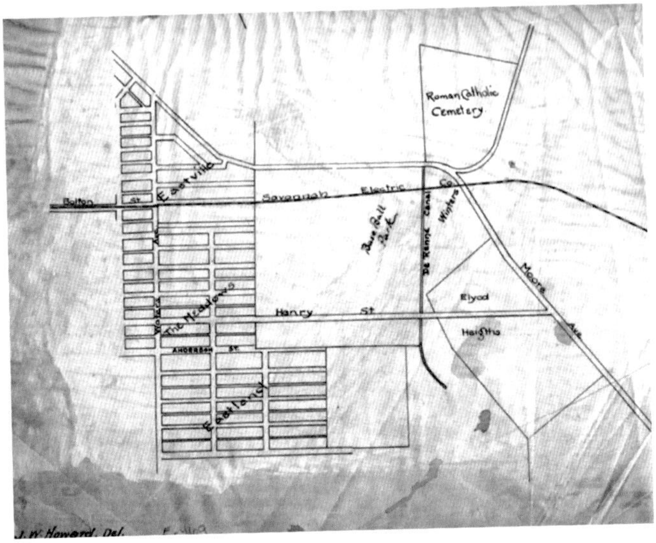


After a few years playing at the Bolton St. Park, professional baseball in Savannah moved to a new facility in 1910. Located near the intersection of Henry Street and Waters Avenue near the Roman Catholic Cemetery, the new Savannah Athletic Field hosted the Savannah Indians and Savannah Colts through the end of 1915. (Courtesy of the City of Savannah, Research Library, and Municipal Archives.)

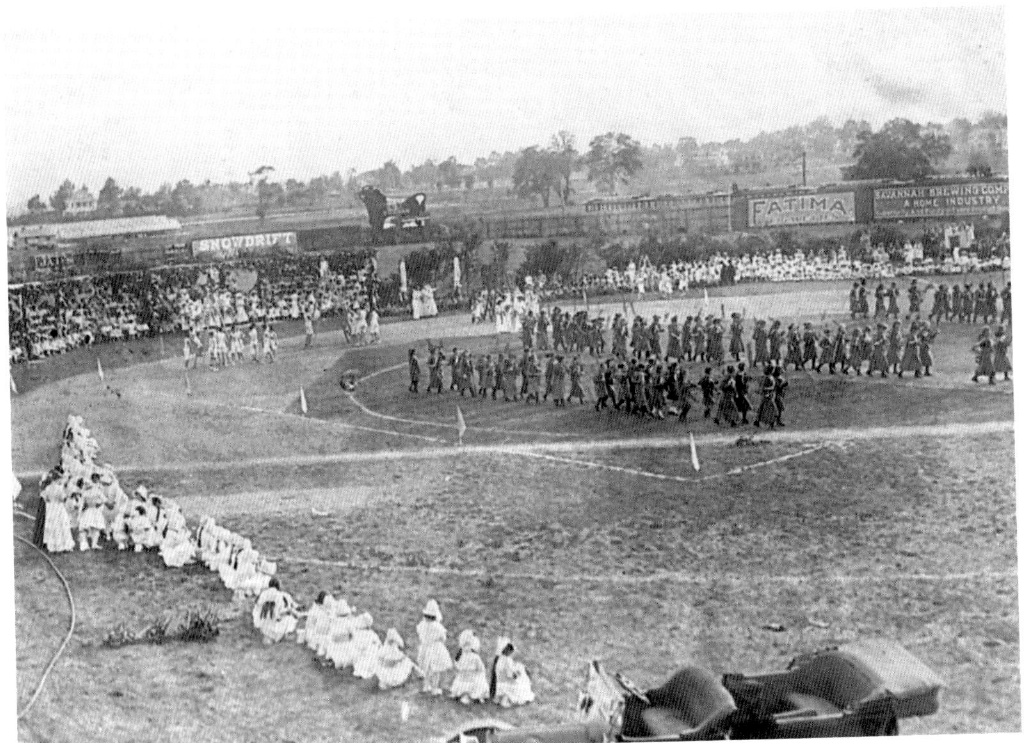


This photograph offers one of the best known views of the Savannah Athletic Field. Although this image does not show a baseball game in progress, the diamond is clearly visible. Covering the infield in the photograph is one of the earliest Girl Scout troops. The Savannah Athletic Field and other public venues hosted a variety of civic events. (Courtesy of the Juliet Gordon Low Birthplace.)

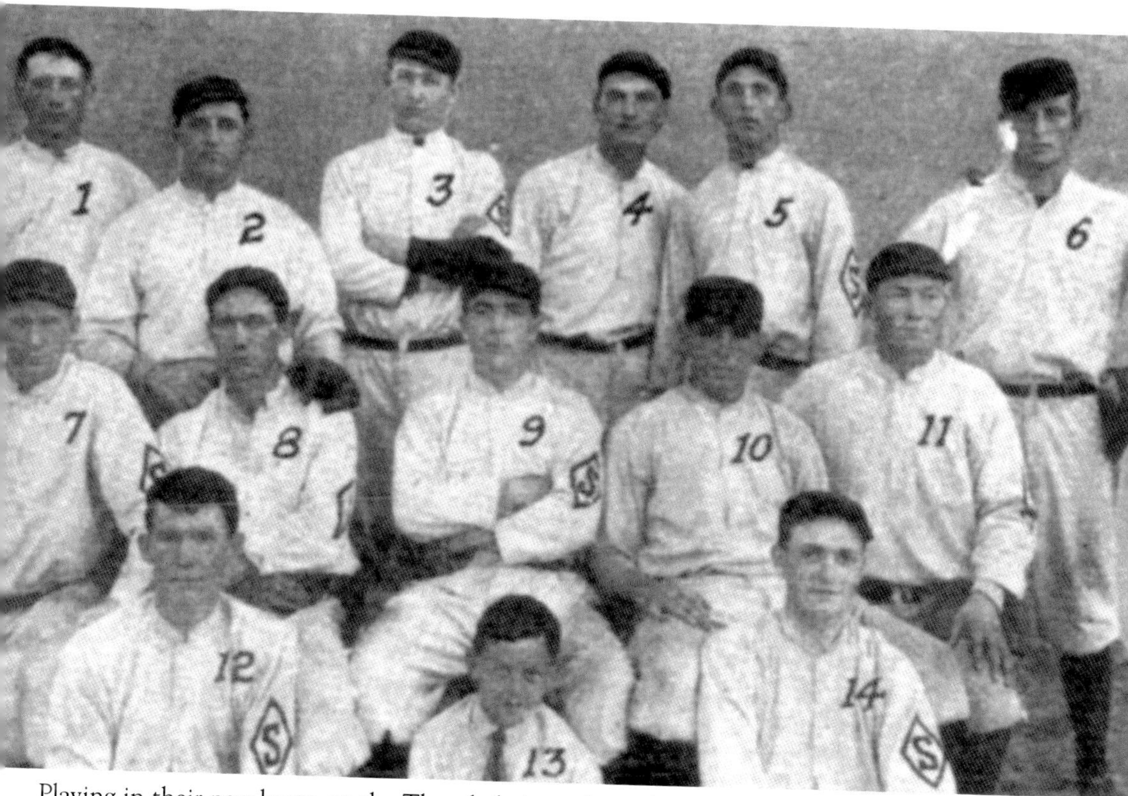


Playing in their new home on the Thunderbolt car line, the 1910 Savannah Indians began the year looking to improve on their fourth place finish in the South Atlantic League the previous year. With star player Joe Jackson now with the New Orleans Pelicans, longtime Savannah veteran and Ernie Howard became the Indians' leader at the plate, although hitting 80 points less than Jackson the previous year. The Indians of 1910 featured four players with major league talent: third baseman Mike Baltenti, outfielder and team manager George Magoon, pitcher John Martina, and first baseman George "Possum" Whitted. Compared to the previous season, the 1909 Savannah Indians improved one spot in their quest for their second Sally pennant, finishing the year in third place.

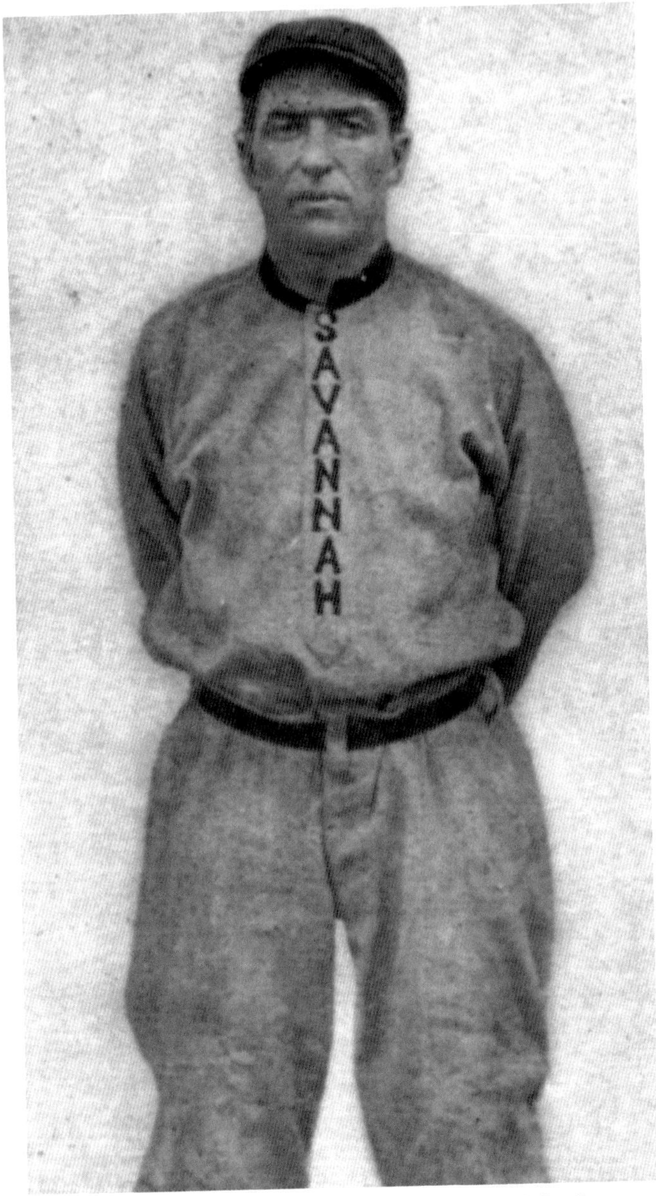


Nearing the end of his professional career, George Magoon joined the Savannah Indians in 1910 as a player and manager. Beginning his career in 1896 with Portland of the New England League, Magoon made his major league debut in 1898 with the Brooklyn Bridegrooms. After his big league career was over in 1903, Magoon returned to the minors. After stops in Indianapolis, Toronto, Des Moines, and Trenton, Magoon arrived in Savannah. With his five years in the major leagues and 10 years of experience playing minor league ball, Magoon was a good fit in Savannah as he skippered the Indians. Serving as an outfielder with the club, he collected 66 hits in the 97 games he played in. Even though he guided the Indians to a third place finish, he was replaced the following year as manager. Magoon managed one more year in 1913 and then retired from baseball. (Courtesy of the Richard B. Russell Library for Political Research and Studies.)

One of the four players for the 1910 Indians who played in the majors was right hand pitcher John "Oyster Joe" Martina. With the Indians for only one year, Martina won 14 games for Savannah. Although he only spent one year in the majors with the 1924 Washington Senators, Oyster Joe enjoyed a long professional career, playing 21 seasons of baseball. (Courtesy of the Richard B. Russell Library for Political Research and Studies.)

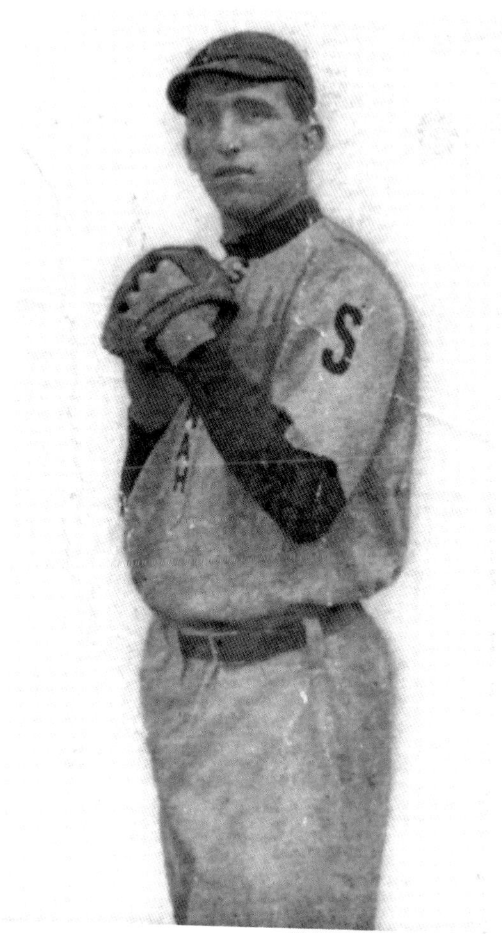

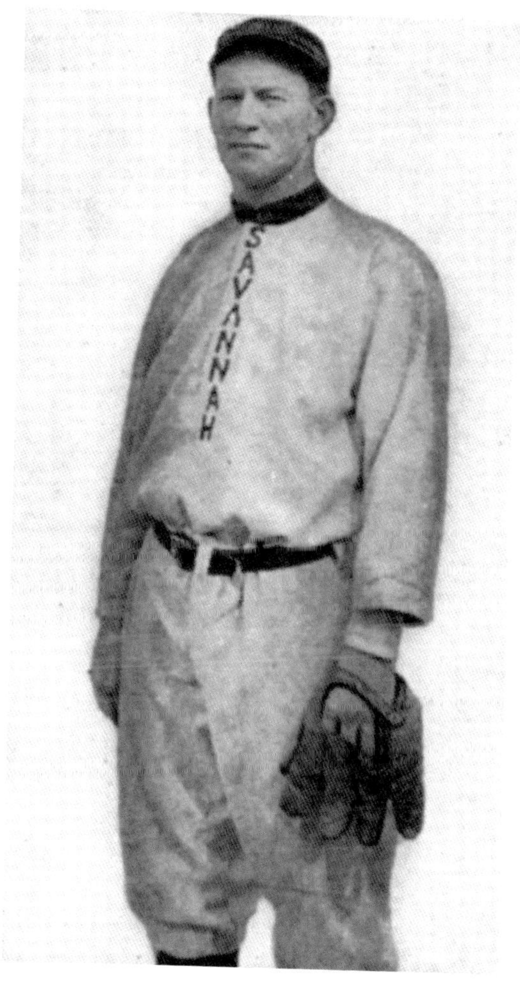

Mike Balenti began his professional career with the 1910 Savannah Indians at the age of 23. Through a professional career stretching from 1910 to 1917, Balenti spent two years in the majors. He disappeared from baseball after the 1917 season, only to resurface eight years later as a player and manager for the Blackwell Glassers. (Courtesy of the Richard B. Russell Library for Political Research and Studies.)

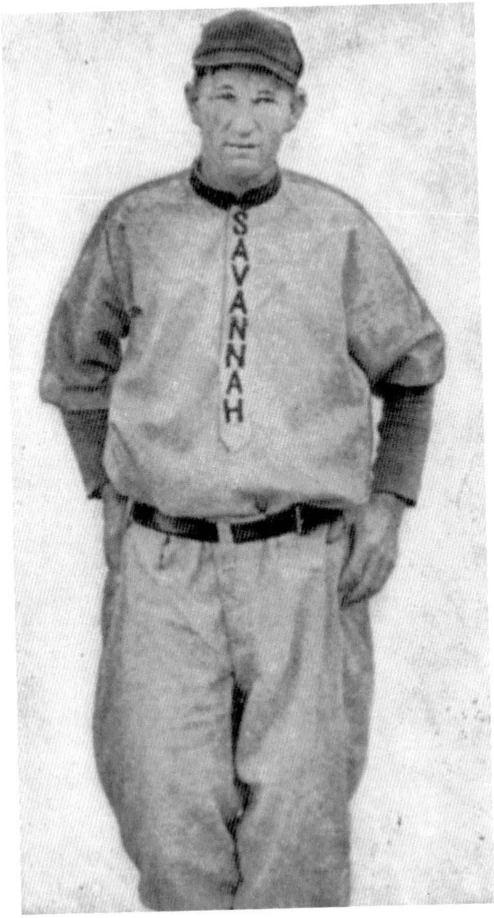

Eddie "Rip" Reagan was another career minor league player who stopped by Savannah for part of the 1910 season. Appearing in 101 games, Reagan hit for a paltry .189 average. Playing mostly shortstop and some second base, Reagan's closest step toward the majors was his stint in class A New Orleans at the end of the 1910 season. (Courtesy of the Richard B. Russell Library for Political Research and Studies.)

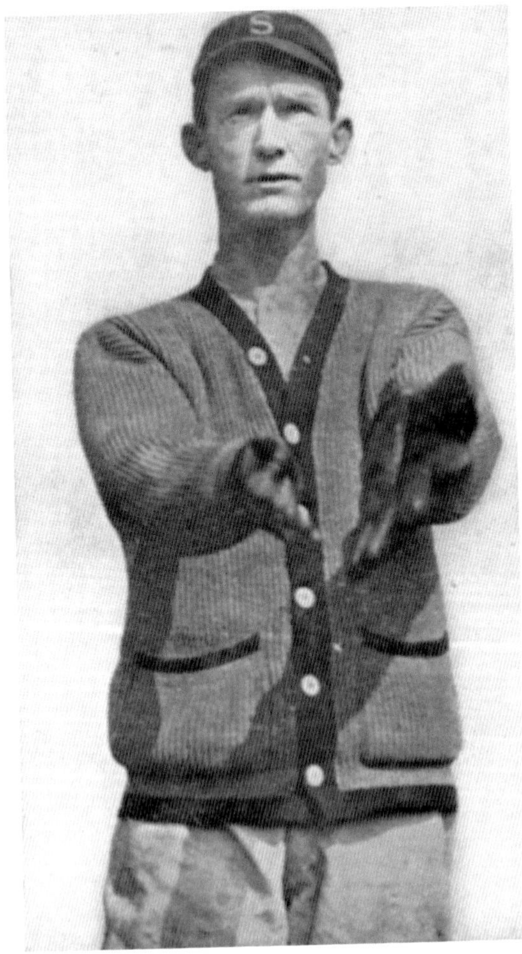

In a wonderful year that saw the defending World Series champion Philadelphia Athletics return to Savannah for training in the spring and Savannah native Nicholas Corish elected as South Atlantic League president, 1911 was somewhat of a disappointment for the Savannah Indians. Ending the year in 6th place, the Indians were led by "Big" Red Murch, who was playing his third and final year in Savannah. (The Richard B. Russell Library for Political Research and Studies.)

Pres. William Howard Taft visited Savannah in May 1912 as the keynote speaker at the Hibernian Society banquet, which was postponed from St. Patrick's Day in his honor. While in town, Taft attended the second game of a doubleheader along with Gov. Joe Brown, Judge Peter W. Meldrini, Hibernian president Shelby Myrick, and other dignitaries. Although the Indians lost the game in Taft's presence, they rebounded to win 66 games that season, finishing in second place.

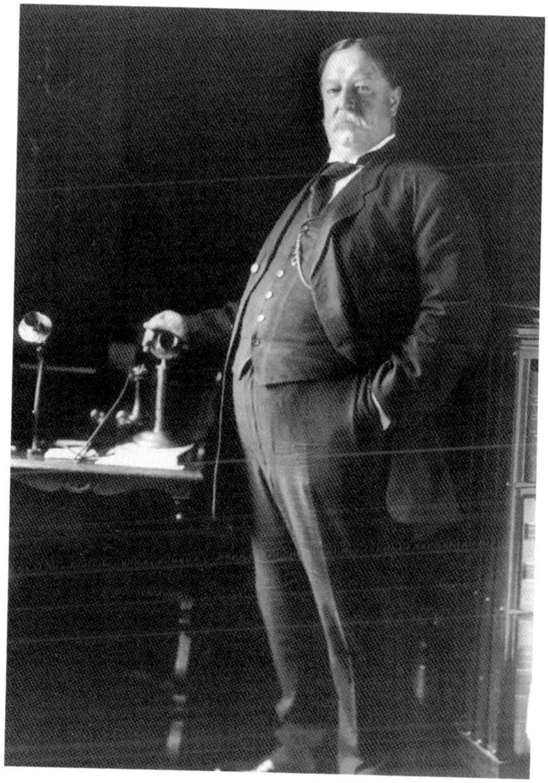

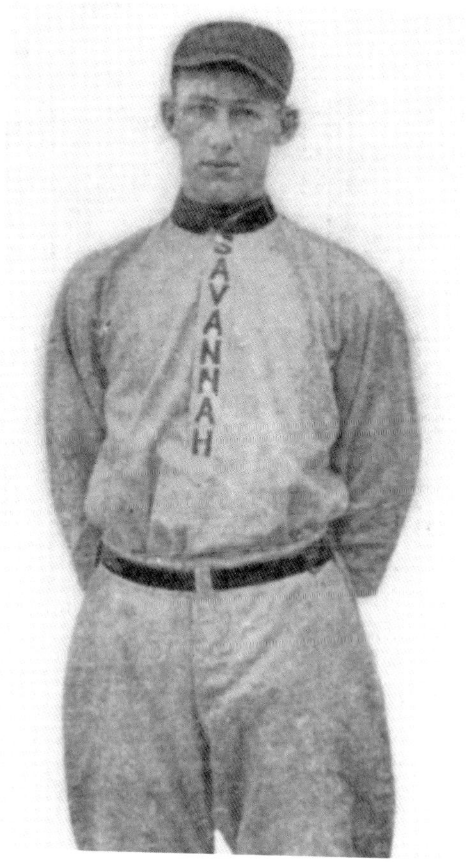


Leading the 1912 Indians, Al Shulz won 25 of the 43 games that he appeared in. Three of his six seasons spent in the minor leagues were with the Savannah Indians. Among his five seasons in the major leagues, three were with the New York Yankees. After his big league career was spent, Shulz played out his professional career with the Toledo Iron Men and the AA Milwaukee Brewers. (Courtesy of the Richard B. Russell Library for Political Research and Studies.)

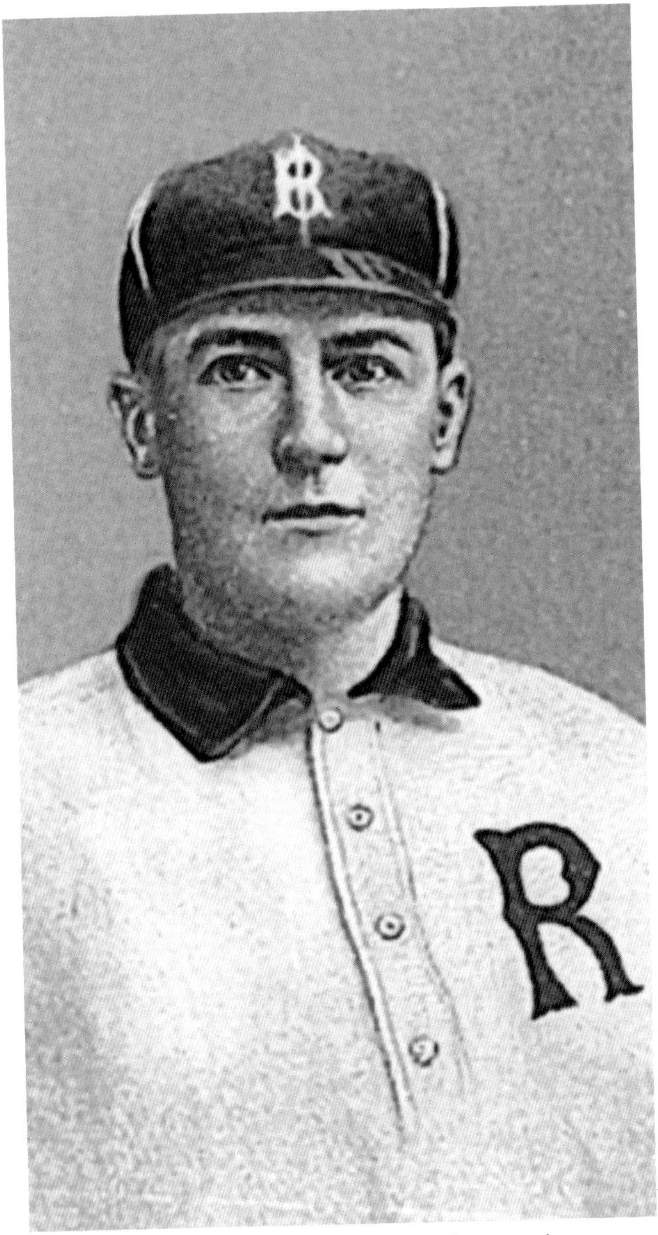

The teams under the tenure of Perry Hamilton Lipe as player and manager for the Savannah Indians and after 1912 the Savannah Colts are remembered as the pinnacle of early Savannah professional baseball. Although remembered for committing multiple errors while playing third base while President Taft was in attendance, Lipe is mostly known for developing a winning ball club in Savannah. Based on his team building efforts, the "Lipesmen" of 1913 won both halves of the Sally League season and were awarded their second pennant based on their 78 win season. Lipe began his professional career when he was 26 years old for the Memphis Egyptians. After bouncing around the minor leagues throughout the south, including stops in Greenville, Macon, and Richmond, Lipe arrived in Savannah for the first of his four seasons.

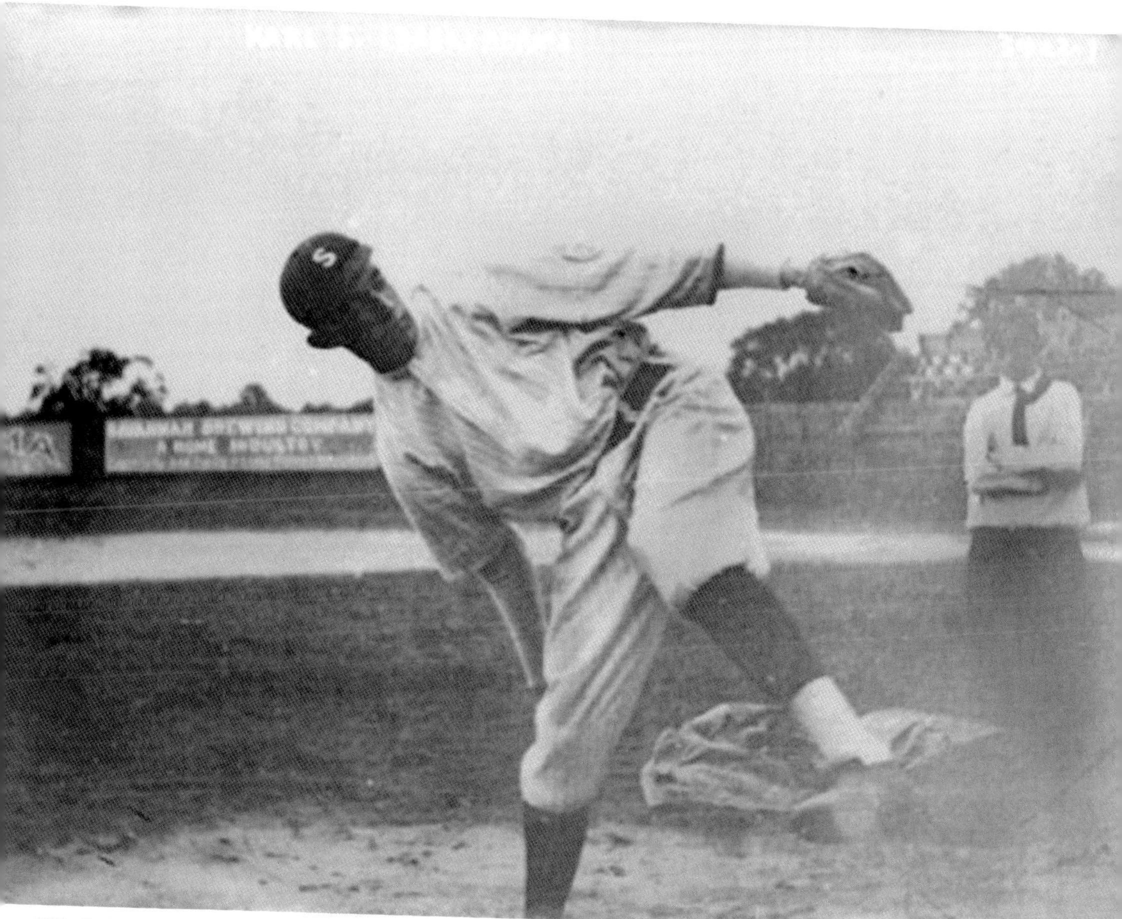

While Perry Lipe was the leader of the team, 23-year-old right hander Karl Adams helped lead the pitching staff of the 1913 Colts toward their second championship. Adams won 20 of 33 games for Savannah in his first year of professional baseball. After playing in 26 games for the Indianapolis Indians, he was promoted to the major leagues in 1914. Only pitching in four games for the Cincinnati Reds, he did not record any wins or losses, yet earned an ERA of 9.00. The following year playing for the Chicago Cubs, Adams appeared in 26 games. Earning a record of one win and nine losses, Adams's big league career came to a close. He returned to the minors, where he played six more seasons. Unique to this photograph of Adams is the view it offers of the Savannah Athletic Field.

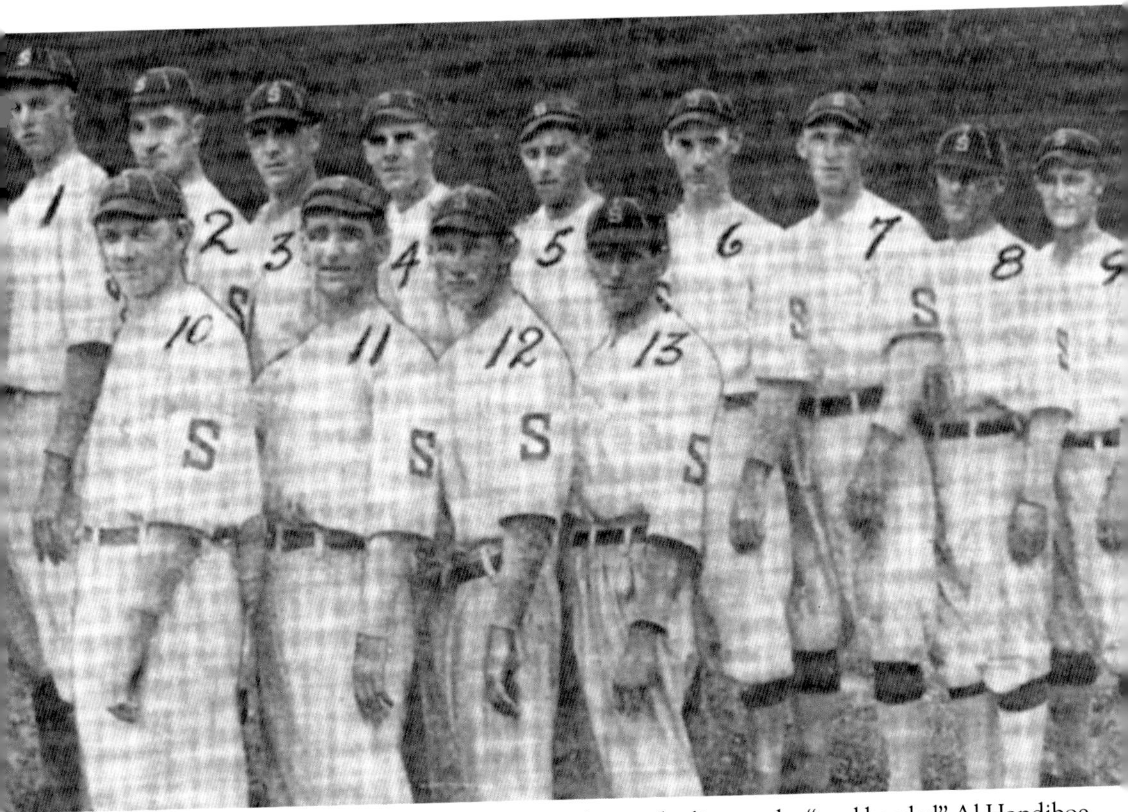


Old timers remembered this team well. Batting first in the lineup, the "cool headed" Al Handiboe would usually draw a walk or hit a single. Lipe would hit next and sacrifice himself to move Handiboe to second. Sammy Mayer then would hit a hard single or double that advanced Handiboe to third. According to memory, the big "Red" Gust would then either hit a triple or home run, scoring himself, Handiboe, and Mayer. If he did not produce the RBIs, the books were wrong. While this is certainly legend, the 1914 Savannah Colts won the first half of the season and ended up clinching their third Sally League title over the Albany Babies, four games to one in the playoffs. The Savannah club's success, however, soon helped bring about their demise; fans were becoming accustomed to the local club winning so much that attendance was beginning to decline.

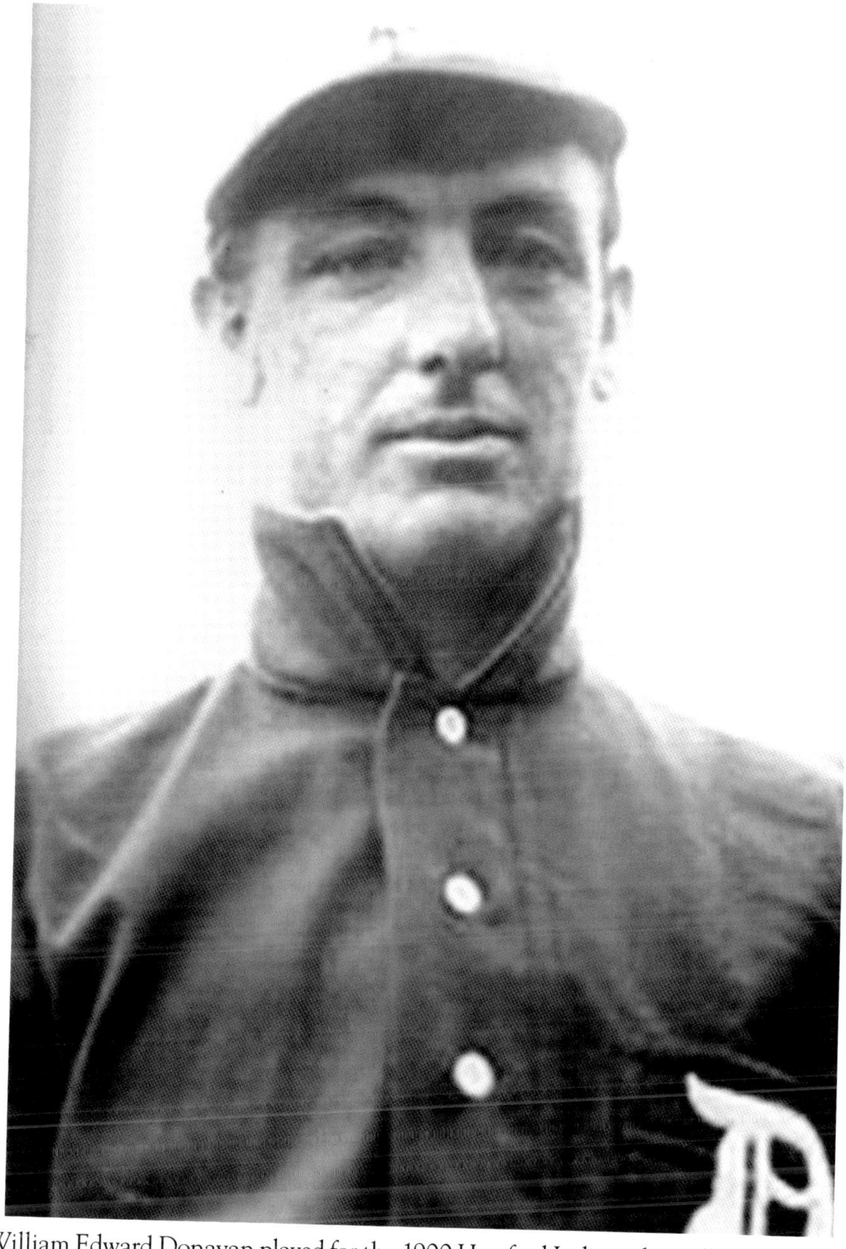

When William Edward Donavan played for the 1900 Hartford Indians, he walked nine consecutive batters and earned himself a new nickname. "Wild" Bill Donovan played 18 seasons in the major leagues and spent three years as the New York Yankees manager. Despite his lack of control on the mound, he won a stellar 186 games as a pitcher with the Washington, Brooklyn, Detroit, and New York Yankee teams. He also led the National League with 25 wins in 1901 and led the American League in complete games with 34 wins in 1903. In fact, he ranks number 50 on the major league all-time complete games list. While he was a manager he brought his 1915 Yankees to Savannah to train in the spring for the upcoming season. Donovan spent three years as the head of the Yankees and one year managing the Philadelphia Phillies.

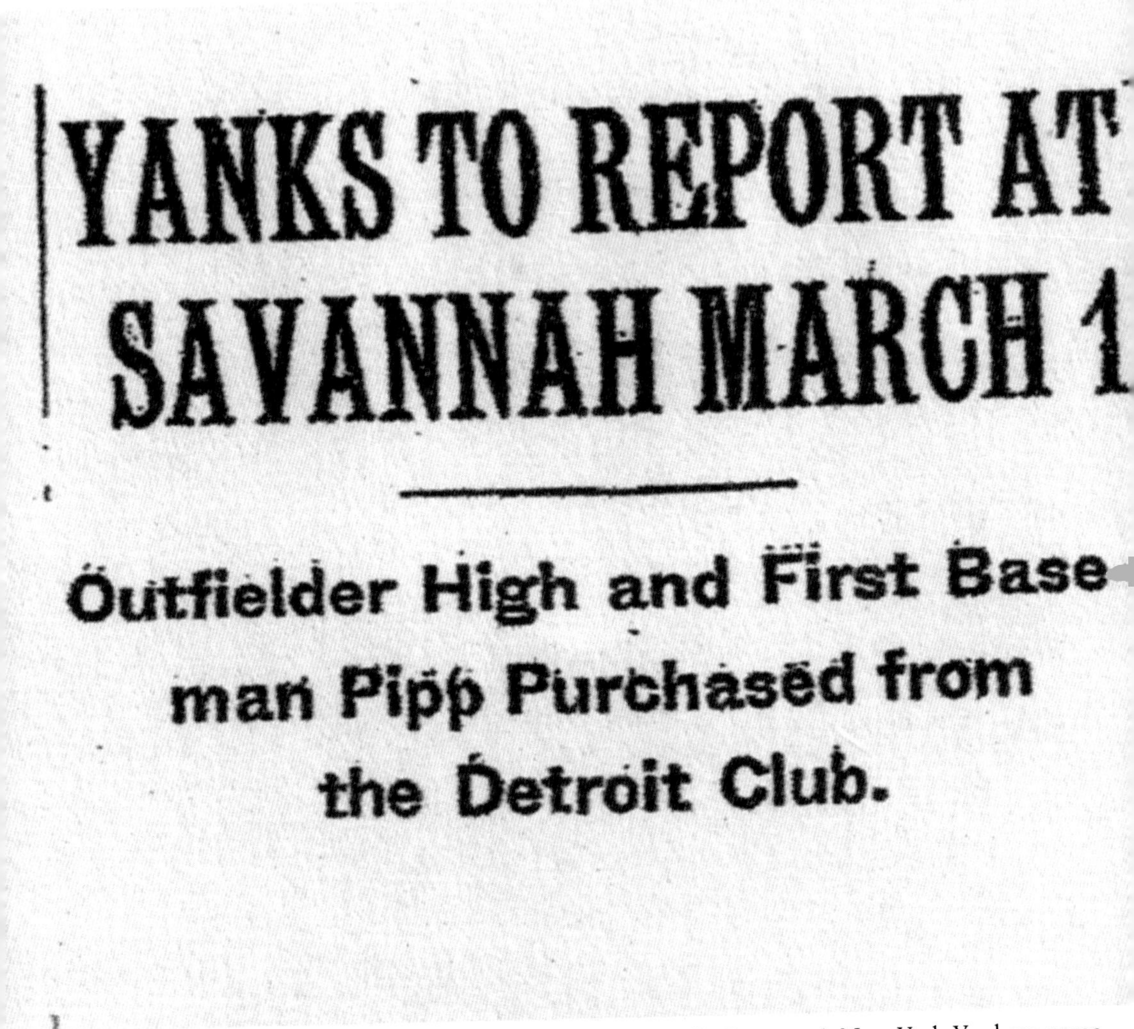

YANKS TO REPORT AT SAVANNAH MARCH 1

Outfielder High and First Baseman Pipp Purchased from the Detroit Club.

The baseball season of 1915 began in high fashion as Billy Donovan's New York Yankees came to Savannah for their spring practice. The Yanks were coming off a disappointing 1914 season where they finished in seventh place in the American League. The year 1915 would not be much better for Donavan's club. Although they improved to a fifth place standing, they finished a disappointing 32.5 games behind first place in the American League. Notable about this image, however, is the new first baseman they acquired. From 1915 through 1925, Wally Pipp was a solid player for the Yankees. As the American League home run champion in 1916 and 1917, Pipp also won a World Series with the Yankees in 1923. He also helped groom a young first baseman named Lou Gherig. Enjoying a solid career, Pipp is best known as the player Gherig replaced in the lineup for the game on June 2, 1925. That game was the first of Gherig's 2,170 consecutive games played. (Courtesy of *The New York Times.*)

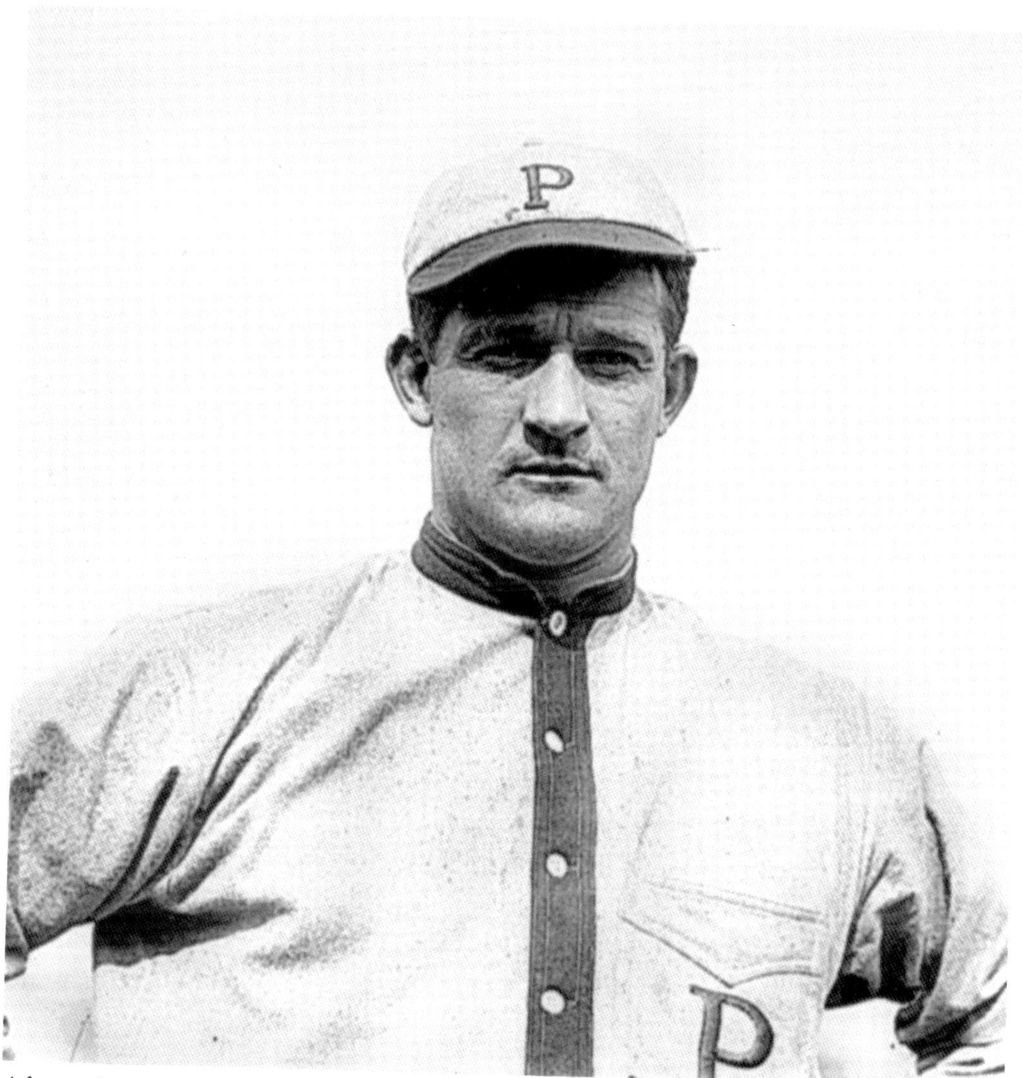

After eight seasons of playing professional baseball, right handed pitcher Harry Camnitz was wrapping up the final year of his professional career in Savannah for the Savannah Colts in 1915. With stops in the Ohio-Pennsylvania League, Eastern League, Ohio State League, and South Atlantic League, Camnitz acquired a record of 99 wins and 88 losses. After spending the 1909 and 1911 seasons playing in the majors, Camnitz provided 12 wins and losses for Savannah. The 30-year-old Camnitz and the 1915 Savannah Colts only won 34 games during the shortened season while losing 52 contests. Not only did his career come to a close after the 1915 season ended, so did professional baseball in Savannah. Poor attendance and the onset of World War I forced the Savannah franchise to give up its spot in the South Atlantic League.

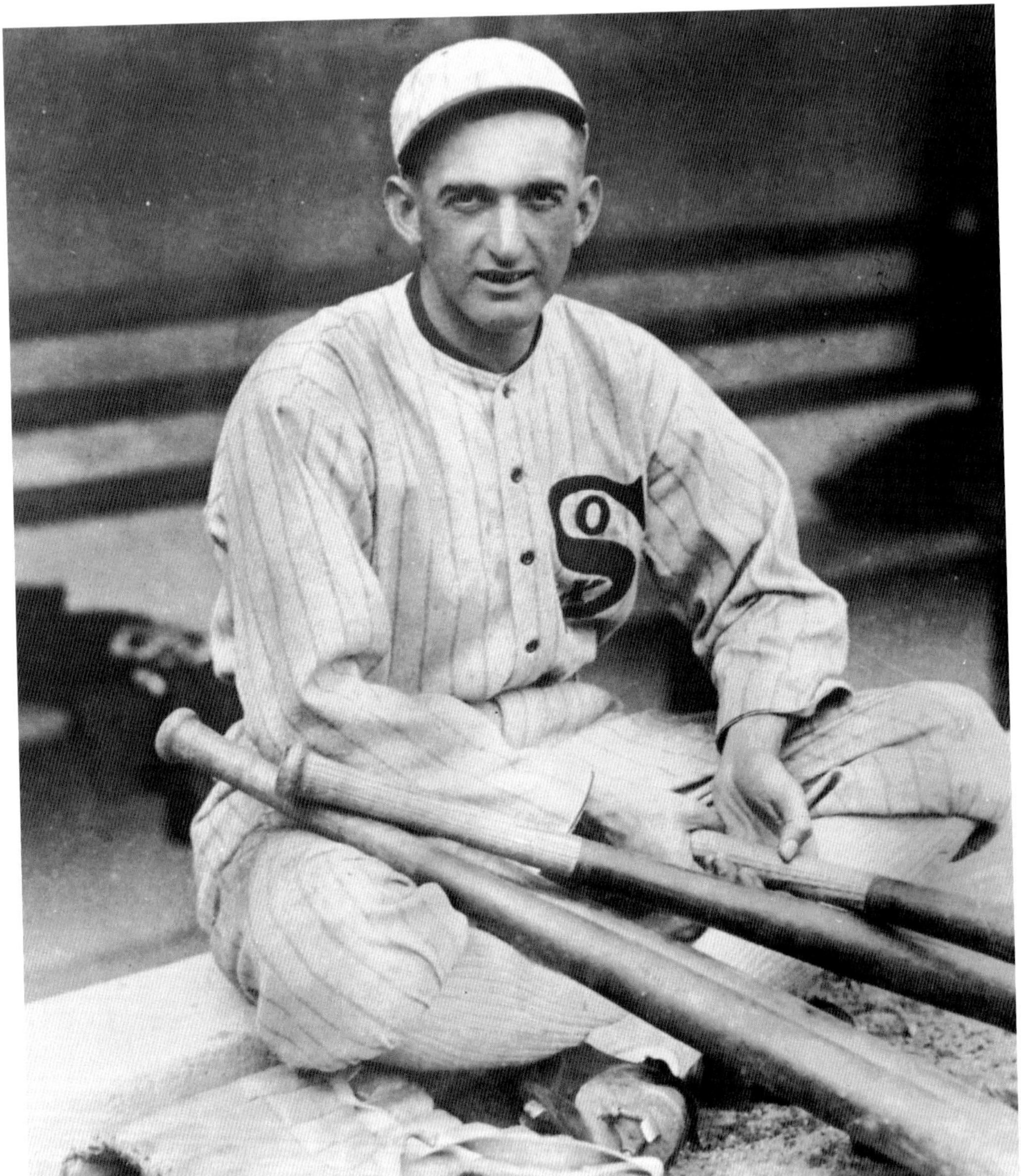

Adding to the displeasure of Savannah's baseball fans following the loss of a professional team, the dramatic fall of the greatest player who had ever played for a Savannah club seemed to rub salt in the wounds. Shoeless Joe Jackson advanced from Savannah to play in the major leagues for the Cleveland Naps and later the Chicago White Sox. His batting average of .408 as a rookie for the 1911 Naps stands as a record today. His World Series ring from 1917 and his career average of .356 make him Hall of Fame worthy. It is his alleged involvement in the 1919 Chicago Black Sox scandal, however, that furthered the disappointment of Savannah's baseball fans. Despite an acquittal and evidence of his innocence, Jackson was banned from professional baseball after the 1920 season. In 1922, he opened a dry cleaning business in Savannah.

# 2

# THE GOLDEN AGE

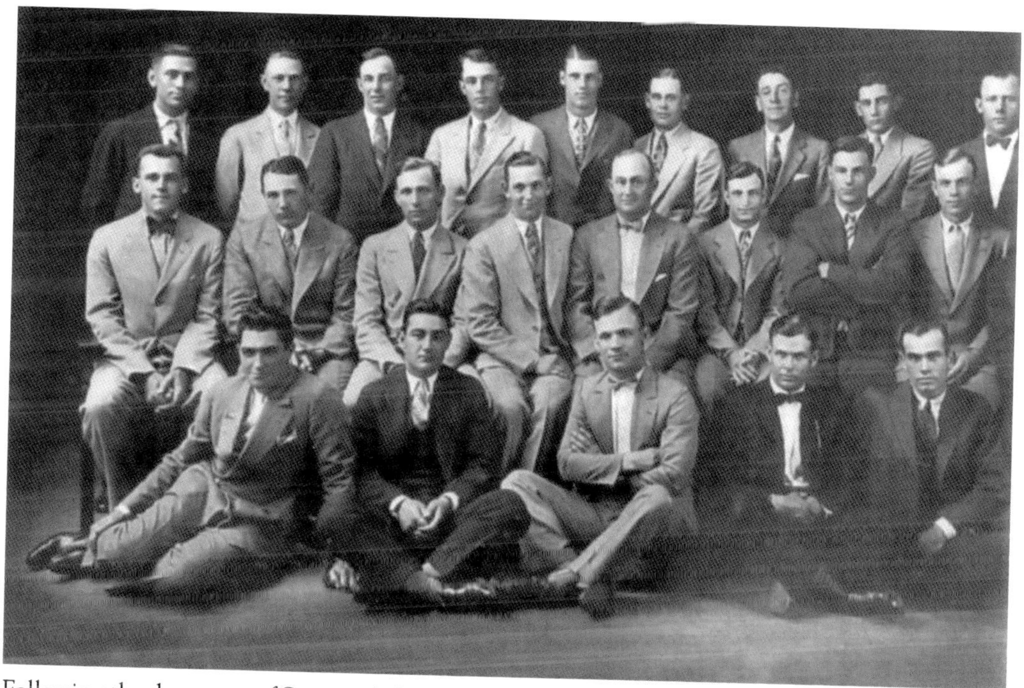

Following the departure of Savannah from the South Atlantic League in 1915 and the subsequent folding of the league in 1917, professional baseball returned to Savannah in 1923 when the Washington Senators trained in Savannah followed by the Detroit Tigers (pictured here) in 1924. Managed by the aging Ty Cobb who returned to Savannah, the 1924 Tigers finished third in the American League with a record of 86 wins and 68 losses. While Savannah was still several years from receiving another professional team, Detroit's spring training in Savannah was shared by the Rochester Tribe, New York Yankees, and St. Louis Cardinals. Although the Detroit club is pictured above, the arrival of the Yankees garnered the most interest throughout the Savannah area. Their plan to train in Savannah was viewed as the leading sporting event of the year.

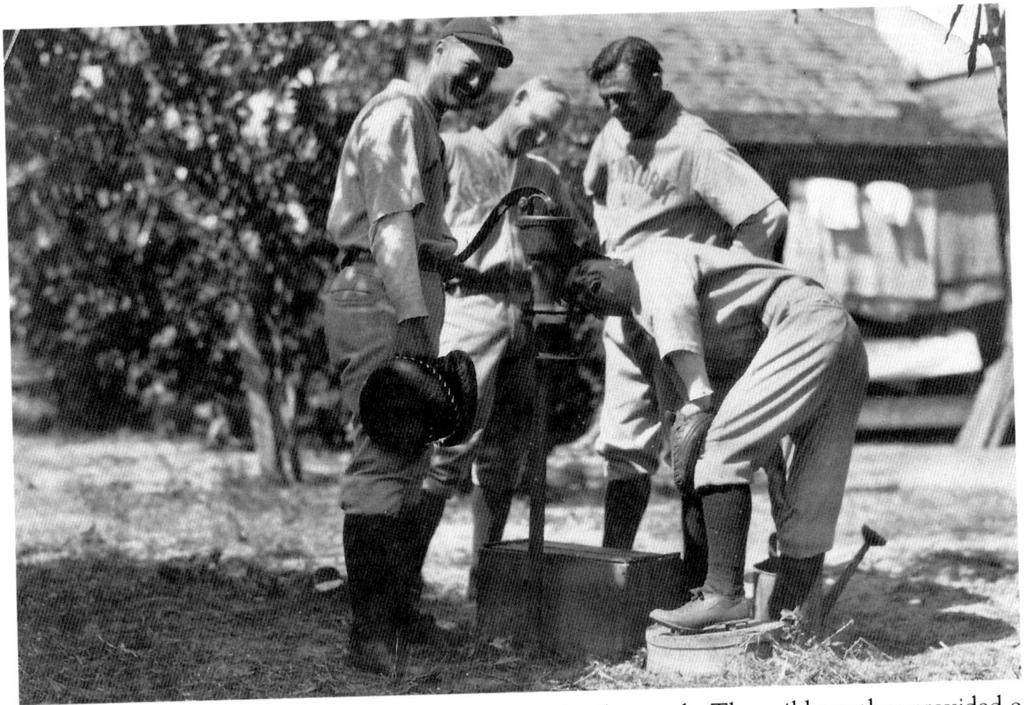

Players from northern cities enjoyed their training in the south. The mild weather provided a pleasant experience for the players. Although much of their time was spent preparing for the upcoming season, players often had down time. Cities in the south such as Savannah provided a lot of recreation opportunities. The beach, golf courses, and bowling allies were among the popular choices. These photographs show members of the 1924 New York Yankees fooling around on a farm. The player looking at the camera in the above photograph was a young catcher in his rookie year with the Yankees. Martin "Chick" Autry only spent one year with the Yankees, with stops in Cleveland and Chicago following. (Both, courtesy of Tom Autry.)

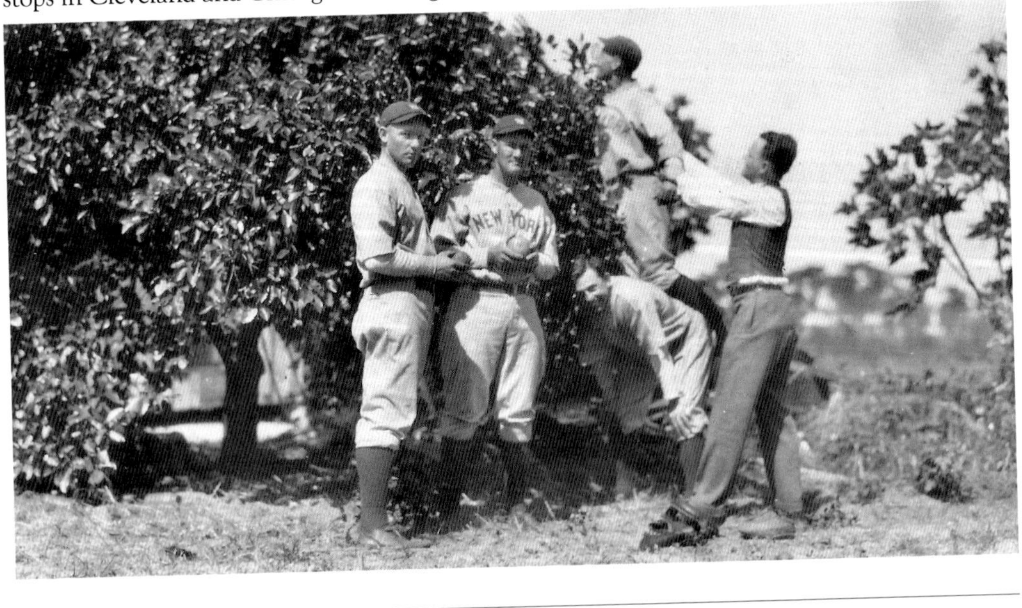

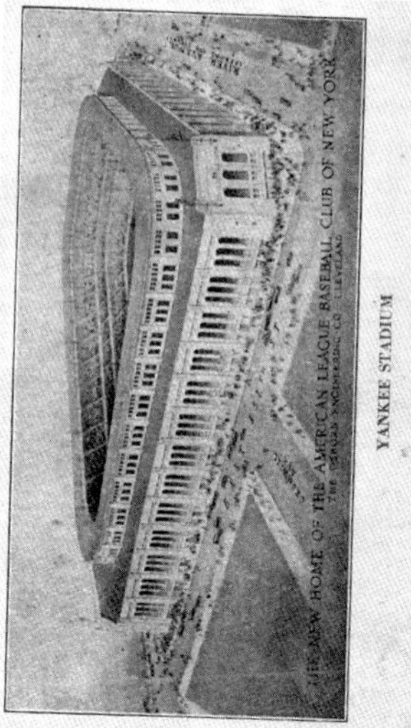


ITINERARY

New York Yankees

SPRING EXHIBITION TOUR

1925

After finishing in second place behind the Washington Senators in the American League in 1924, one year after winning the World Series in 1923, the 1925 Yanks were looking to get back to their championship ways. This schedule and itinerary laid out the plans for the Yankees' return trip south for spring training. Savannah continued to be a popular destination and was to be their first stop, with an exhibition game against the Rochester Tribe. Despite their training in Savannah and around the South, the Yankees regressed, only winning 69 games and finishing in seventh place. (Both, courtesy of Tom Autry.)

SCHEDULE OF GAMES

| | | | | | |
|---|---|---|---|---|---|
| At Savannah, Ga. | March | 27th | with | Rochester | Club |
| " Jacksonville, Fla. | " | 28th | " | Brooklyn | " |
| " Montgomery, Ala. | " | 29th | " | " | " |
| " Birmingham, Ala. | " | 30th | " | " | " |
| " " | " | 31st | " | " | " |
| " Nashville, Tenn. | April | 1st | " | " | " |
| " " | " | 2nd | " | " | " |
| " Atlanta, Ga. | " | 3rd | " | " | " |
| " " | " | 4th | " | " | " |
| " Chattanooga, Tenn. | " | 5th | " | " | " |
| " Knoxville, Tenn. | " | 6th | " | " | " |
| " Asheville, N. C. | " | 7th | " | " | " |
| " Greenville, S. C. | " | 8th | " | " | " |
| " Charlotte, N. C. | " | 9th | " | " | " |
| " Richmond, Va. | " | 10th | " | " | " |
| " Brooklyn, N. Y. | " | 11th | " | " | " |
| " " | | 12th | " | " | " |

In addition to the above schedule the Yankees will also play eight games in St. Petersburg. Five with the Boston Braves and one each with the Cincinnati, Brooklyn and Philadelphia National League Clubs.

BAGGAGE

All personal trunks will be sent direct to New York from St. Petersburg. They must be packed and ready to ship by noon on Wednesday, March 25th.

HOTELS

| | | | |
|---|---|---|---|
| At St. Petersburg, Fla. | The | Hotel | Princess Martha |
| " Savannah, Ga. | " | " | Savannah |
| " Jacksonville, Fla. | " | " | Seminole |
| " Montgomery, Ala. | " | " | Exchange |
| " Birmingham, Ala. | " | " | Tutwiler |
| " Nashville, Tenn. | " | " | Hermitage |
| " Atlanta, Ga. | " | " | Atlanta-Biltmore |
| " Chattanooga, Tenn. | " | " | Patten |
| " Knoxville, Tenn. | " | " | Farragut |
| " Asheville, N. C. | " | " | Battery Park |
| " Greenville, S. C. | " | " | Imperial |
| " Charlotte, N. C. | " | " | Charlotte |
| " Richmond, Va. | " | " | Murphy |
| " New York, N. Y. | " | " | Alamac |

The Princess Martha Hotel at St. Petersburg is conducted on the American plan and no bills excepting for laundry shall be charged to the Ball Club.

MEALS

Cash will be advanced for all meals on the trains and in the different towns on the trip North. No accounts of any kind to be charged on this trip.

TRAINS

☞ See Club Bulletins in the hotel lobby in each town for the time of arrival and departure of trains.

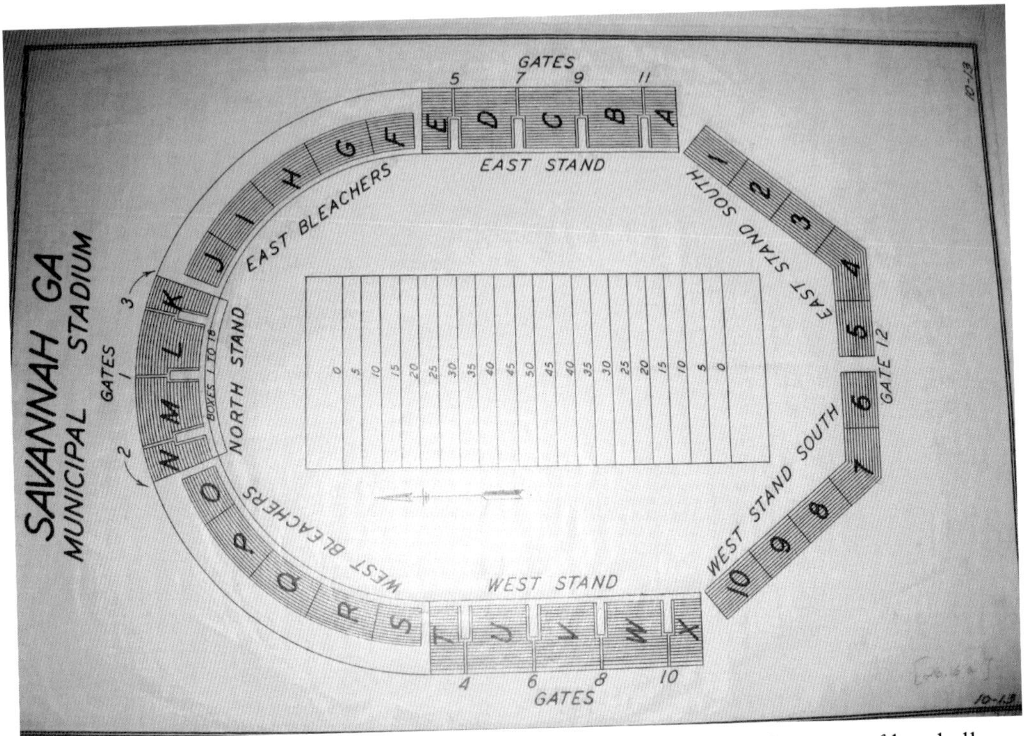


Although Savannah was still without a professional team of its own, the sport of baseball was continuing to grow in popularity. Gaining on baseball was the rise of football. Savannah leaders felt the city needed an adequate stadium that could accommodate both sports. Choosing Daffin Park as the site, construction began on the new project in 1925. By the spring of 1926, the $100,000 stadium was ready to welcome the return of the Savannah Indians. Playing in the Southeastern League, the Indians finished in sixth place. (Courtesy of the City of Savannah, Research Library, and Municipal Archives.)

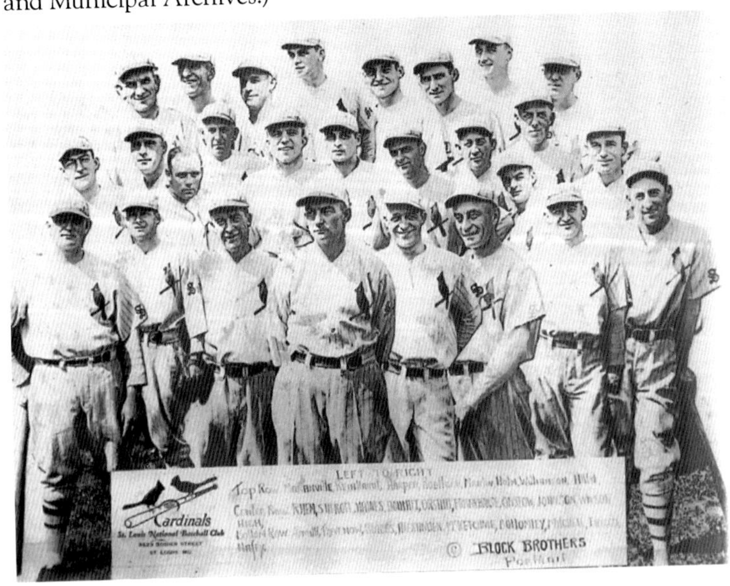


In 1927, the 15,000 fans who could fit into the new Municipal Stadium were treated to a rematch of the 1926 World Series. Led by manager Rogers Hornsby and MVP Bob O'Farrell, the World Series champion St. Louis Cardinals stopped by Savannah to play the defending American League champion New York Yankees.

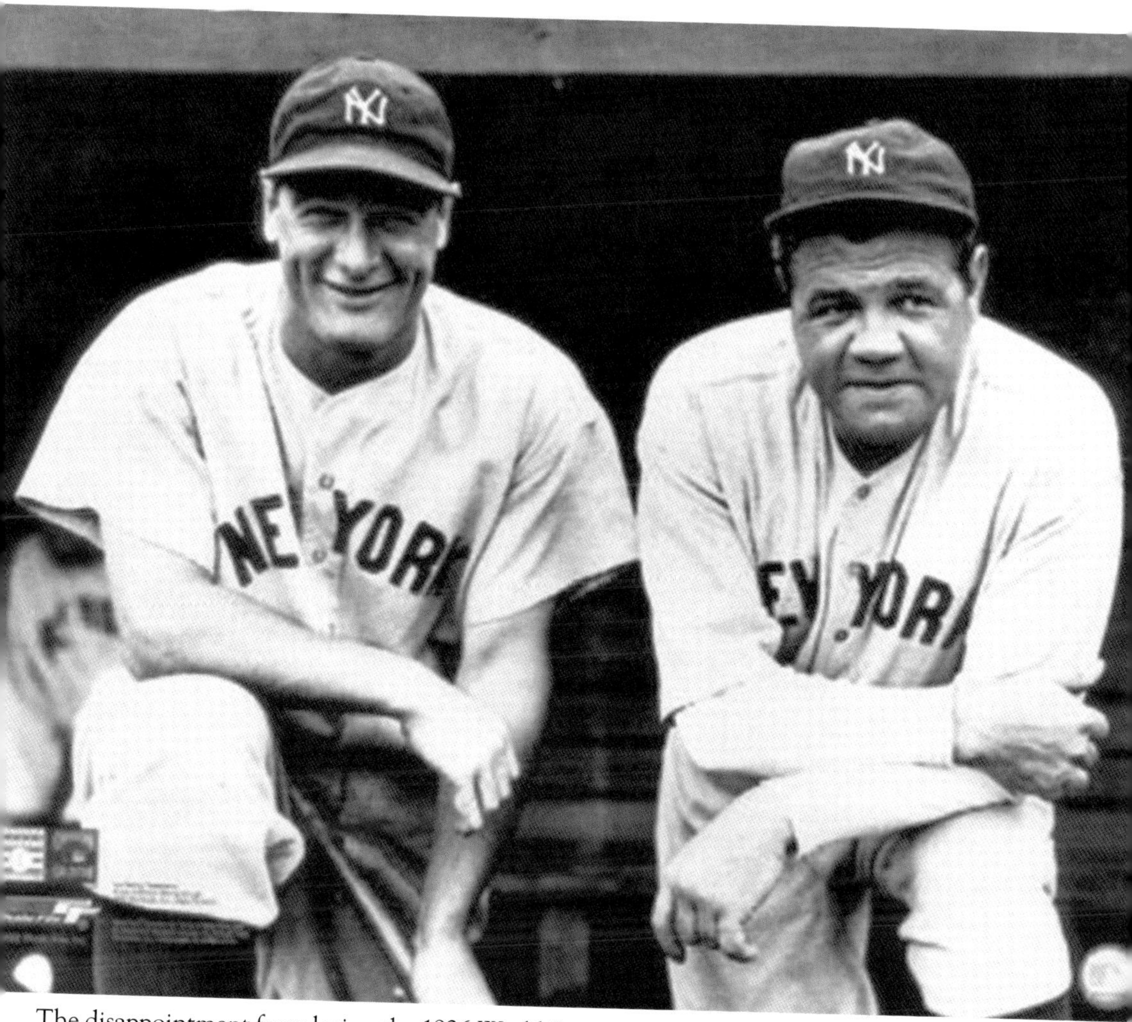


The disappointment from losing the 1926 World Series in the ninth inning of the seventh game carried over for the Yankees in the spring of 1927. Looking to redeem themselves, the 1927 Yankees traveled to St. Petersburg in Florida to train for the upcoming season. Playing their way back north to begin the year, the Yankees stopped over in Savannah once again for an exhibition game. With the *Savannah Morning News* providing plenty of coverage, Savannah baseball fans turned out in plenty to watch the game. In front of an enthusiastic crowd at Municipal Stadium, Babe Ruth and Lou Gherig led the Yankees once again, yet lost 20-10 to the St. Louis Cardinals. While the crowd enjoyed the preseason game, the upcoming Savannah Indians season would not be as satisfying for the Savannah crowd. The Indians finished in fifth place in 1927.

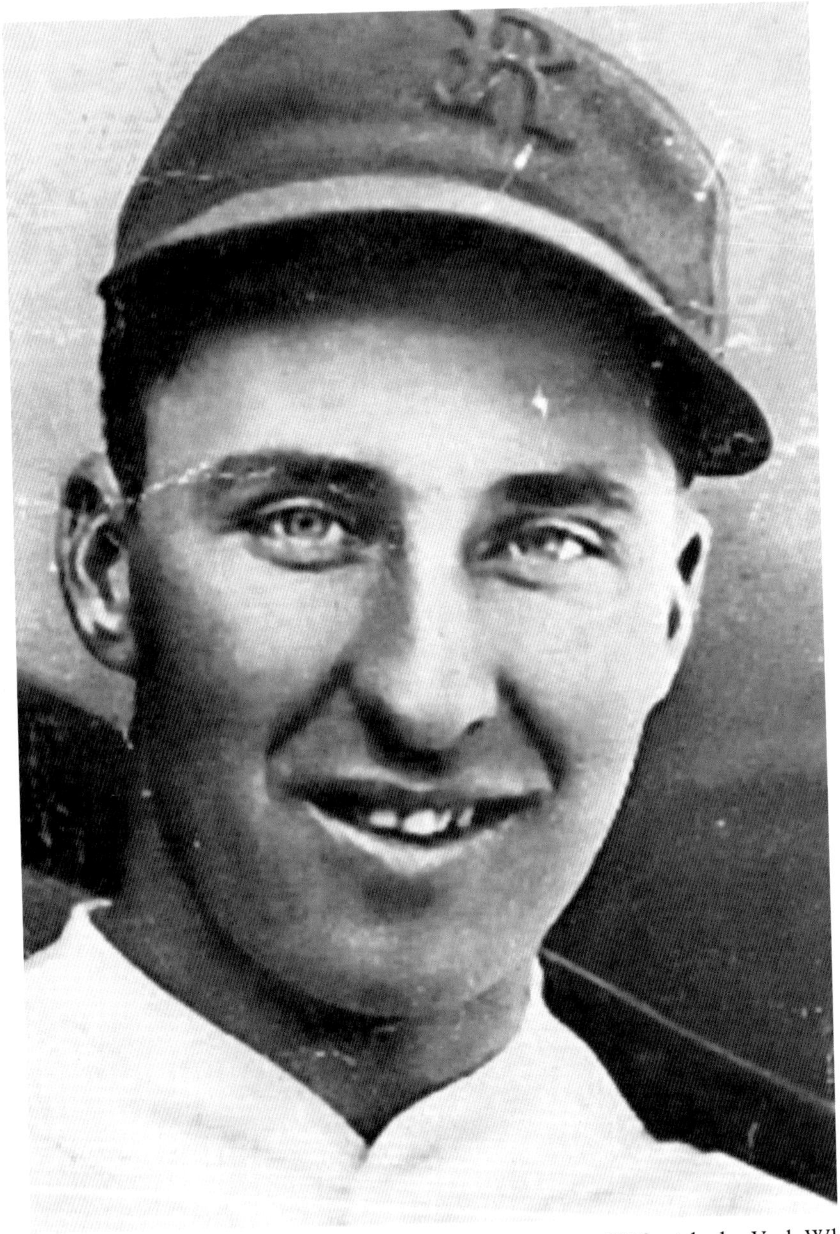

James Anthony "Ripper" Collins began his professional career in 1923 with the York White Roses in the New York–Penn League. Two seasons later, Collins arrived in Savannah to play for the Indians. Playing in the outfield in 96 games for the 1927 Indians, Ripper Collins hit for a decent .282 average. Although Collins did not put up impressive numbers during his stay in Savannah, his talent carried him to the major leagues. Playing for the "Gashouse Gang" St. Louis Cardinals in 1931, Collins helped the Cardinals win the World Series over the Philadelphia Athletics. His big league career lasted nine years, playing for the Chicago Cubs and Pittsburgh Pirates after his time with the Cardinals. After his big league days were over, Collins returned to the minor leagues, playing for the Albany Senators and San Diego Padres. Collins retired after the 1947 season.

With a record of 49 wins and 65 losses, the 1928 Savannah Indians suspended operations with one month left in the season and were dropped from the Southeastern League. The onset of the Great Depression in 1929 meant Savannah would once again be without a professional baseball team until the revival of the South Atlantic League in 1935. On April 4, 1935, fans packed into Municipal Stadium to watch another spring exhibition game. Returning to Savannah, 40-year-old Babe Ruth and the Boston Braves were facing the squad from the Georgia Teachers College, now known as Georgia Southern University. In his first at bat of the game, Ruth smacked a line drive home run over the right field fence, giving the Savannah crowd exactly what they came to see. The Braves beat the teachers 15-1. (Below, courtesy of Dight Oliff.)

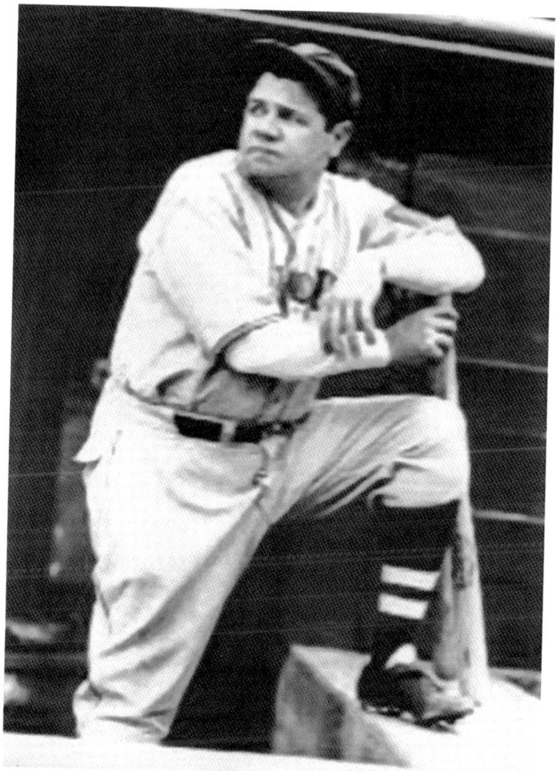

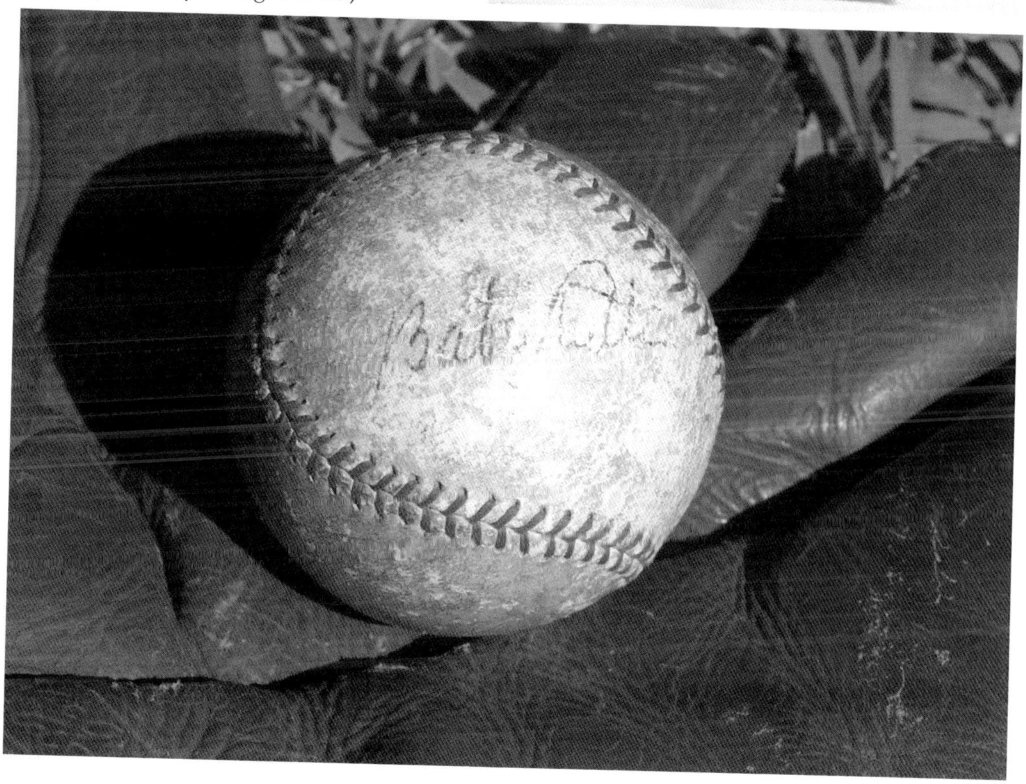

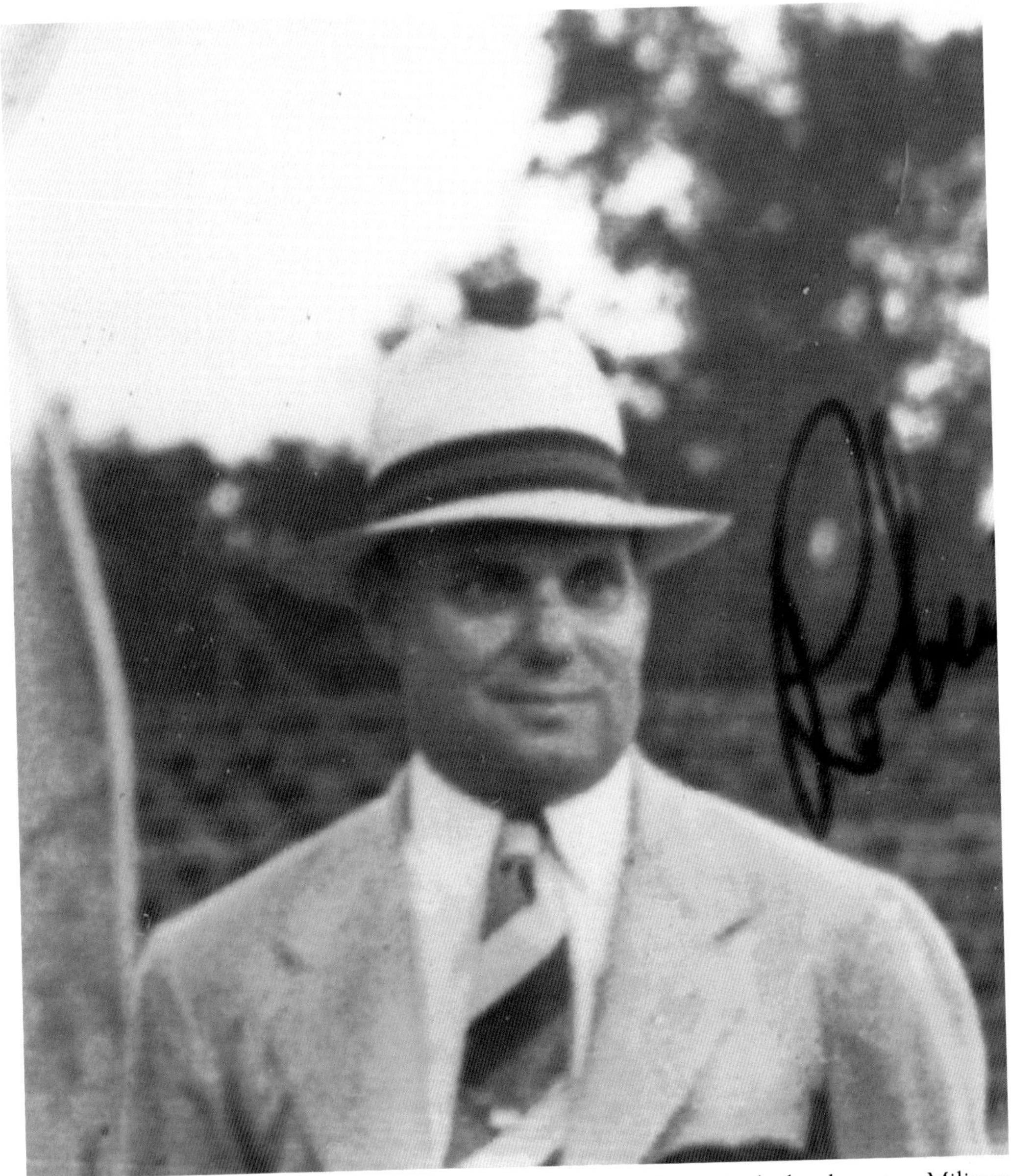

Savannah native Robert E. LaMotte began his baseball career playing in the local amateur Military League and City Leagues. After gaining fame in these leagues, LaMotte began his professional career in 1919 with the Tampa Smokers. The 22-year-old LaMotte broke into the major leagues with the 1920 Washington Senators. Spending three years in Washington, LaMotte finished his big league career with the St. Louis Browns. After a long career that included 11 seasons of minor league ball and five seasons in the major leagues, Bobby LaMotte returned home in 1935 and helped revive baseball in Savannah. With the help of other prominent Savannah baseball fans, LaMotte succeeded in getting baseball to return. Serving on the board of directors for the South Atlantic League, LaMotte also managed the 1936 Indians. In 1938, the *Sporting News* named LaMotte "Mr. Baseball of the Minors."

On April 21, the Savannah Indians beat the Jacksonville Tars 7-1 to begin the 1936 season and end the eight-year absence of baseball. In fact, more than 99,000 fans packed Municipal Stadium throughout the 1936 season to welcome baseball and the Indians back to Savannah. The Indians finished the year in fourth place. (Courtesy of Tom Autry.)

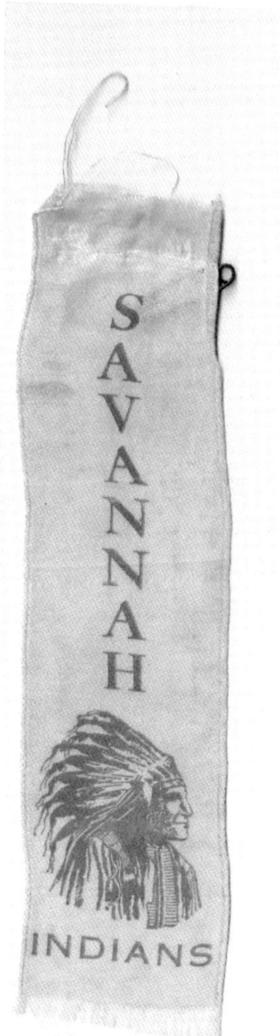


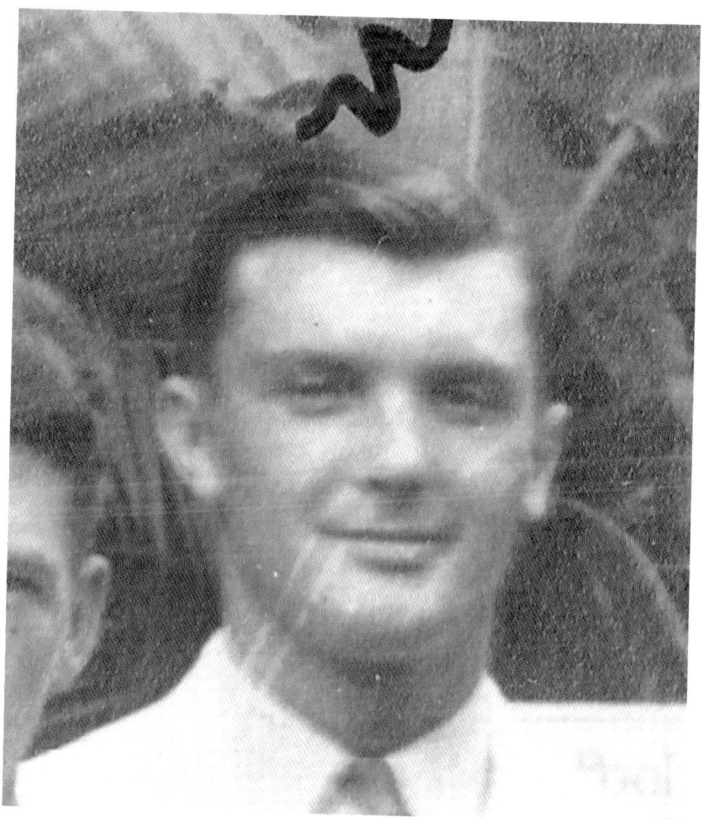

Starring for the 1936 Indians, outfielder Nick Etten hit .328 in 153 games. His first of two seasons in Savannah, Etten was one of six players with major league talent. Etten spent nine seasons in the big leagues, playing for the World Series champions, the Yankees, in 1943 and 1947. (Courtesy of Tom Autry.)

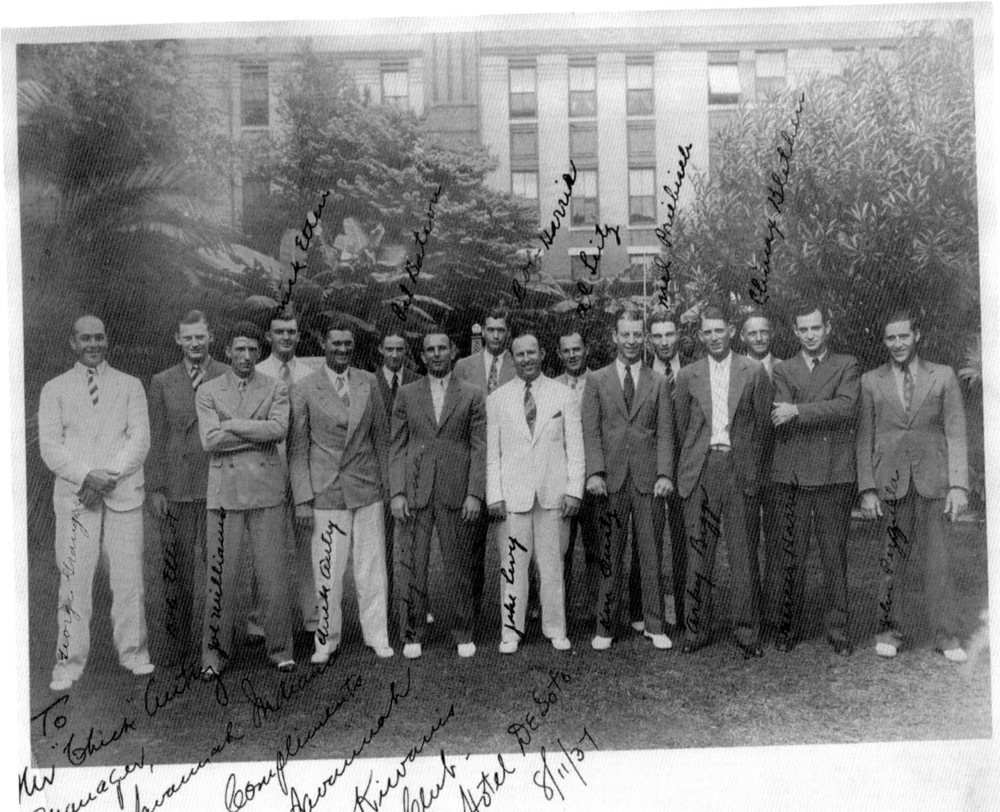


Beginning an affiliation with the Pittsburgh Pirates, the 1937 Savannah Indians were one of the most talented teams ever assembled in Savannah. Over 192,000 Savannah fans came out to see player/manager Chick Autry's dapper squad. With eight players who had or would spend time in the majors, the Indians won their fourth championship over Macon three games to one. (Tom Autry.)

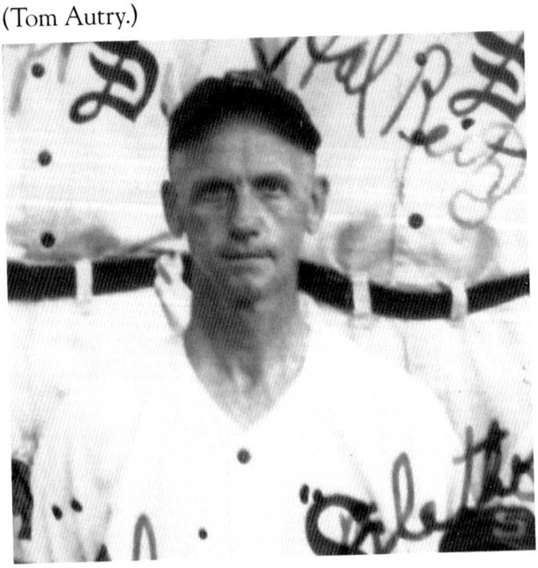

Clarence "Climax" Blethen spent most of his 19-year professional career in the minor leagues. Savannah was the last destination for Blethen, who joined the 1937 Indians at the age of 43. Despite his advanced age for a ballplayer, Blethen led the South Atlantic League with an ERA of 2.29. He retired from baseball following the 1938 season. (Courtesy of Tom Autry.)

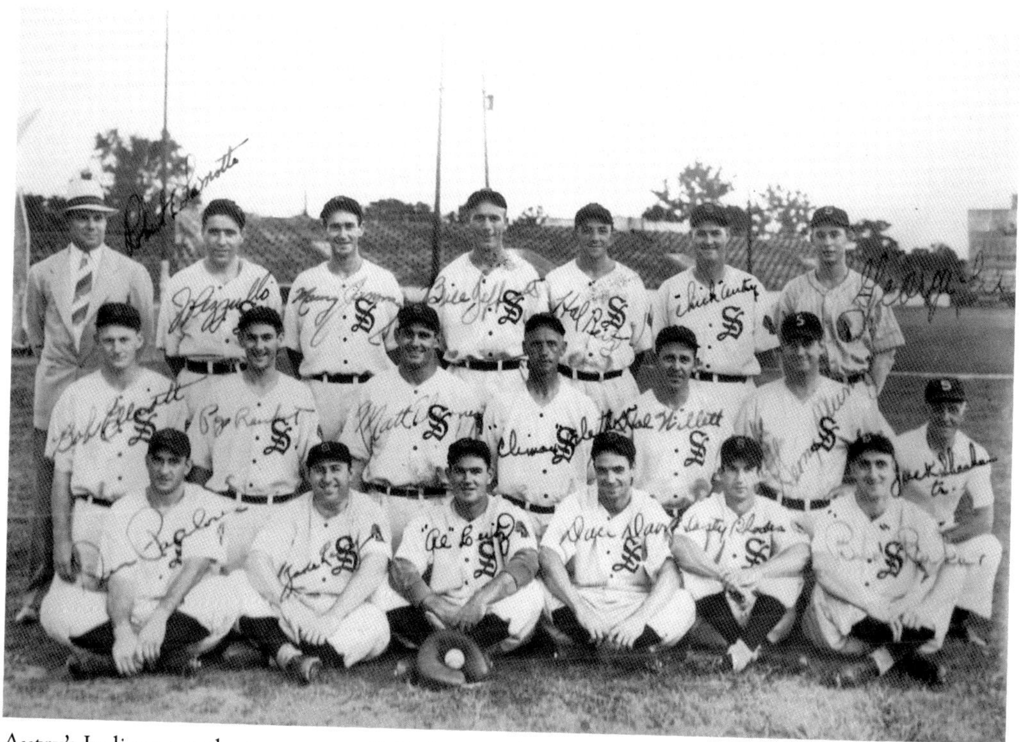

Autry's Indians sought to repeat as Sally League champions in 1938. With only a handful of guys who had some major league experience, the Indians found themselves back in first place with 81 wins at the end of the season. The Macon Peaches, however, were looking to avenge their defeat in the previous year's playoffs and beat Savannah three games to one to clinch the 1938 pennant. (Courtesy of Tom Autry.)

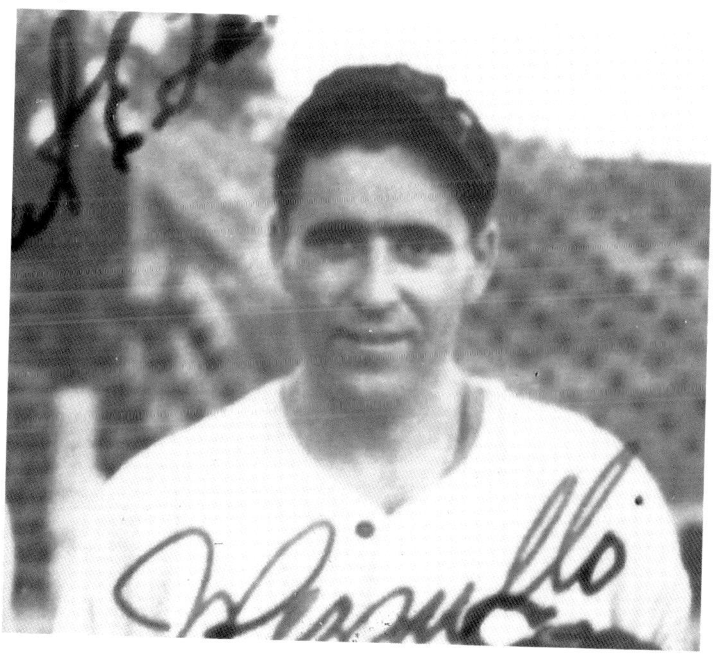

John "Pretzel" Pezzullo played seven seasons of professional ball, including two brief stops in the majors with the Philadelphia A's. He spent two years with the Savannah Indians in 1937 and 1938. His second season in Savannah was stellar, leading the league with 26 wins and 218 strikeouts. Pezzullo retired from baseball after the 1941 season. (Courtesy of Tom Autry.)

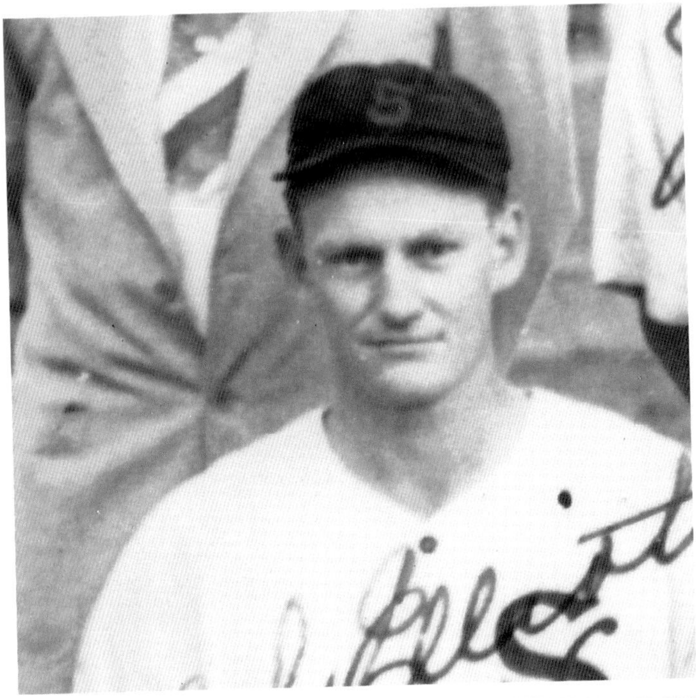

Known as "Mr. Team," Bob Elliott spent the first three years of his professional career with the Savannah Indians. With a .321 average and 12 home runs for the 1938 Indians, Elliott advanced to the majors the following year and spent the next 15 seasons in the big leagues. He spent the last five years of his baseball career managing several different minor league clubs and the 1960 Kansas City Athletics. (Courtesy of Tom Autry.)

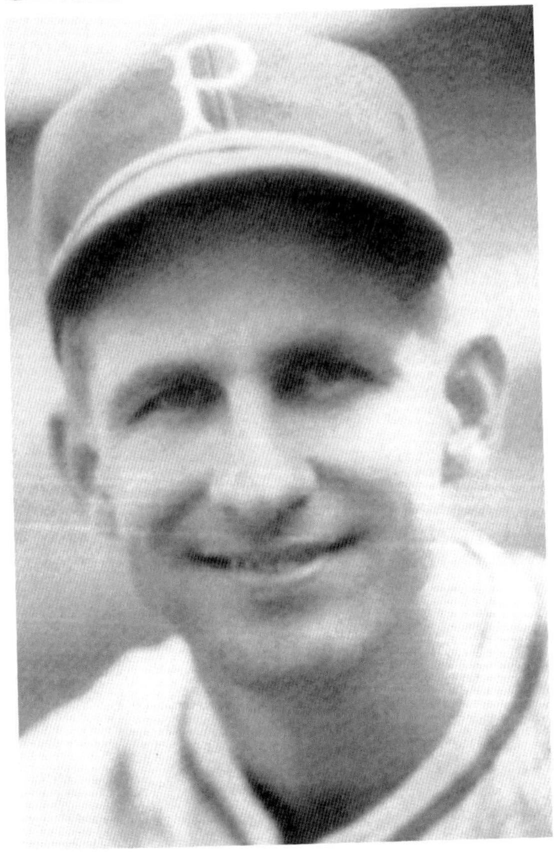

Alf Anderson and his .331 batting average helped lead the 1939 Savannah Indians to an 80-59 record and a return trip to the Sally League playoffs. For the third year in a row, the Indians reached the final round but were swept by the Augusta Tigers in four games. Anderson eventually went on to play three years in the major leagues with Pittsburgh.

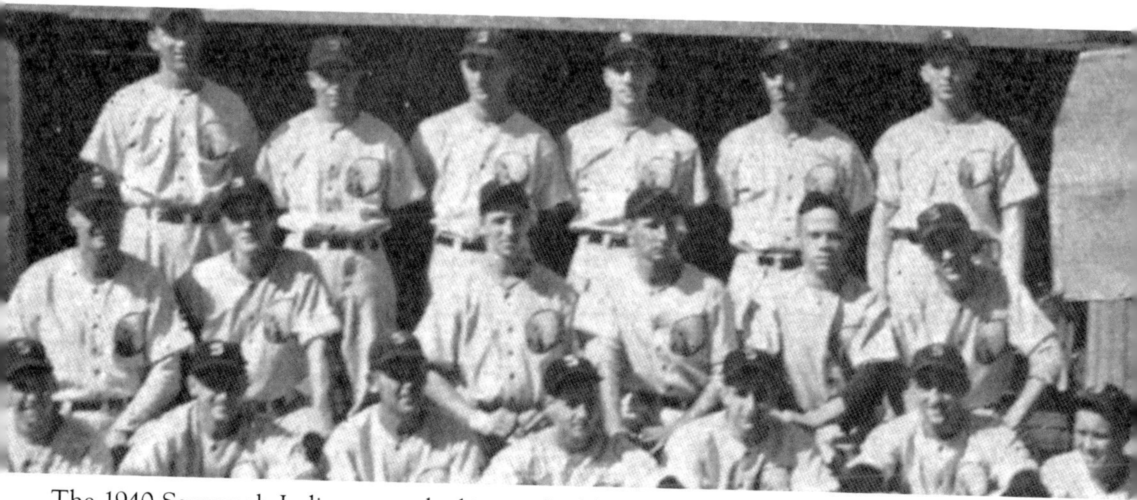

The 1940 Savannah Indians were looking to build on the success of the previous year, when they finished in third place but lost in the final round of the playoffs to the Augusta Tigers. The Indians would come close to that goal, finishing in first place with 94 wins but losing in the first round of the playoffs to the Macon Peaches. Wanting to continue this success, the Savannah Indians wound up with what seemed like a long season. Even with having future major leaguers Bob Chipman, Herb Crompton, Jim Mertz, and Connie Ryan, the Indians of 1941 would fall to last place in the Sally League standings with a record of 57 wins and 80 losses. The good news for the Indians of 1941 was that they were able to play in a brand new ballpark. (Skip Jennings.)

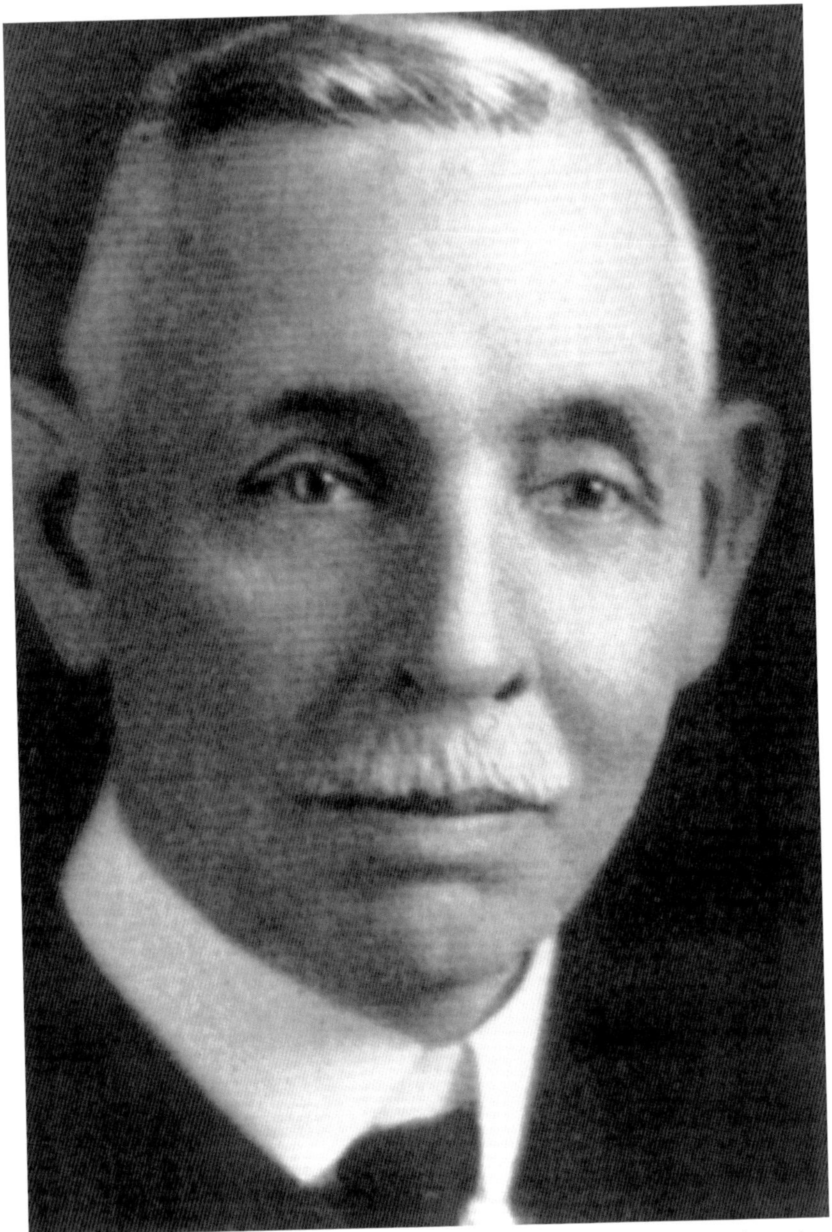

A hurricane that came through Savannah in August 1940 destroyed the grandstand and most of the bleachers of Municipal Stadium. Causing tens of thousands of dollars in damage, a new stadium had to be constructed, as there was no chance of repairing the old stadium. Leading the efforts in Savannah for a new park, Spanish American War general William L. Grayson helped raise the $150,000 needed to rebuild the ballpark. With local citizens contributing to the fundraising efforts, about half of the money was acquired from the Works Progress Administration. The Savannah City Council passed a resolution naming the new stadium in honor of all of Grayson's civic duties in April 1941. Honoring his military heritage, Grayson also served as commander in chief of the United Spanish American War Veterans. (Courtesy of Eugene Beals.)

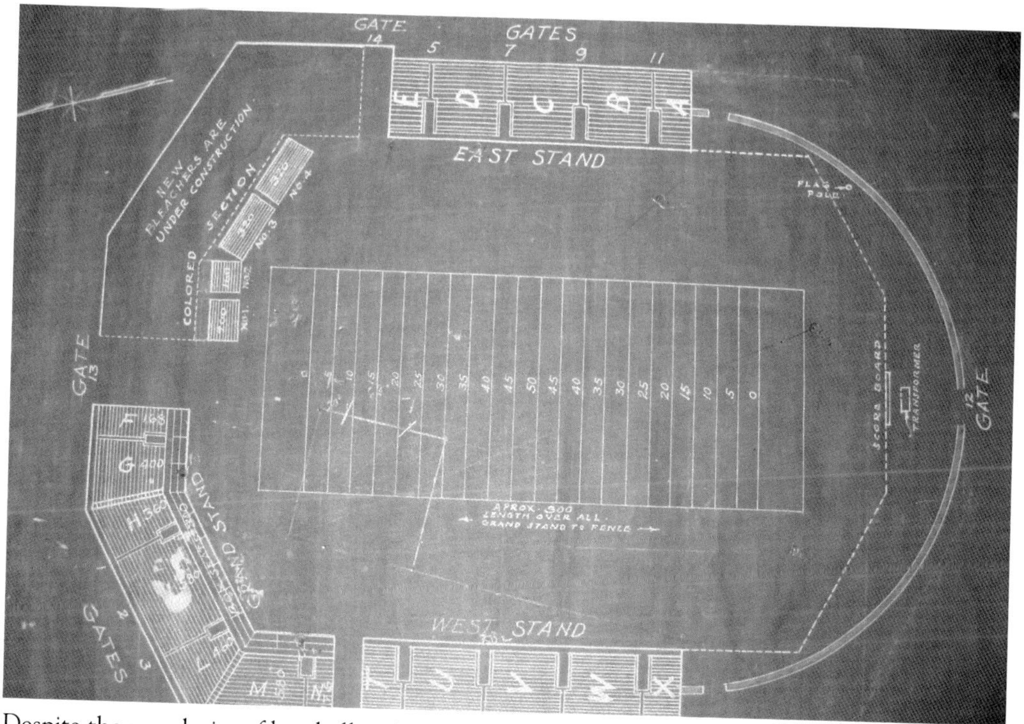


Despite the popularity of baseball in Savannah, the plans for the new stadium still included the option of allowing football games to be played. In fact, from 1927 through 1959, Municipal and Grayson Stadiums hosted the annual Thanksgiving football game between Benedictine Academy and the Savannah High School. The press box above the west stands was used for football purposes. (Courtesy of the City of Savannah, Research Library, and Municipal Archives.)

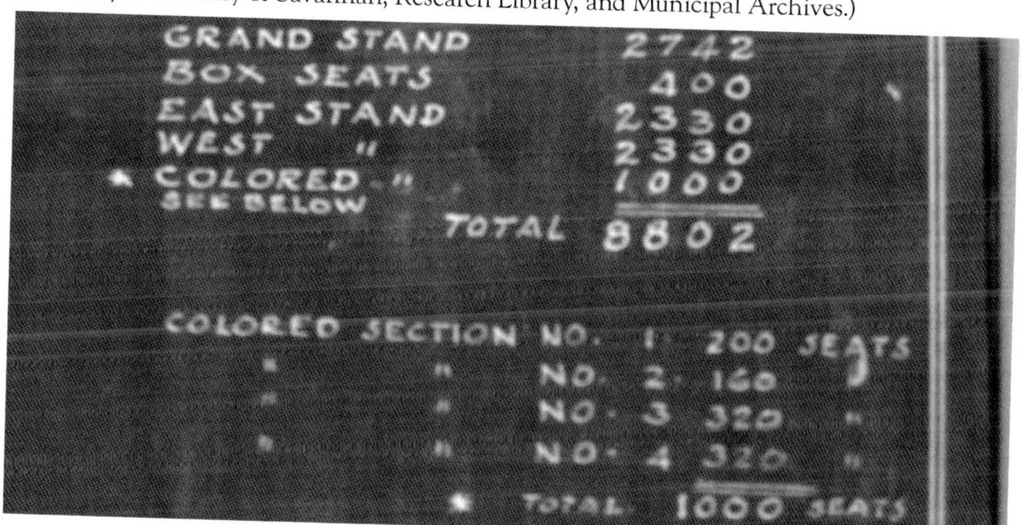


Grayson Stadium was smaller than Municipal Stadium. Where Municipal could hold 15,000 patrons, Grayson could only seat 8,802. Located along the third base line, the colored section only allowed 1,000 fans. A view of the colored section can be found on the left-hand side of the image above. (Courtesy of the City of Savannah, Research Library, and Municipal Archives.)

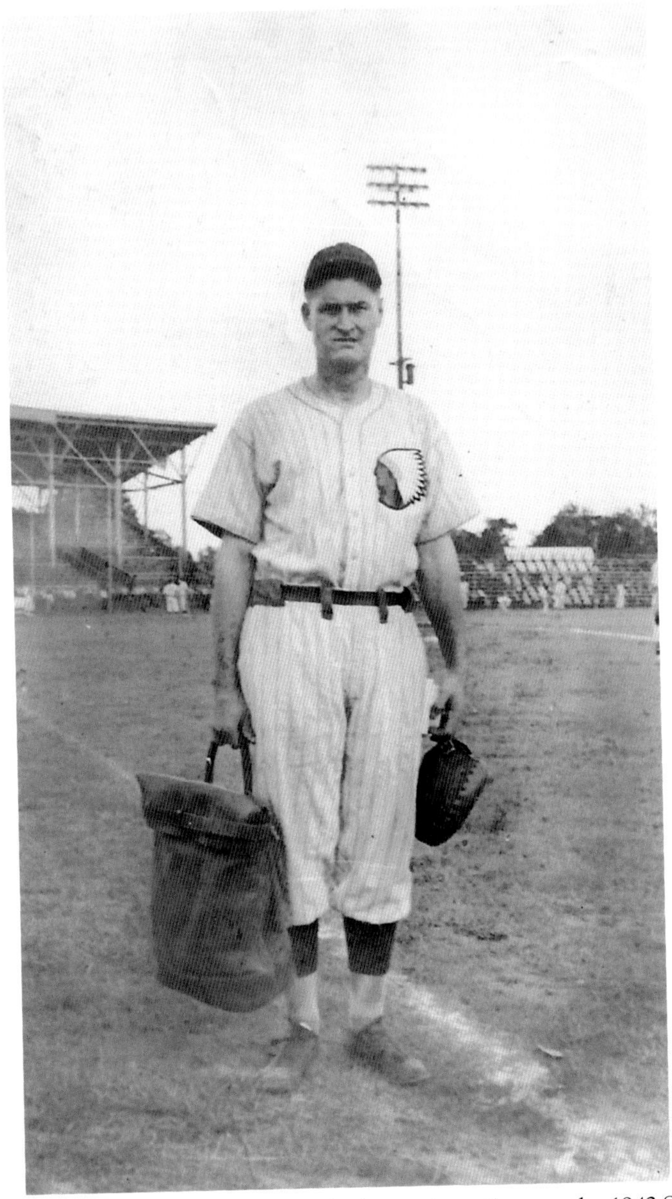

Even with right-hander William Ayers leading the league in strikeouts, the 1942 Savannah Indians finished the year with a losing record and in fifth place. That year would also be Chick Autry's last year as Savannah's skipper. Under his guidance for six years, the Savannah Indians won one Sally League championship and had four playoff appearances. Autry left Savannah with 446 wins and 387 losses during his tenure. After a four year hiatus from professional baseball, he returned to managing with the 1947 Charleston Rebels. In 1948, he spent two seasons managing the Beaumont Explorers, a farm team of his old New York Yankees. Autry's six seasons in the major leagues and 16 seasons of minor league baseball are not remembered by most casual baseball fans, but to Savannah, he remains one of the most treasured managers the city has seen. (Courtesy of Tom Autry.)

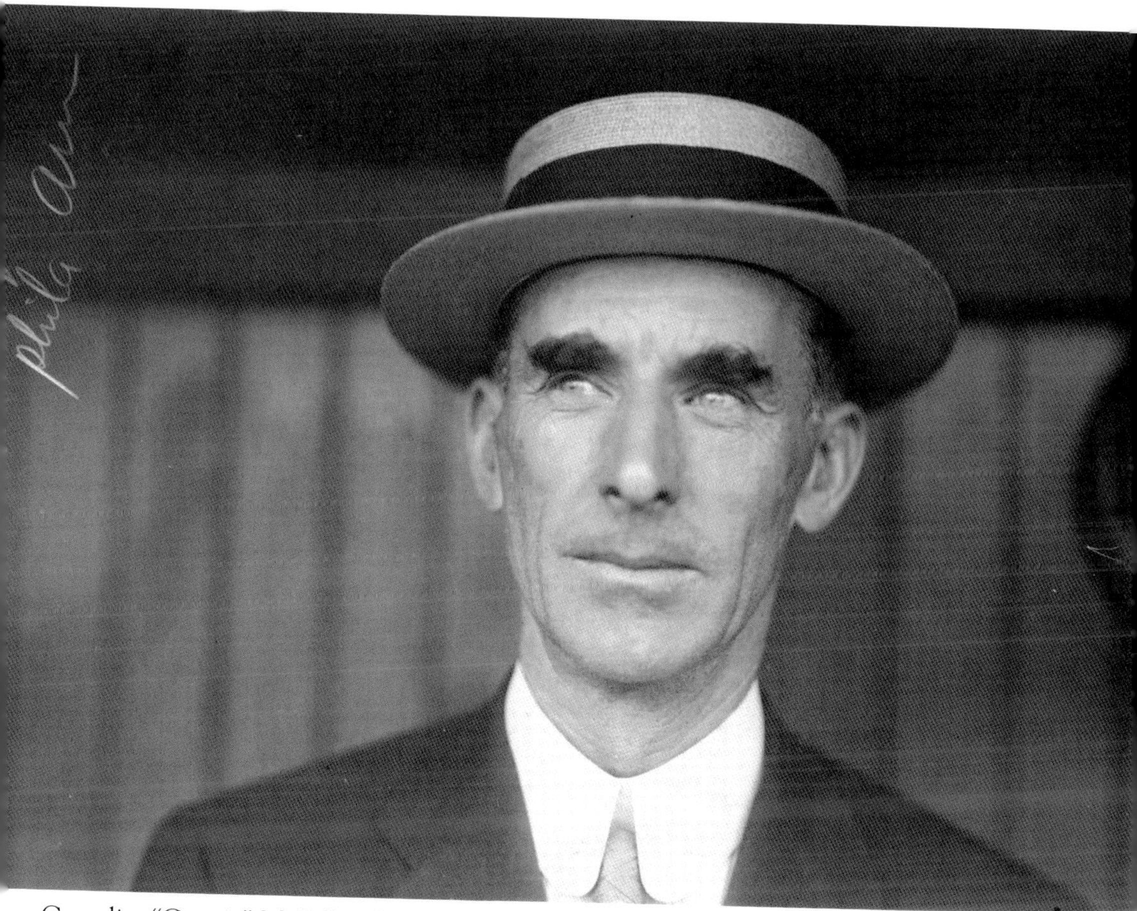

Cornelius "Connie" McGillicuddy enjoyed one of the longest and most successful careers that professional baseball has ever seen. Playing 11 years and managing for 53 years, he is largely associated with the Philadelphia Athletics organization. As a catcher, first baseman, and outfielder, "Mack," as he was better known, played for the Washington Nationals, Buffalo Bisons, and Pittsburgh Pirates. His managerial career began in 1894 with the Pirates and ended in 1950. A five time World Series champion, he has the most victories in major league history. Owning the A's outright from 1936 through 1954, Mack purchased the Savannah Indians and made the club an affiliate of the A's in 1946. Savannah's affiliation with the Philadelphia and later Kansas City A's lasted until 1955. Mack was elected into the Baseball Hall of Fame in 1937.

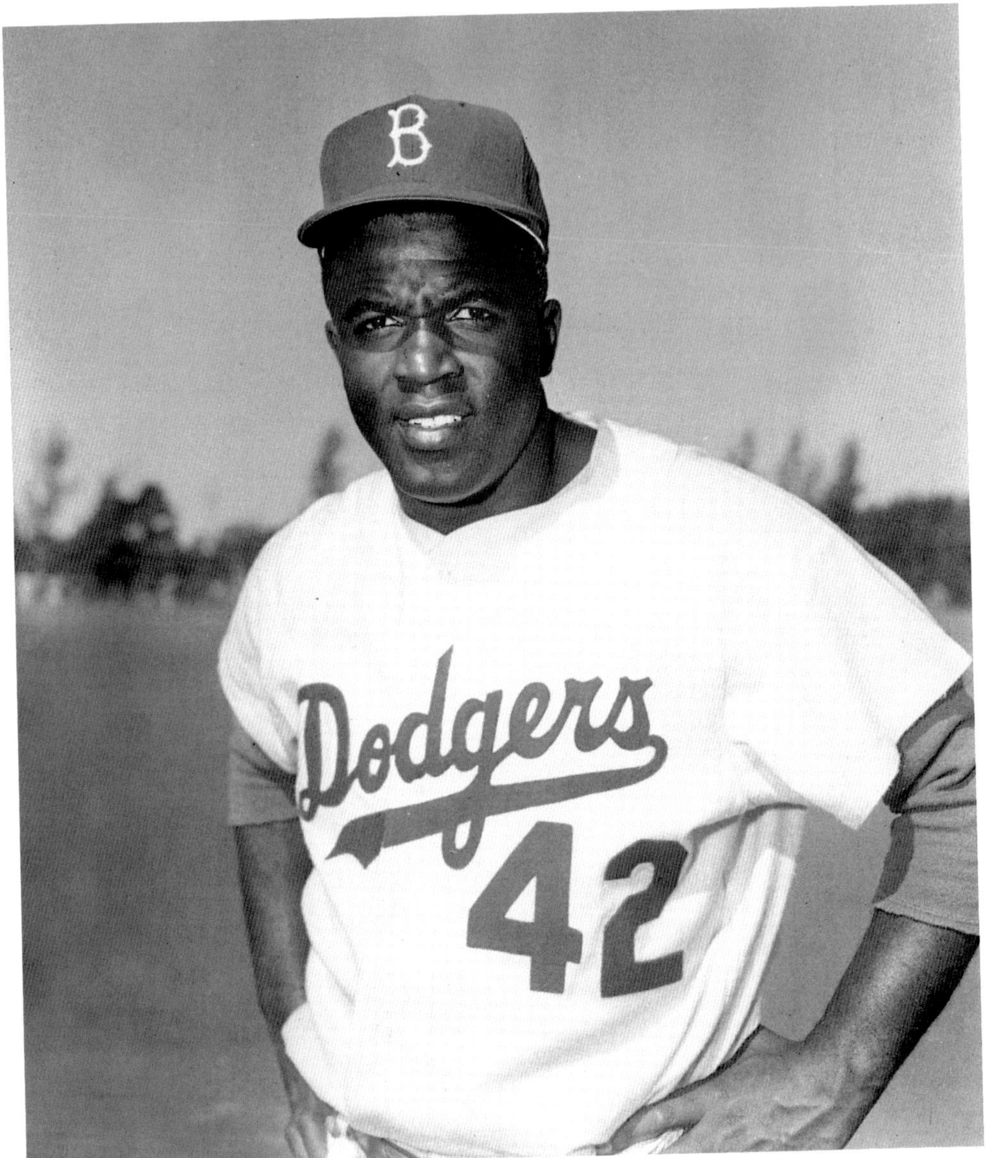


Becoming a multisport star for the University of California at Los Angeles, Jackie Robinson served his country during World War II. Upon his discharge, Robinson resumed his baseball career with the Kansas City Monarchs in the professional Negro Leagues. After becoming dismayed at the gambling involved in the Negro Leagues and the strain of travel, Robinson entertained offers to play in the major leagues. Signing with the Los Angeles Dodgers organization in 1945, Robinson joined the Dodgers farm team in Montreal. In April 1946, the Montreal Royals were scheduled to play the Savannah Indians in a spring exhibition game, yet the contest was cancelled. A spokesman for the Indians declared the reason as "circumstances beyond our control." Even though the spokesman claimed that the cancellation was with mutual consent from both the Indians and Royals, he refused to elaborate. In the Jim Crow south, however, no explanation was needed. The Royals were the only club in organized baseball using black players at the time.

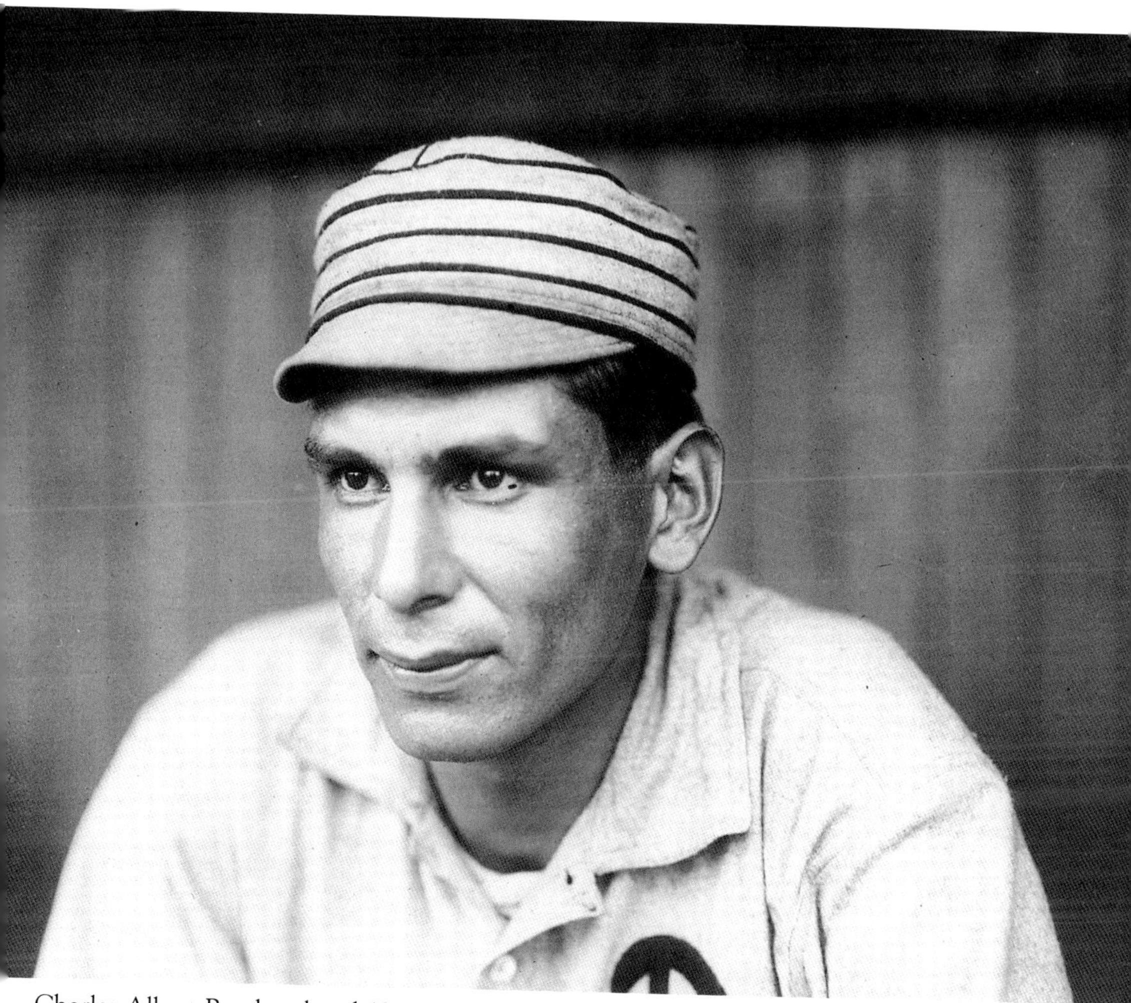

Charles Albert Bender played 12 seasons with the Philadelphia A's from 1903 through 1914. Nicknamed "Chief" because of his lineage to the Native American Ojibwa tribe, Bender twice won 20 games with the Philadelphia A's. In addition to his high career winning percentage, Bender pitched a no hitter in 1910. Winning three World Series titles with the A's, Bender spent 16 seasons in the major leagues. After retiring as a player in 1925, Connie Mack hired Bender in 1926 to serve the A's organization as a scout, coach, or manager. When Mack bought the Savannah Indians in 1946, Bender was installed as the club's manager. Bender only stayed in Savannah for one year as his Indians finished in eighth place in 1946. In 1953, Chief Bender was elected to the Baseball Hall of Fame. He died in 1954 at the age of 70

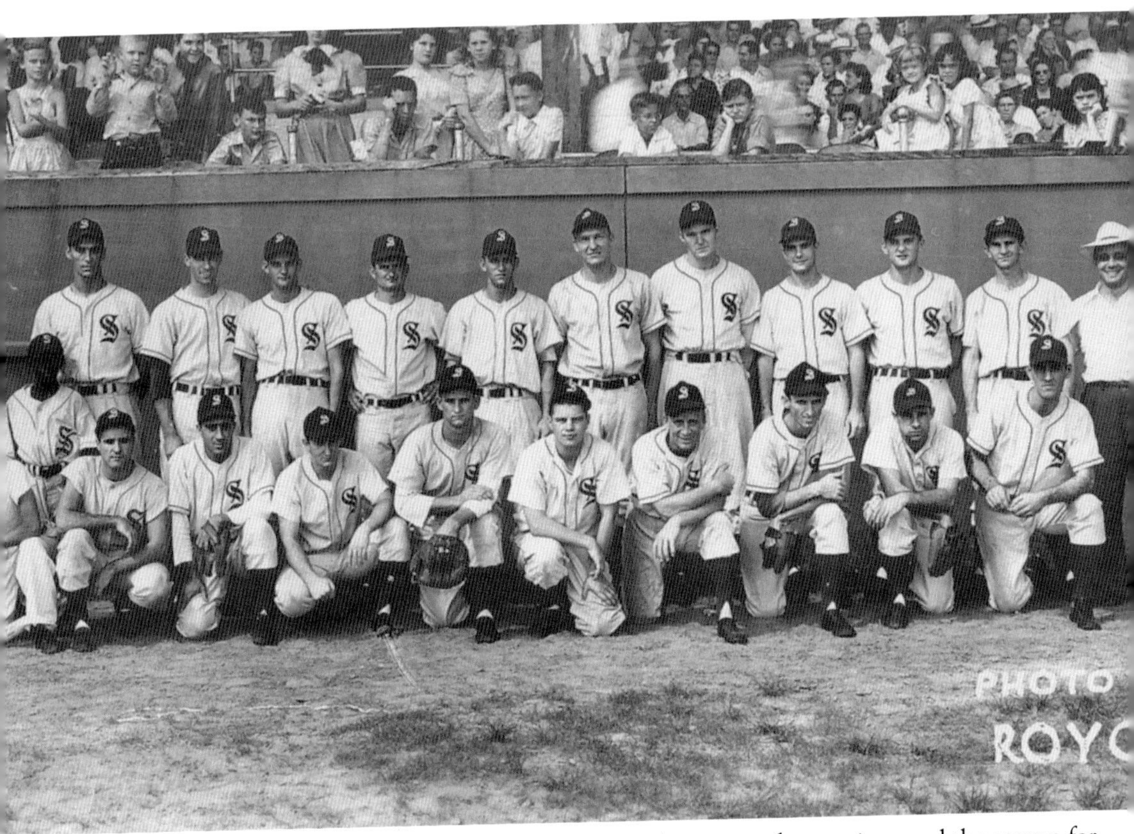


On February 2, 1943, the South Atlantic League voted to suspend operations and the season for the duration of World War II. With the Sally League resuming operations in 1946 and the team having a disappointing season, the 1947 Indians were looking for their situation to improve, and it did. More than 192,000 fans came out to Grayson Stadium to watch the Indians bring another pennant to Savannah in 1947. Featuring seven players with futures in the big leagues, the Indians did not disappoint. Although they won 85 games, the Indians finished in second place but advanced to the playoffs. Savannah advanced past Charleston in seven games to reach the finals against the Augusta Tigers, and then knocked them off in five games to clinch their fifth Sally championship. (Courtesy of Skip Jennings.)

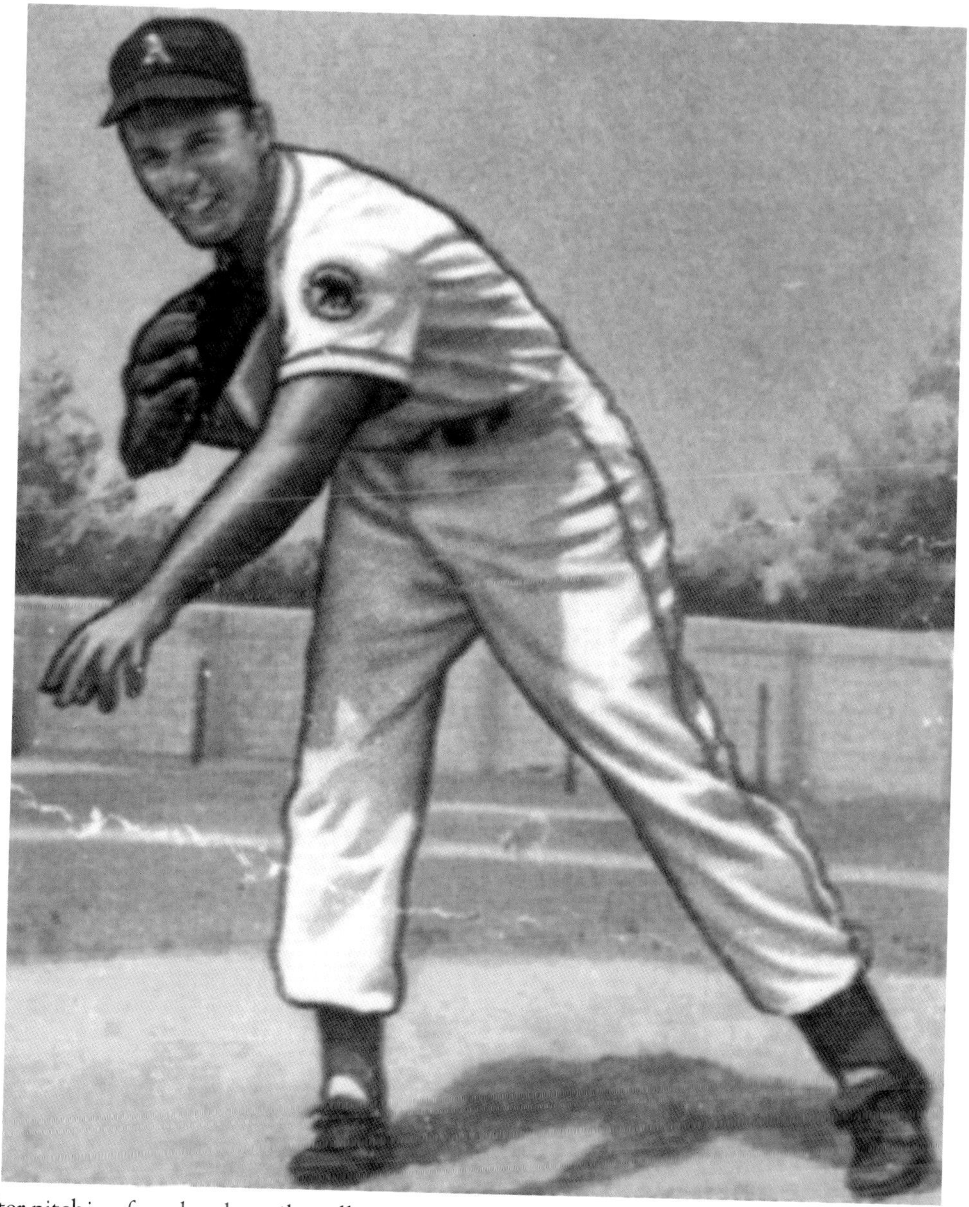

After pitching for a local textile mill team in South Carolina, Lou Brissie was signed by Connie Mack's Philadelphia A's after graduating high school. Serving in World War II as a paratrooper in Europe before he began his professional career, Brissie suffered severe leg injuries. After multiple surgeries, he was still disabled in 1946, yet was awarded a contract by Connie Mack. Fans flocked to Grayson Stadium when he pitched. Regular attendance often doubled or tripled when Brissie was on the mound. Winning 23 games with an ERA of 1.91 and 278 strikeouts, Brissie fascinated local fans when he pitched, basically on one leg. He went on to play seven seasons in the majors for the Philadelphia A's and Detroit Tigers. For his service in the war, Brissie was awarded the Bronze Star medal and two Purple Hearts. For his service that magical year in Savannah, Brissie was endeared to the hearts of Savannah's baseball fans. (Courtesy of Skip Jennings.)

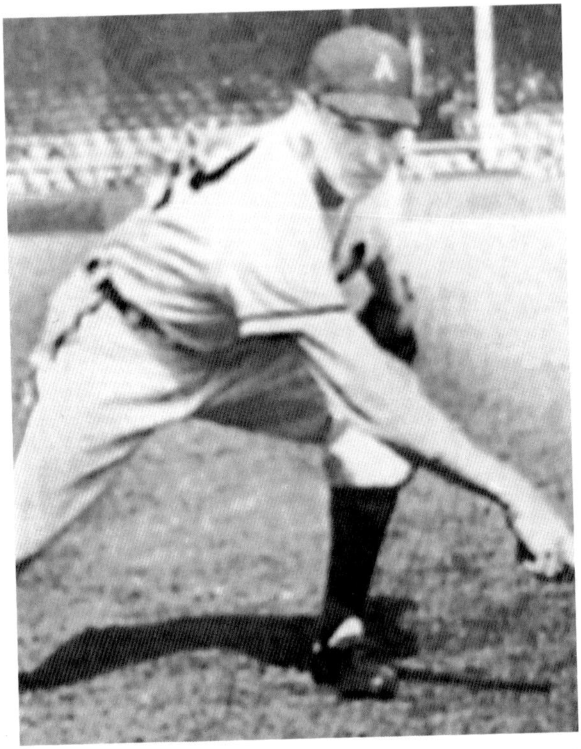

The 1947 season was the first of three for Bill Hockenbury. From the third base position, Hockenbury only hit for a .256 average, yet he led the South Atlantic League with 19 home runs. Spending nine years traveling through the minors, Hockenbury never reached the major leagues, yet his contribution to the 1947 Indians left a major impression on Savannah baseball fans.

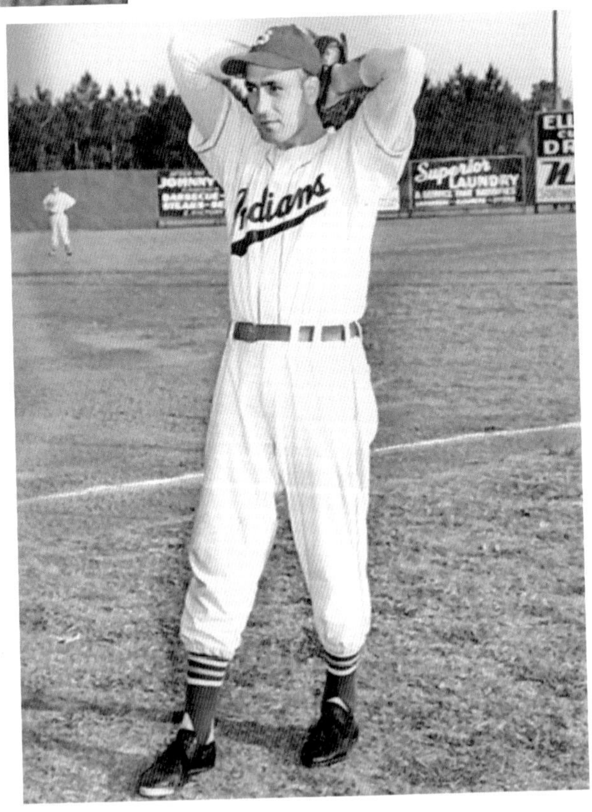


Sanford Silverstein played his first year of minor league baseball with the 1948 Savannah Indians. The Indians, coming off a high from the magical Lou Brissie season the year before, suffered a letdown in the standings, falling from second place in 1947 to eighth place in 1948. The number of fans coming out to Grayson Stadium also fell, dropping to just over 107,000.

The Indians rebounded in 1949, winning 84 games and climbing back to finish in second place in the South Atlantic League once again. Roaming the outfield for the 1949 Indians was 23-year-old William Benton. Benton only played four seasons of professional baseball and hit .260 with 14 home runs with the Indians that year.

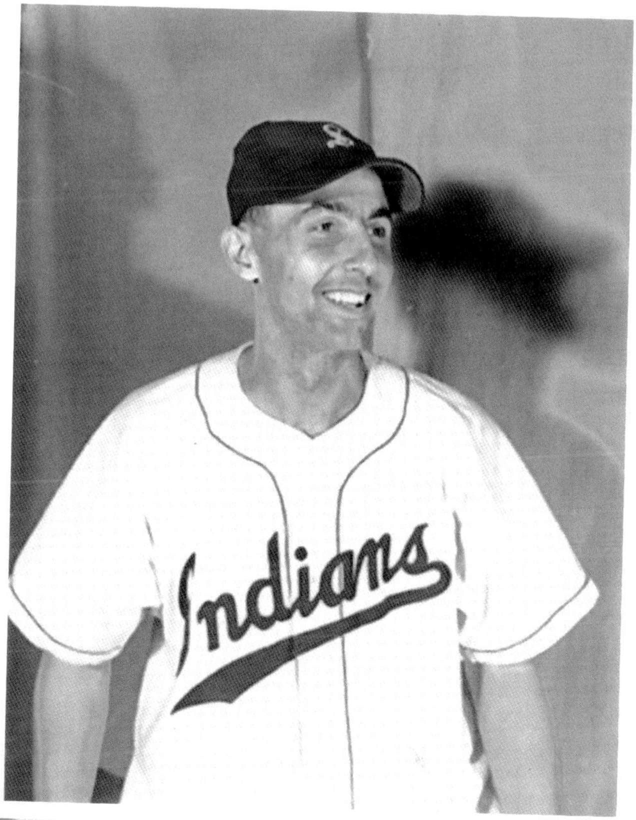


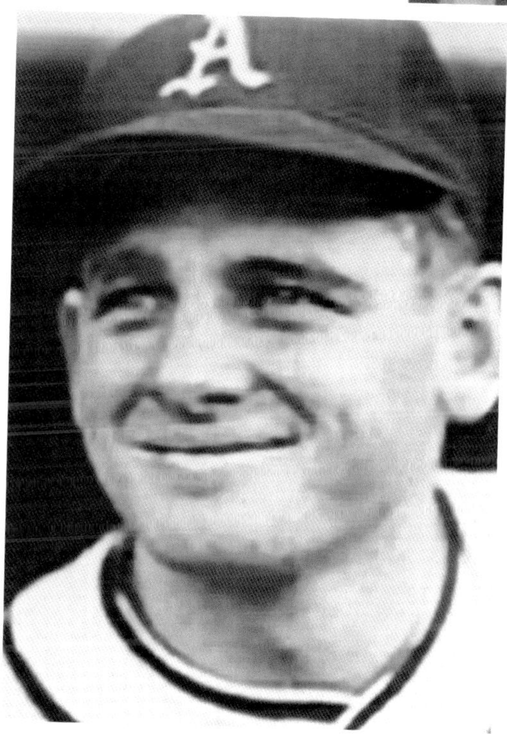

The 1950 Indians departed their spring training home in West Palm Beach, looking to build on their success from the previous season. Featuring three players with major league talent, the Indians would again finish in second place with an 83-70 record. One of those future major leaguers, Skeeter Kell, appeared in the final 22 games with the Indians after being promoted from Cordele.

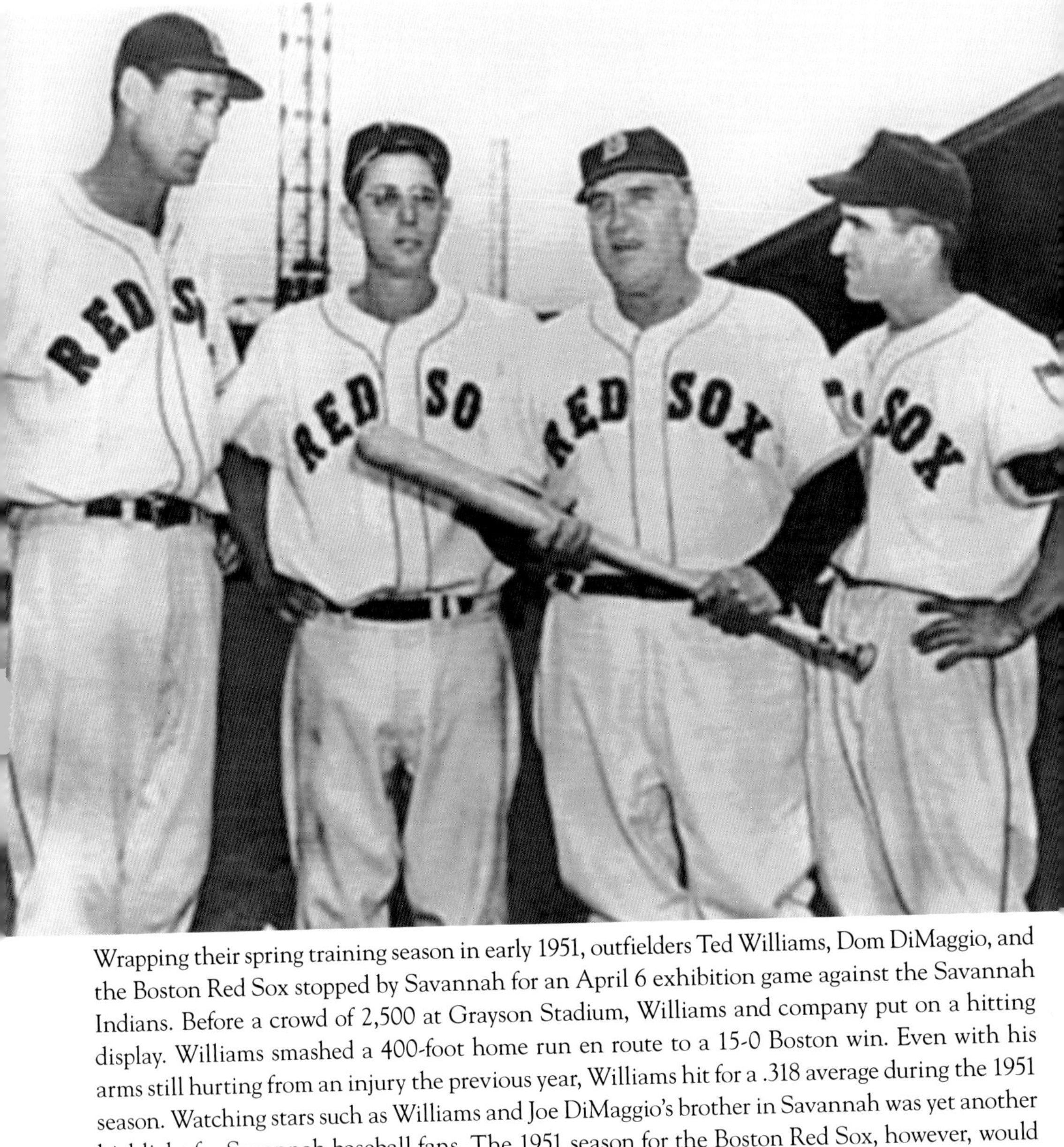


Wrapping their spring training season in early 1951, outfielders Ted Williams, Dom DiMaggio, and the Boston Red Sox stopped by Savannah for an April 6 exhibition game against the Savannah Indians. Before a crowd of 2,500 at Grayson Stadium, Williams and company put on a hitting display. Williams smashed a 400-foot home run en route to a 15-0 Boston win. Even with his arms still hurting from an injury the previous year, Williams hit for a .318 average during the 1951 season. Watching stars such as Williams and Joe DiMaggio's brother in Savannah was yet another highlight for Savannah baseball fans. The 1951 season for the Boston Red Sox, however, would be another disappointment. For the second year in a row, the Red Sox finished in third place behind the New York Yankees. The following year was worse as the Sox finished in sixth place.

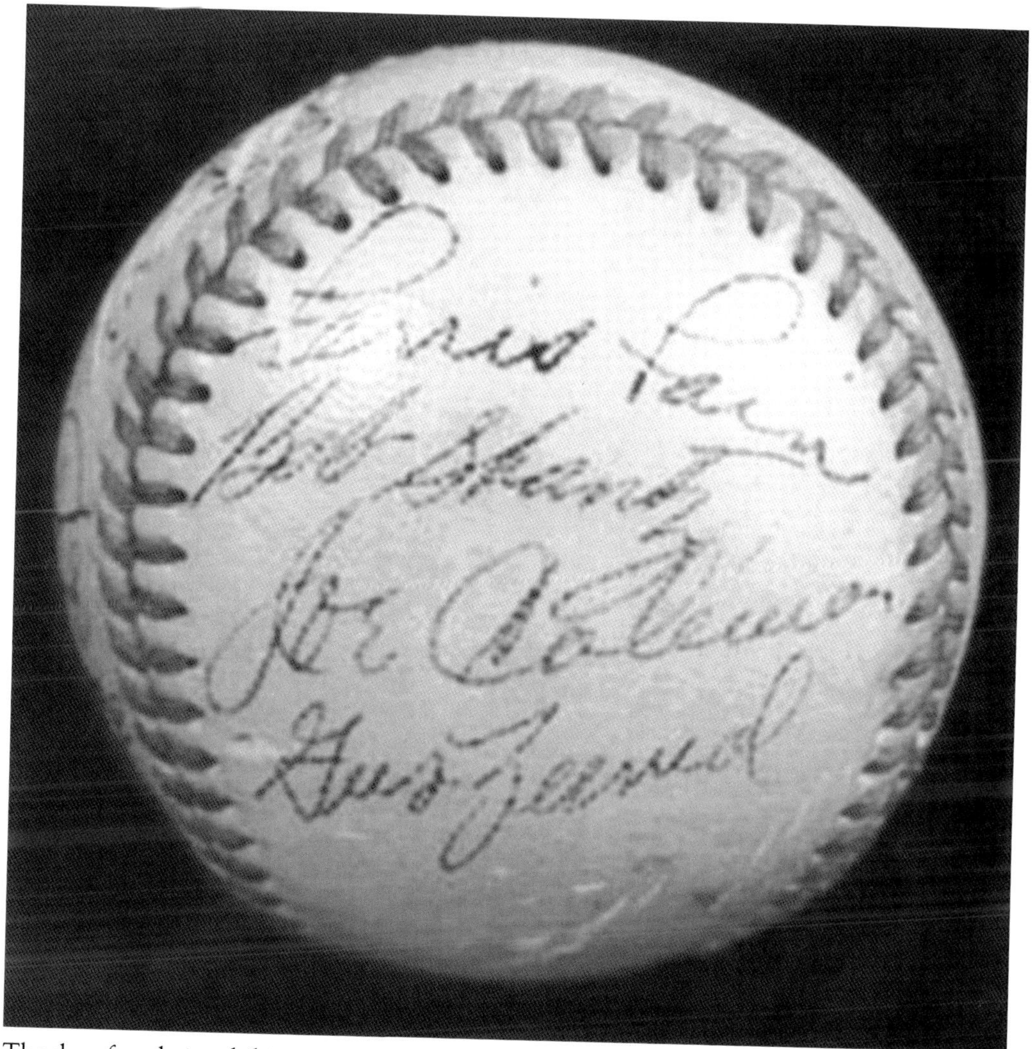

The day after their exhibition game against the Indians, the Philadelphia A's visited Grayson to play a practice game against their Sally League farm team. Unlike the day before, the Indians carried the game. The parent club lost the game by a score of 5-4. One can wonder what went through the minds of Lou Brissie and Moe Burtschy as they watched their former minor league team club beat their current team with major league players. The disappointment of the 1951 A's continued into the regular season. Finishing the year with a record of 70 wins and 84 losses, the A's ended the season in sixth place in the American League. Brissie was traded to the Cleveland Indians near the end of April and finished the season with only four wins. Former Indian Burtschy only played in seven games for the 1951 A's.

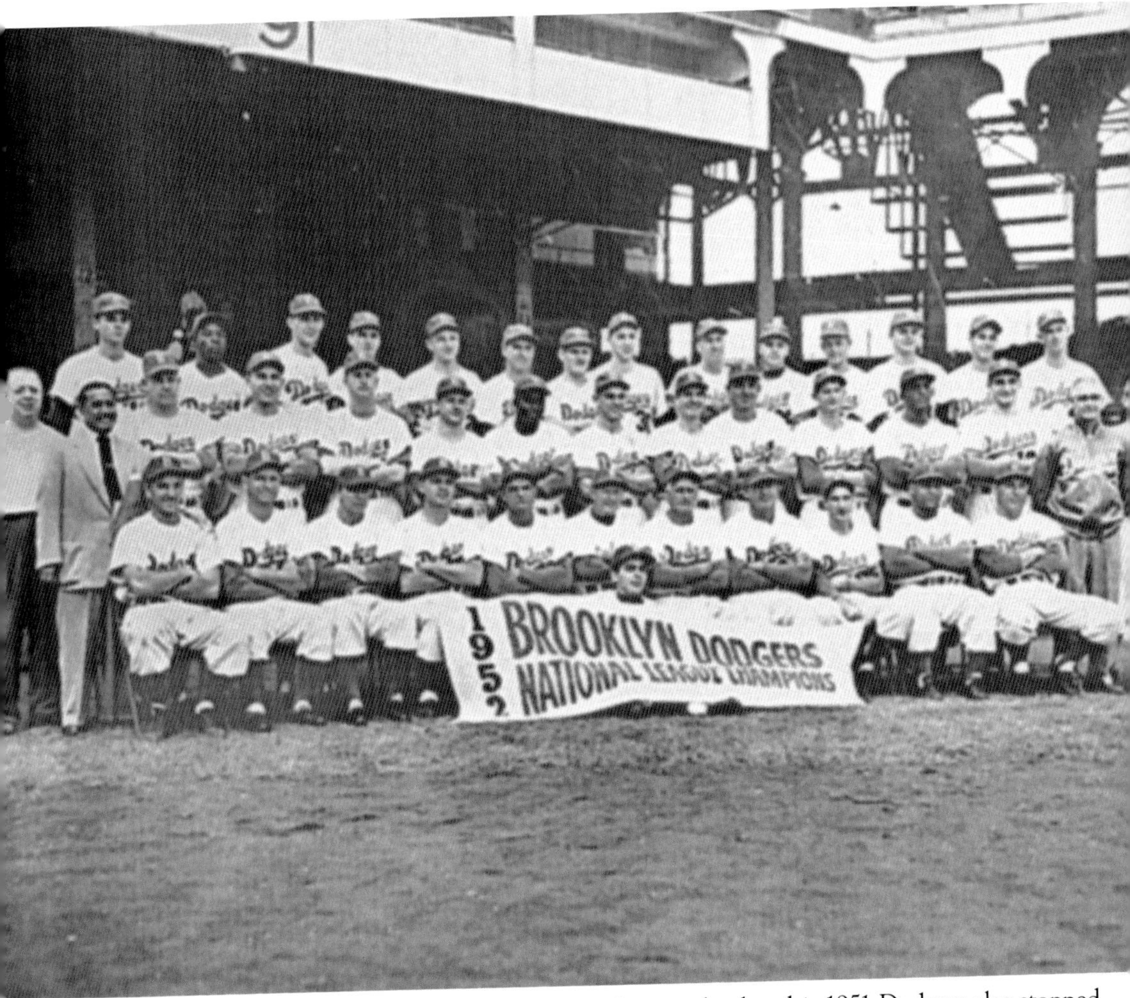


Jackie Robinson finally got his chance to play in Savannah when his 1951 Dodgers also stopped by Savannah for a tune up exhibition game. Led by Robinson, Gil Hodges, and Duke Snider, the Dodgers were looking to build on their second place finish to the Philadelphia Phillies the year before. On April 4, 1951, the Dodgers got a small amount of revenge when they beat the Phillies 5-4, scoring three runs in the last half of the 11th inning. With their season off to a good start, the Dodgers enjoyed a comfortable lead in the standings over the Giants through mid-August. The Giants surged, however, as the Dodgers slumped and the two teams met in a three game playoff. Splitting the first two games, game three ended with the legendary "shot heard round the world" home run by future Savannah resident Bobby Thompson that ended their season. The Dodgers rebounded in 1952 by winning the National League pennant.

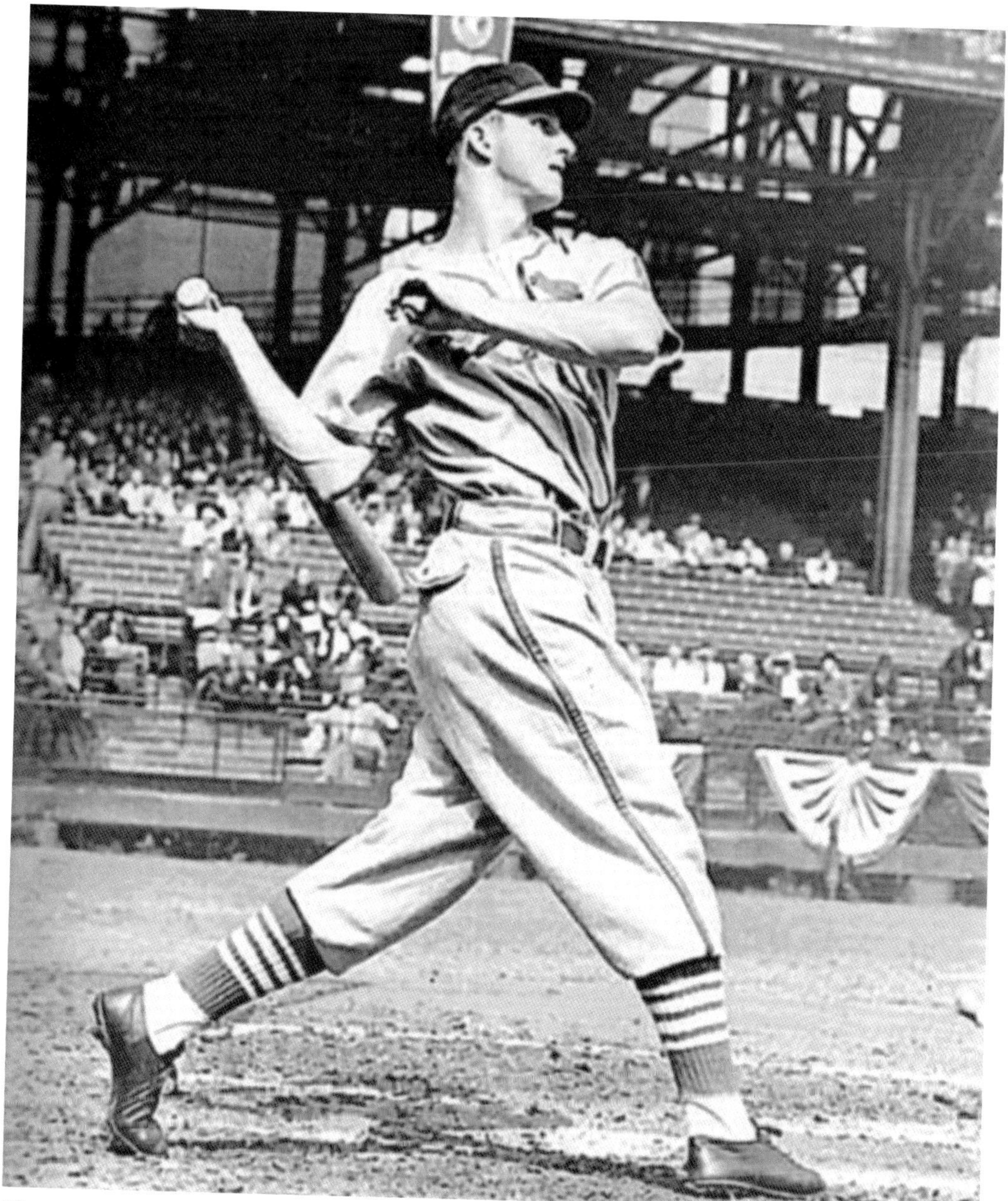

The great Stan Musial and his St. Louis Cardinals stopped by Savannah for an exhibition game against the Philadelphia Phillies on April 4, 1952. In his 11th year in the National League, Musial had already been an eight time all-star, won three World Series, and two National League MVP awards. His accomplishments could have been even greater had Musial not missed the 1945 season while serving in the Navy. Next to Ted Williams, Musial was considered the greatest hitter of his generation. As great a thrill as it was to Savannah fans when Musial and the 1952 Cardinals came to town, the real star of the game was rookie pitcher Steve Ridzik, who threw a no hitter against the Cardinals. After their stop in Savannah, Musial's Cardinals finished in third place while Ridzik and his Phillies finished one game behind them in the standings.

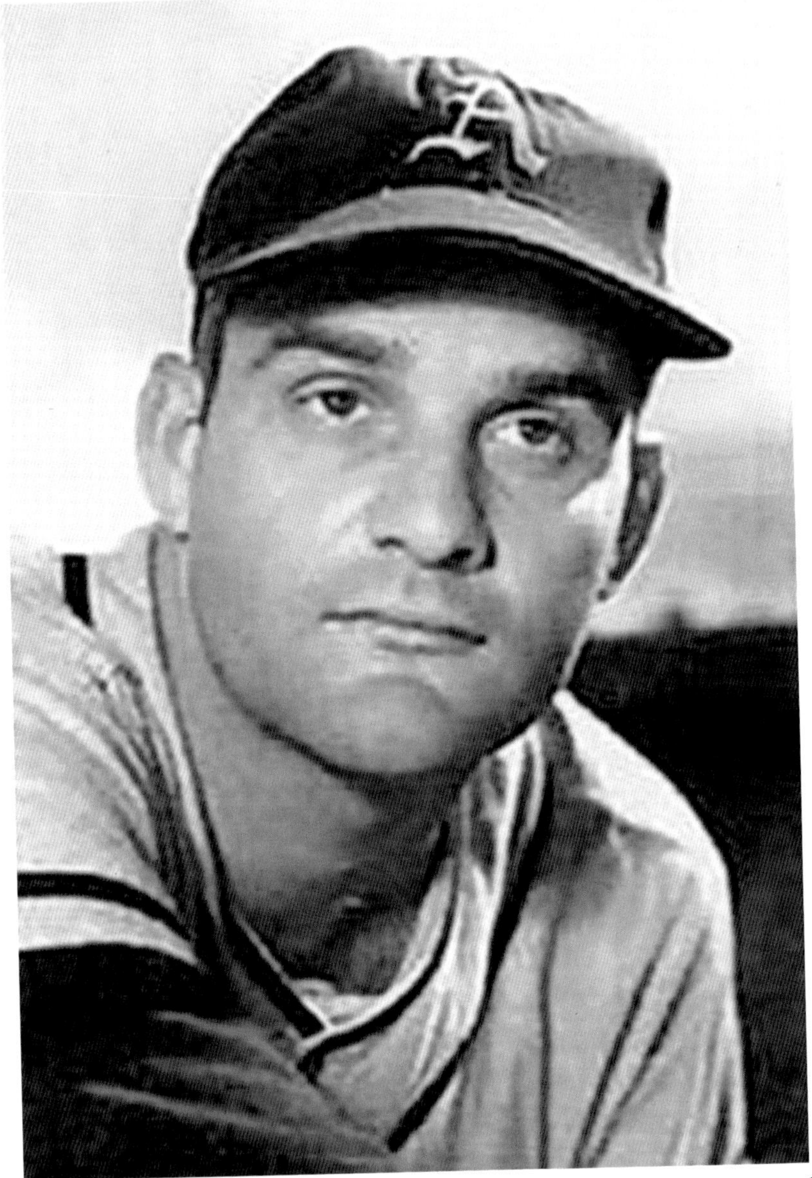

After spending the first four years of his professional career between the Savannah Indians, Martinsville A's, and Buffalo Bisons, right-hand pitcher Harry Byrd's fifth season of professional baseball and fourth season playing in Savannah was in 1951. While Byrd led the Sally League in strikeouts with 180 that year, the Indians regressed, finishing in sixth place and winning only 64 games. Having already gotten a taste of major league action with six games played for the 1950 A's, Byrd arrived full-time in 1952. He would go on to pitch for the New York Yankees in 1954, the Baltimore Orioles and Chicago White Sox in 1955, and the Detroit Tigers in 1957. When his big league days were through, Byrd returned to the minor leagues. He played for five more teams and retired in 1961. Throughout his long professional career, his best season was the 1951 year in Savannah.

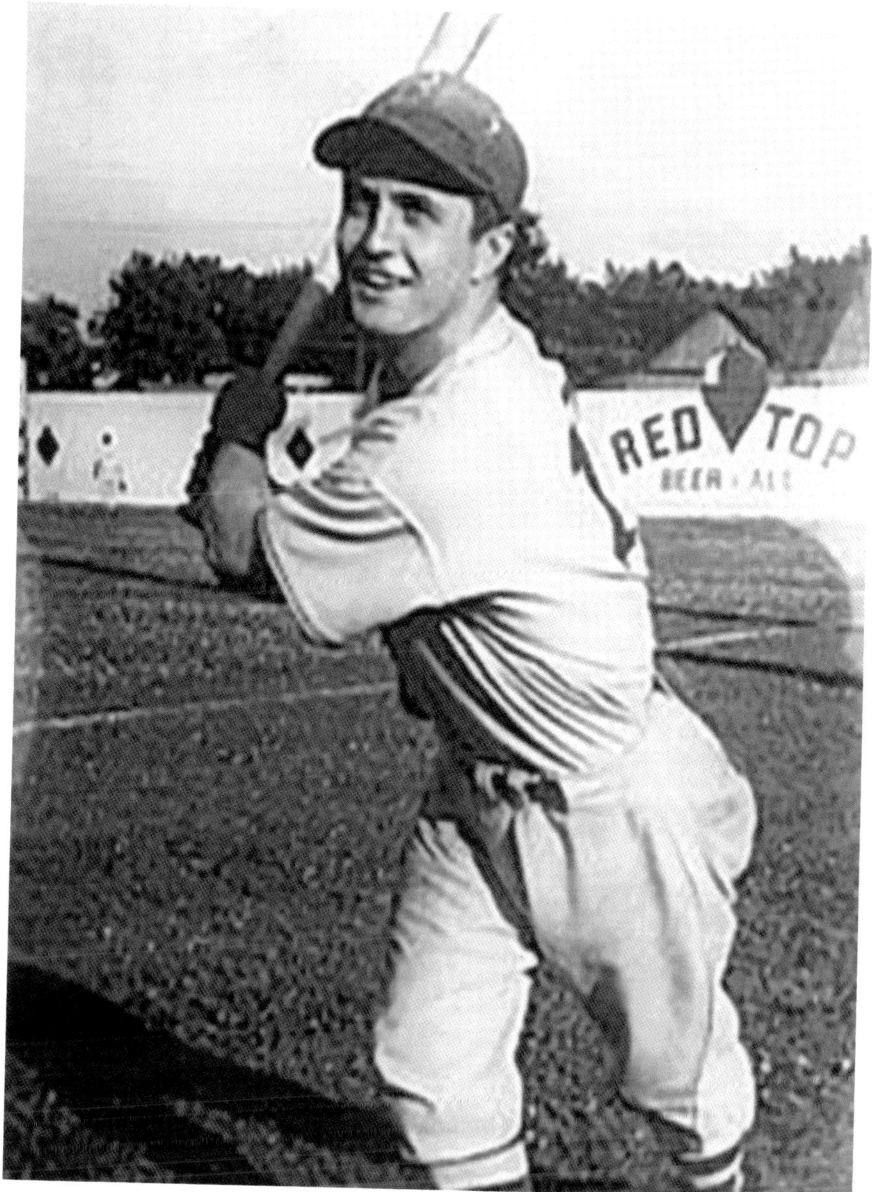


At 36 years old, George Staller was the oldest player on the 1952 Savannah Indians. Although he made a brief appearance in the show with the 1943 Athletics, Staller was a career minor league player. Beginning his professional career in 1937 with the Beatrice Blues of the Nevada State League, he was a player for the Dayton Ducks two years later, and led the Middle Atlantic League with 43 stolen bases. The following year, Staller's .336 batting average and 49 doubles led the Eastern League. Through the 1940s, Staller played for a variety of minor league clubs around the country with two different stops in Montreal. He got a taste of big league action playing right field for the 1943 Philadelphia Athletics. He began serving as manager in 1948 and arrived in Savannah as skipper of the Indians in 1951. His Indians of 1952 finished the South Atlantic League in sixth place, winning 74 games.

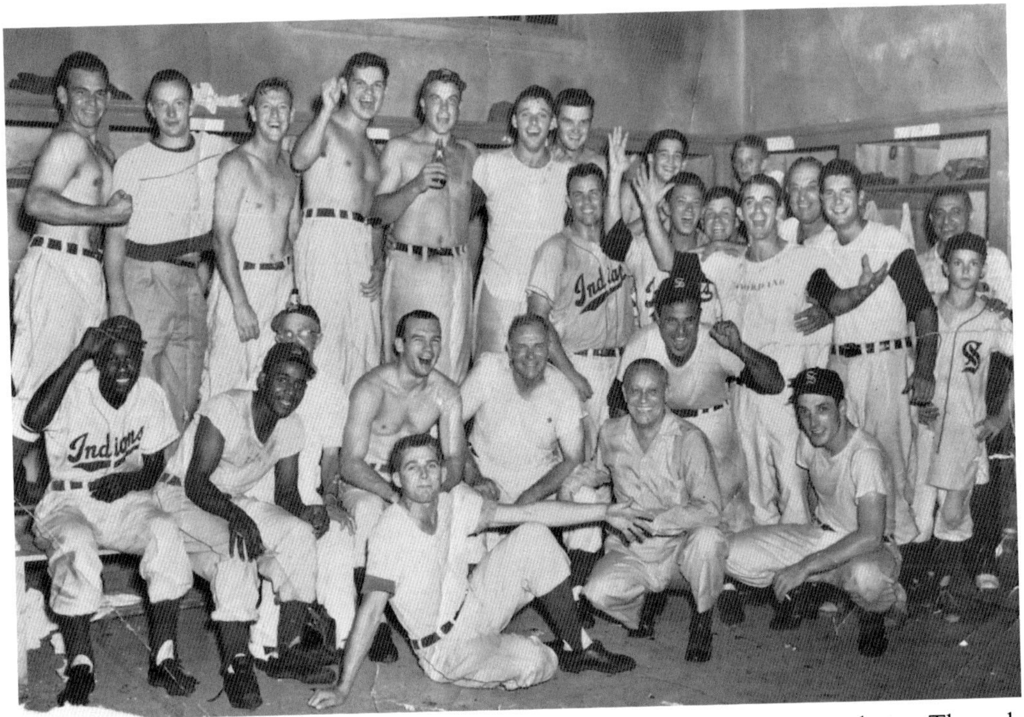

For Savannah baseball and the South Atlantic League, 1953 was a monumental year. Through nearly 50 years, all of the players who came through Savannah and the Sally League had one thing in common, the fact they were all white. Seven years after Jackie Robinson broke the color barrier in the major leagues, the South Atlantic League followed suit in 1953. When Albert Isreal and Junior Reedy started for the Savannah Indians on opening day, they became the first African American players to play in the Sally League. Isreal and Reedy's Indians played in front of a record Grayson Stadium crowd on May 7, as more than 15,000 fans packed into the park for Merchant Appreciation night. The 1953 Indians finished the season in fourth place, winning 68 games. (Above, courtesy of Clarence Watkins; below, courtesy of Lynn Wright.)

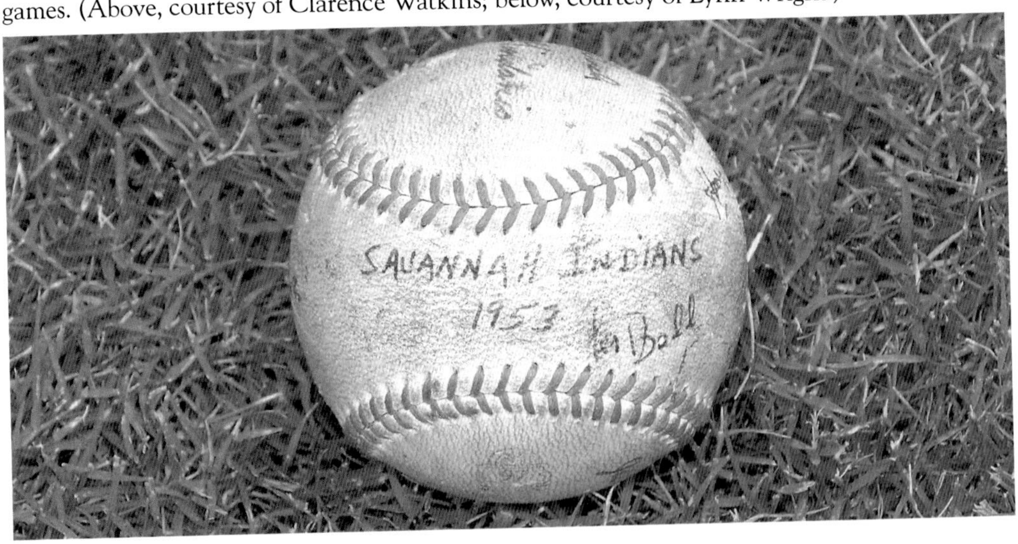

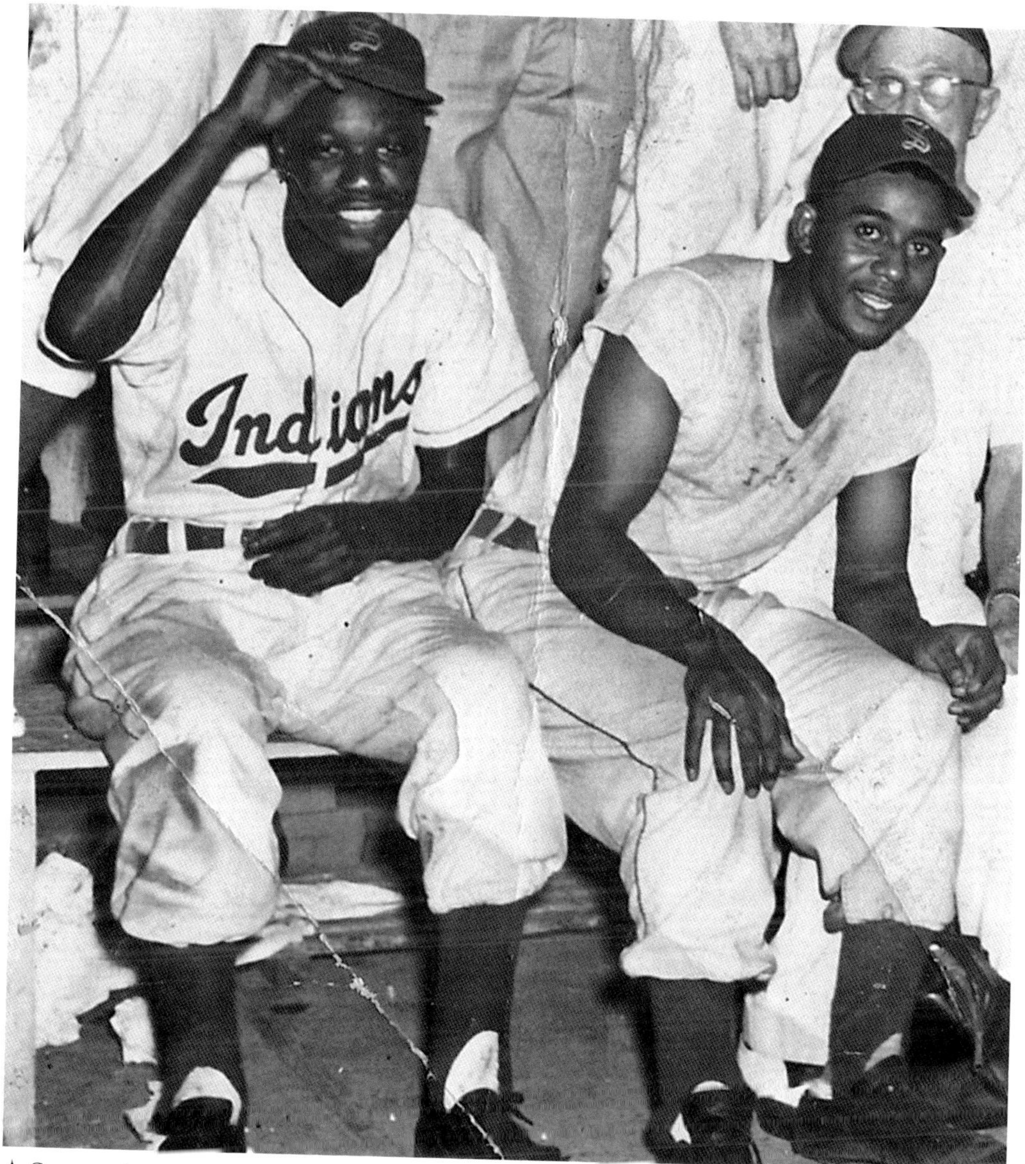

A Savannah native, Junior Reedy had little trouble introducing himself to the local crowd. In a March exhibition game, he hit for the cycle, including an inside the park home run. He also took part in three double plays and drove in three home runs. The 1952 batting leader for the Western League, Reedy played 11 seasons of minor league ball. "Izzy" Isreal also won the batting title in his respective league in 1952. Batting .304 for the Indians in 1953, Isreal only spent five seasons playing professional ball. The seven other teams in the Sally League were paying close attention to how the experiment of using Reedy and Isreal worked. All except for the Montgomery Grays were considering using African American players. The other clubs were not the only ones watching, however: 5,508 fans turned out to Grayson Stadium to watch the opening game against the Jacksonville Braves and witness the historic occasion as the color barrier in southern professional baseball fell on April 15, 1953. (Courtesy of Clarence Watkins.)

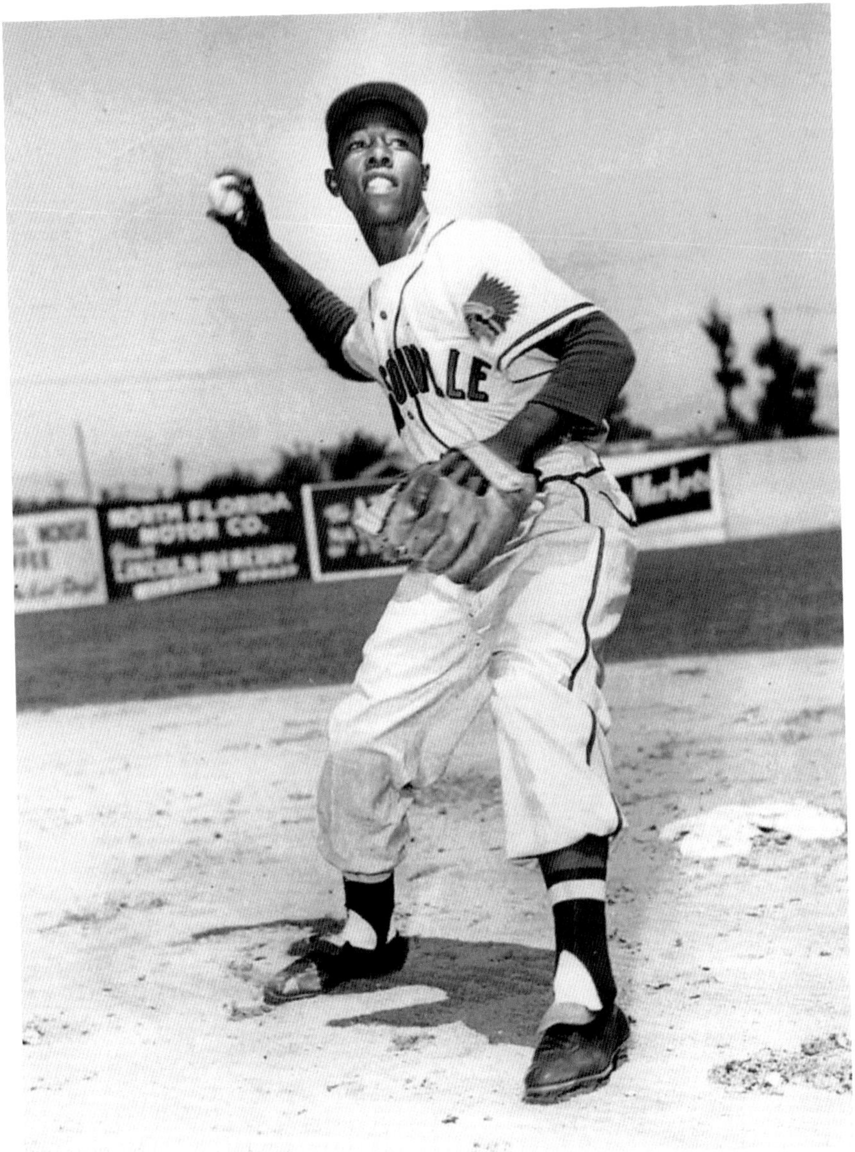

Other South Atlantic League clubs followed the Indians' path and decided to use African American players as well. On opening night in Savannah, the large crowd also saw the Jacksonville Braves' first black player, a 19-year-old second baseman named Henry Aaron. Young Aaron starred for the Braves, hitting 22 homers and a league-high .362 batting average. The Milwaukee Braves called Aaron up the following year, beginning a major league career that few players have rivaled. Named to 25 all-star teams, winning a World Series title, an MVP award, and three Gold Gloves, Aaron cemented his status as one of the greatest players the game had ever seen. His chase of Babe Ruth's home run record vaulted his reputation as a player from great to legendary. As Aaron neared Ruth's record in 1973, he experienced a lot of the racism and bigotry that he saw as a young player in Jacksonville nearly 20 years before. Despite the enormous pressure he faced, Aaron passed Ruth's home run record on April 8, 1974.

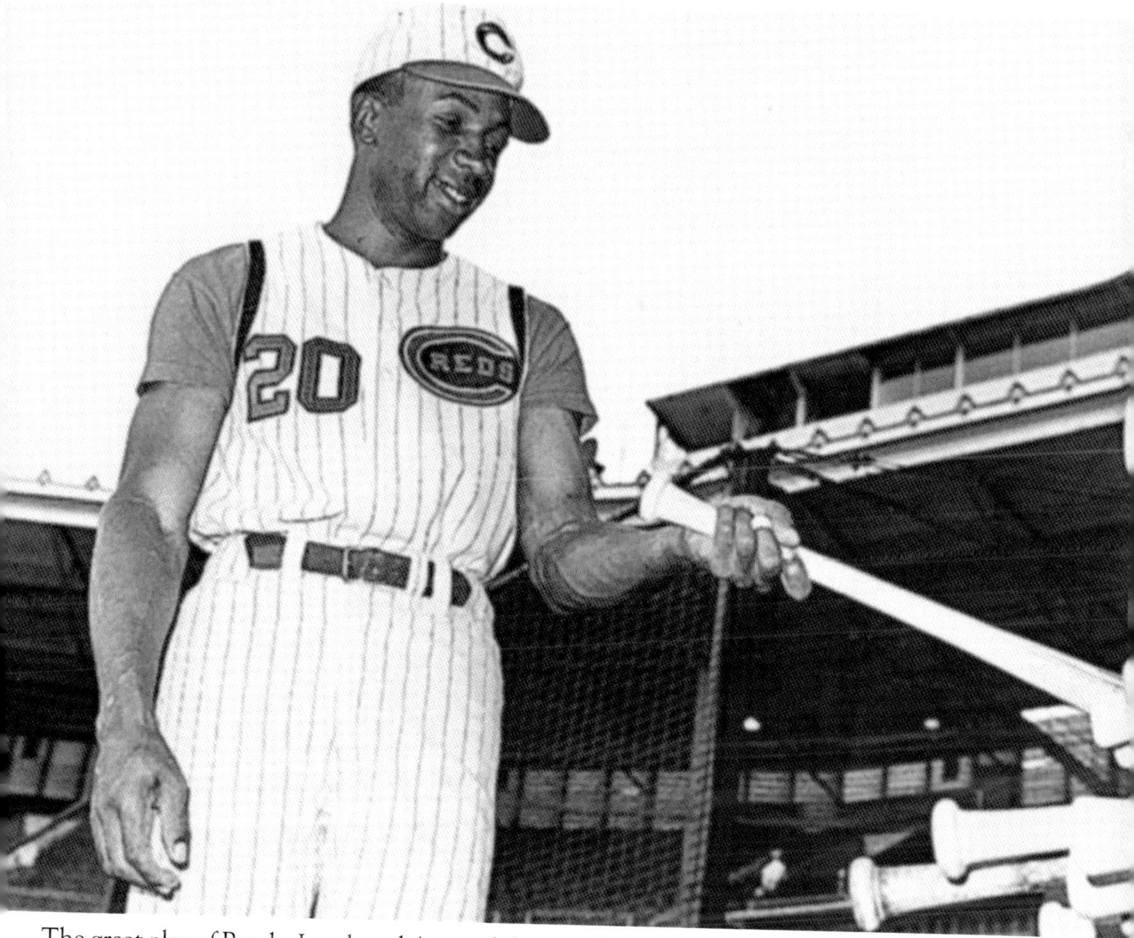


The great play of Reedy, Isreal, and Aaron did not make life easy for them in the Jim Crow south. Facing constant taunts, threats, and segregation from their white teammates in public places, the Sally's first African American players faced a constant struggle. Frank Robinson, who played in Savannah and throughout the South Atlantic League with the 1954 Columbia Reds, was quoted as saying he did not know what racism was until he arrived in the south. Arriving in the major leagues in 1956 with the Cincinnati Reds, Robinson began a professional career that lasted through 1976 as a player and through 2007 as a manager. Some of Robinson's achievements as a player include being named the 1956 Rookie of the Year, being named to 14 all-star teams, and winning two World Series titles and two MVP awards.

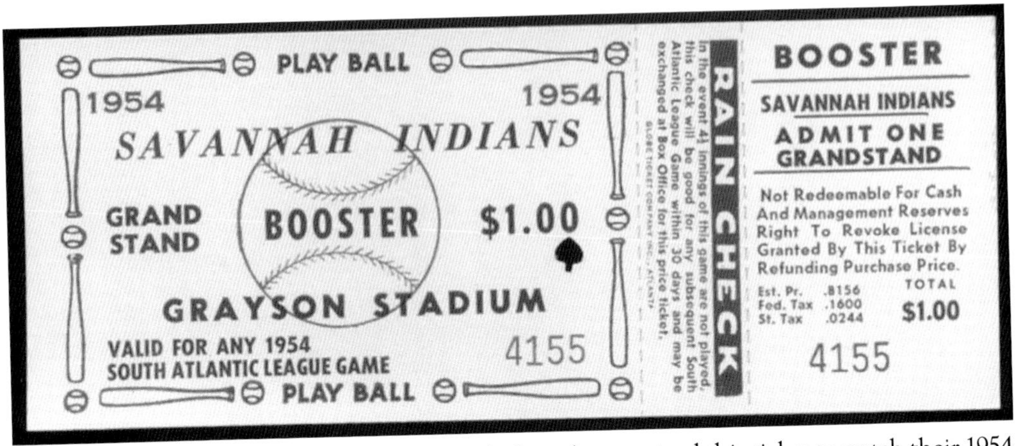


Savannah fans may have been a little confused when they received this ticket to watch their 1954 team. After years of being known as the Indians, the Savannah club decided to change the team name to match their affiliation with the Philadelphia A's. These tickets were apparently printed before the name change. Whatever their name, this ticket enabled fans to watch their team pile up 80 wins on their way to their sixth Sally League championship.

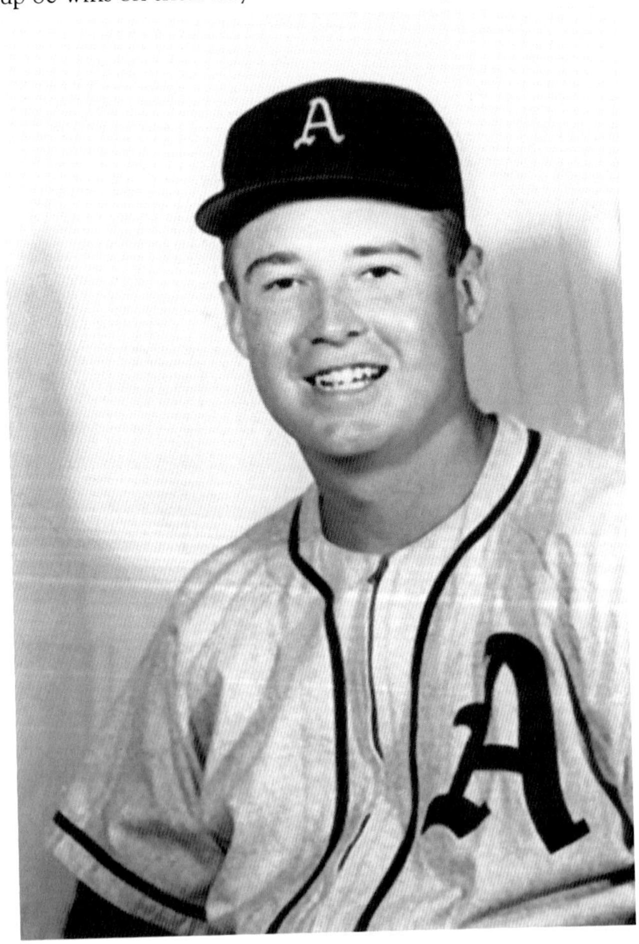

Playing with Al Isreal and Skeeter Kell, who returned to Savannah after a brief stint in the majors, Richard Kirk was a minor part of the Savannah A's success. Only batting .216, Kirk was able to hit 14 home runs and 19 doubles. Dick Kirk played in the minors for four years, with two of them in Savannah.

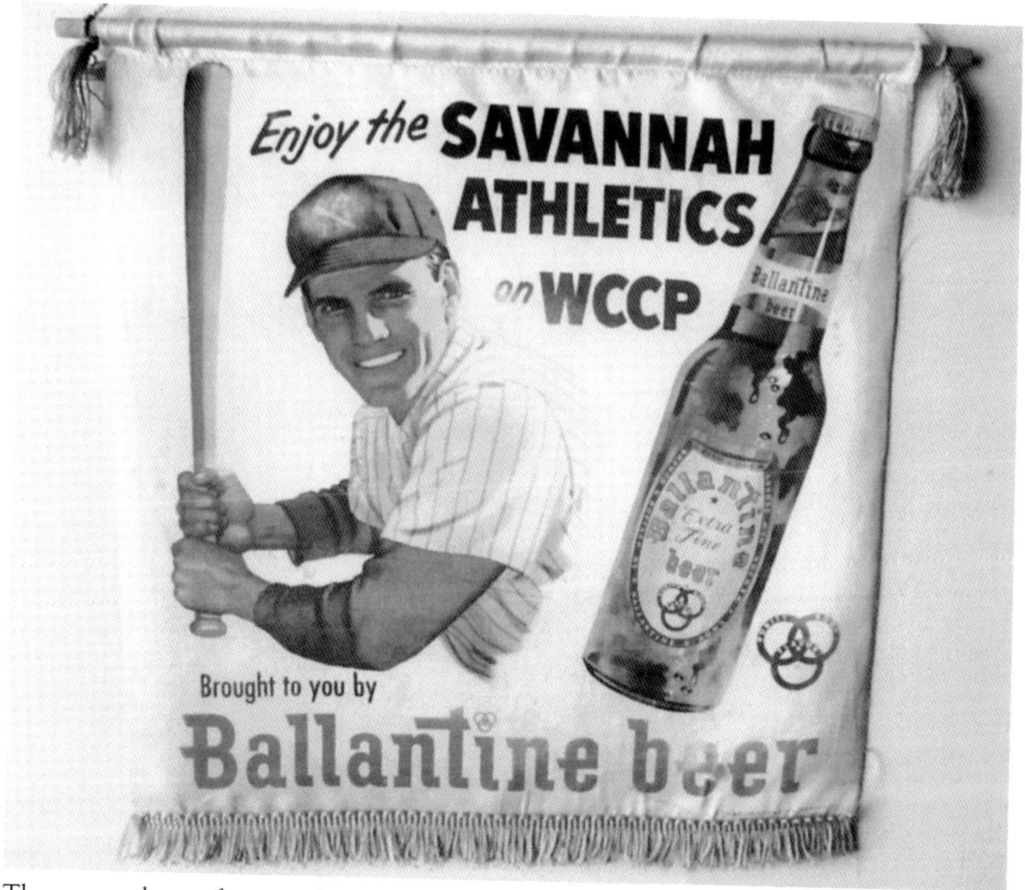


There were plenty of reasons for Savannah fans to break out the Ballantine Beer as the 1955 season began. Fresh memories of the Savannah A's winning the Sally pennant, the parent club Philadelphia A's moving to a new home in Kansas City, and the new Savannah squad that was loaded with talent. The Savannah A's even beat the Kansas City A's at Grayson Stadium in a 9-8 exhibition game. (Courtesy of Dick and Nancy Oyler.)

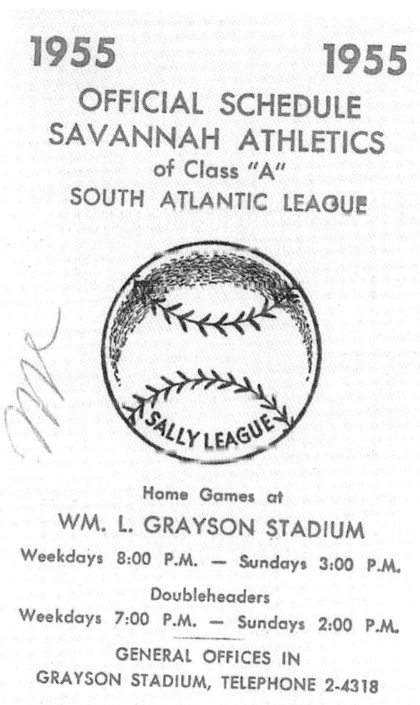


The good times were short lived though, as the Savannah A's finished the year with a losing record. Despite having first baseman Wiley Williams lead the league with 38 home runs and a roster that featured 13 players with major league talent, the A's finished in sixth place. The attendance at Grayson Stadium also fell dramatically in 1955, dropping from more than 82,000 in 1954 to fewer than 49,000 in 1955. (Courtesy of Skip Jennings.)

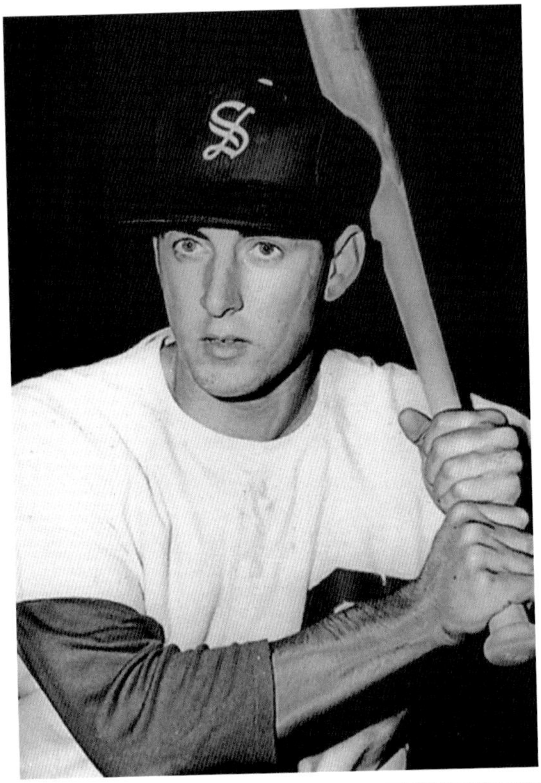

The Kansas City and Cincinnati clubs pulled off an odd trade after the end of the 1955 season. Players were not swapped, but their South Atlantic League franchises were. Savannah now welcomed the Savannah Redlegs to Grayson Stadium. Playing his first of two seasons in Savannah, Drew "Buddy" Gilbert hit .265 while his Redlegs fell a spot in the standings to seventh place. Gilbert eventually made it to the show, playing seven games with the Cincinnati Reds in 1959.

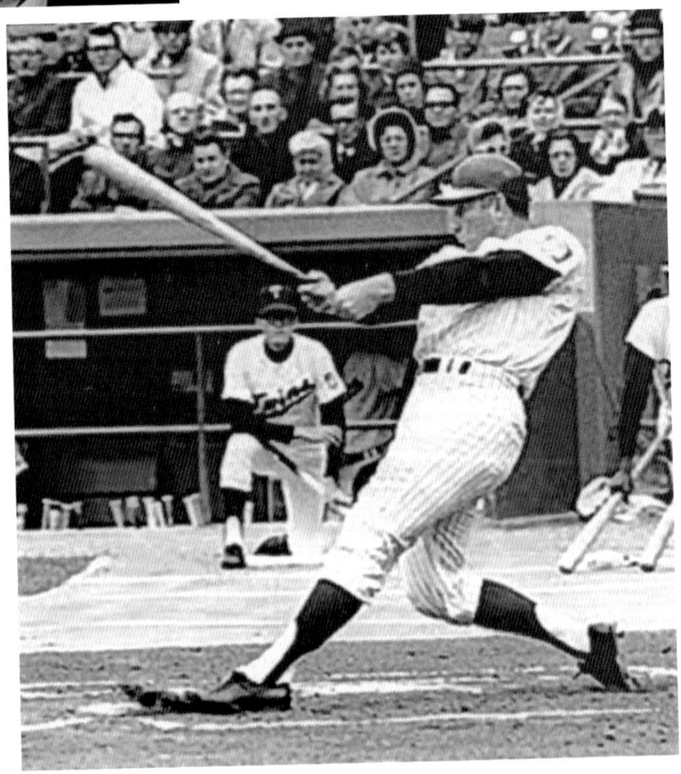

Playing third base for the 1956 Charlotte Hornets, 20-year-old Harmon Killebrew began his professional career showing the talent that suggested a long major league career. In 70 games for the Hornets, many of those played against Savannah, Killebrew batted .325 and hit 15 home runs. After three seasons in the minors, Killebrew was called to the majors, where he played 22 seasons with the Washington Senators and Minnesota Twins.

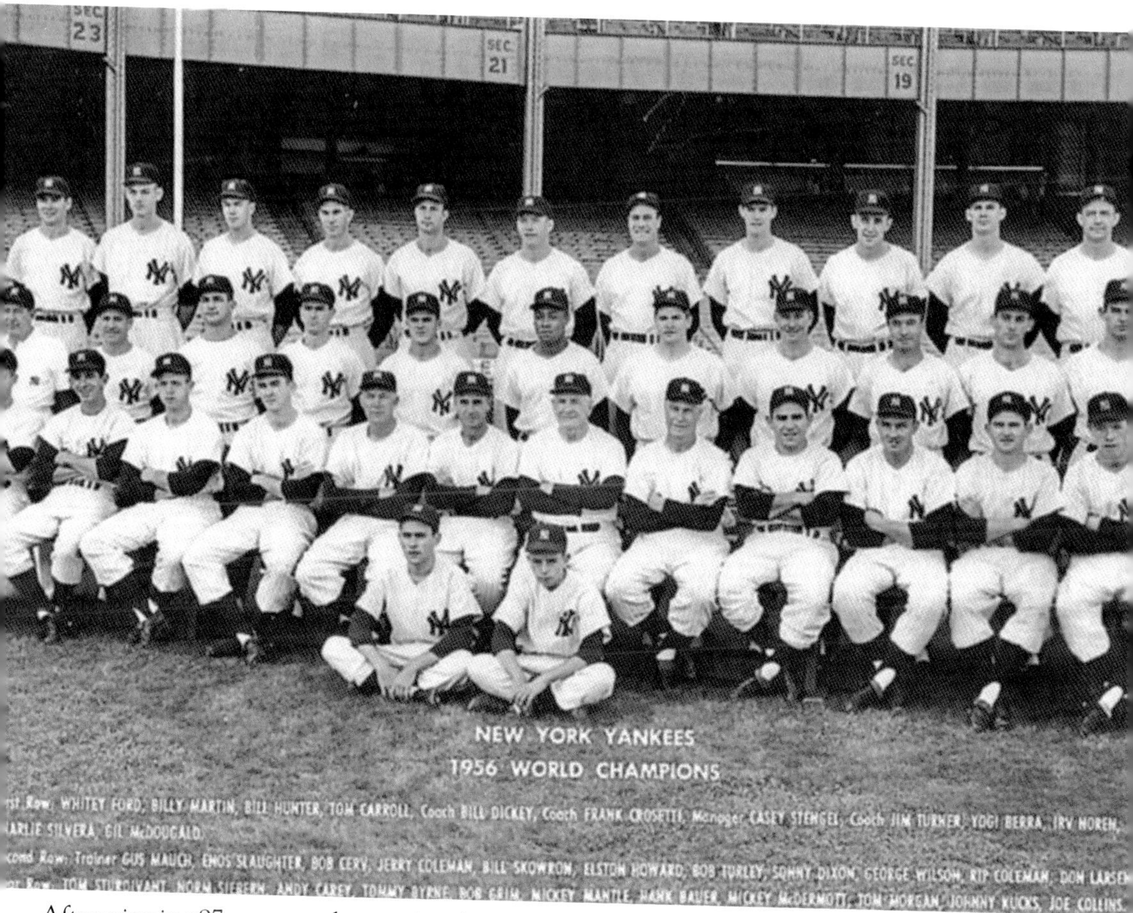


After winning 97 games and capturing their 17th World Series title, the 1956 New York Yankees were clearly the best team in the majors. With a roster of all-time Yankee greats, including manager Casey Stengal, Mickey Mantle, Don Larson, Yogi Berra, Billy Martin, and Whitey Ford, the 1957 Yankees were looking to add another championship to their esteemed history. After leaving their spring training home in St. Petersburg, the Yankees returned to Savannah again for a tune up game, this time against the local Savannah Redlegs. Before a crowd of 4,716 fans, the Bronx Bombers put in a show in front of the Grayson Stadium crowd. Whitey Ford's pitching only allowed four runs by the local Redlegs and the Yankees' bats provided four long home runs. The great pitching and dominant hitting continued for the Yanks as they advanced to the Word Series yet again. The Milwaukee Braves derailed their plans for another title, winning the series in seven games.

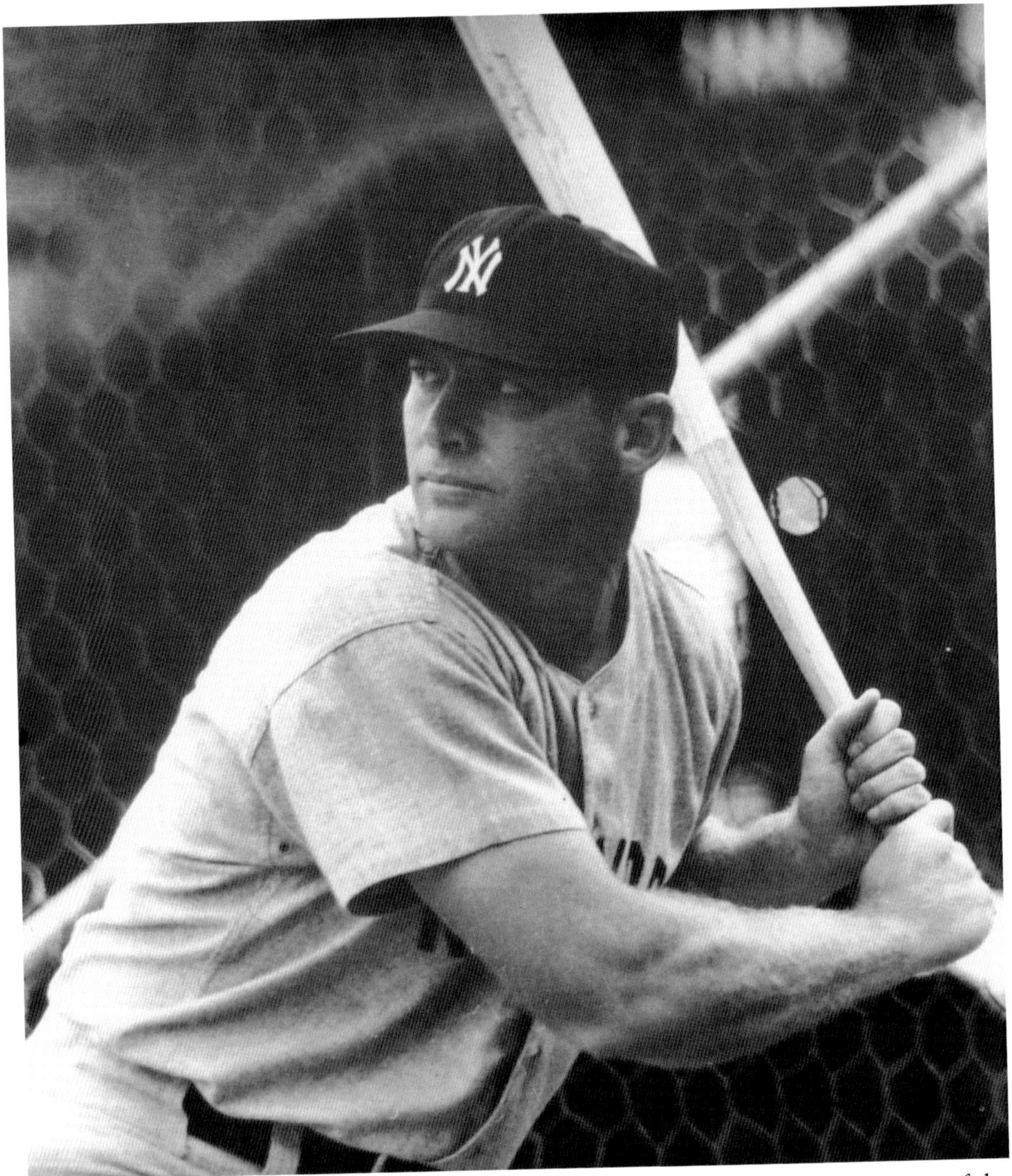

Only in his seventh season as a major league ball player, Mickey Charles Mantle was one of the most popular players in baseball. The *Savannah Morning News* covered Mantle's appearance in the 1957 exhibition game against the Savannah Redlegs in great detail. Describing how Mantle did not drop a fly ball like he did the game before in Jacksonville, the article dedicated to his performance described how he played as if Yankee manager Casey Stengal hadn't forgotten the previous day's error. Mantle had three hits in the game, two singles and a long home run. His success at the plate carried over into the regular season. Mantle ended the 1957 season with a .365 batting average, 34 home runs, and 94 RBIs. He was also awarded his second straight MVP award in 1957.

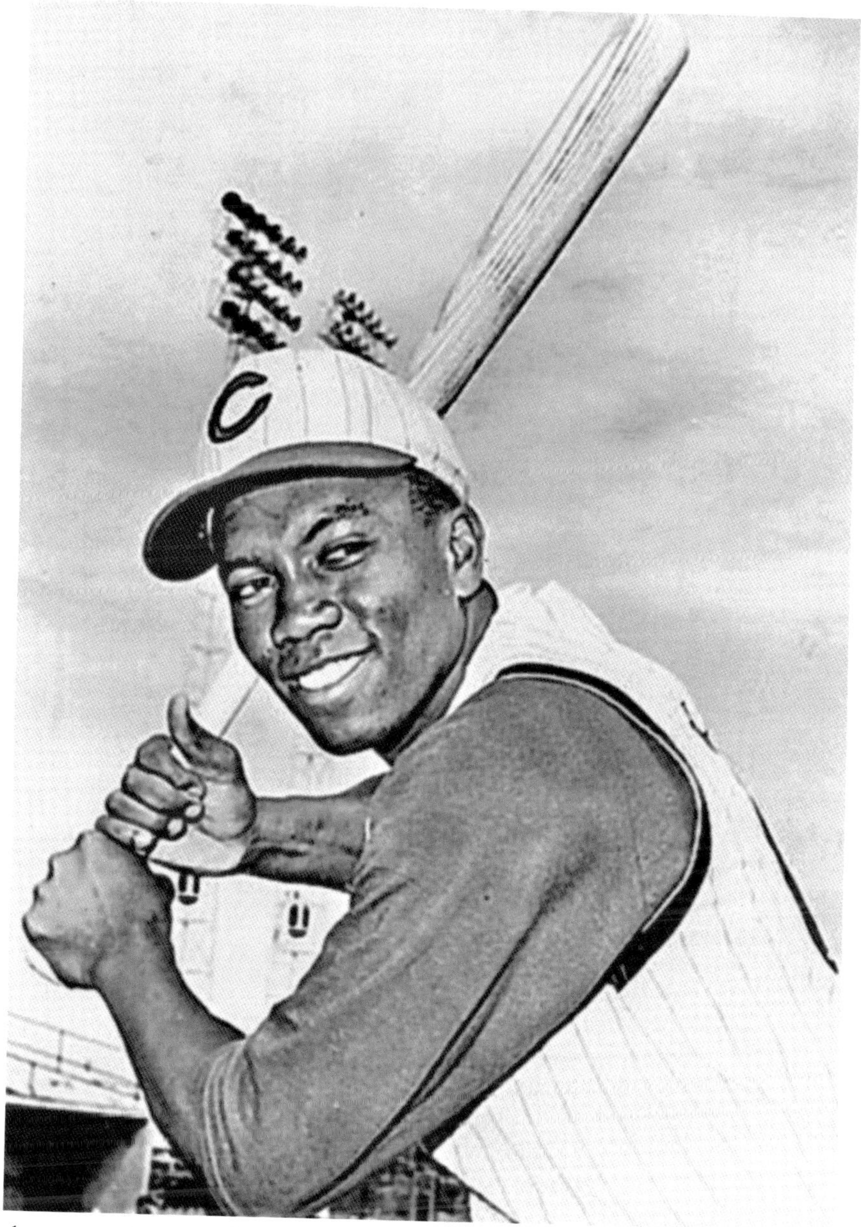

Despite the strong pitching of Whitey Ford in the 1957 exhibition game, 17-year-old Savannah Redleg Chico Cardenas drew two walks and collected two singles against the Yanks. Even with his solid play, the Redlegs lost to the defending champs 8-4. In 1960, Cardenas was called up to play for the Cincinnati Reds, where he hit for a disappointing average of .232 while playing in only 48 games. In 1961, his average climbed to a nice .308 through 74 games. He got a chance at a rematch with the New York Yankees when Cardenas's Reds met the Yanks in the 1961 World Series. The Yankees prevailed again over Cardenas, winning the series in five games. One of his best seasons came in 1966 as he hit 20 home runs and drove in 81 runs. Cardenas went on to become a five-time all-star during his 16-year career.

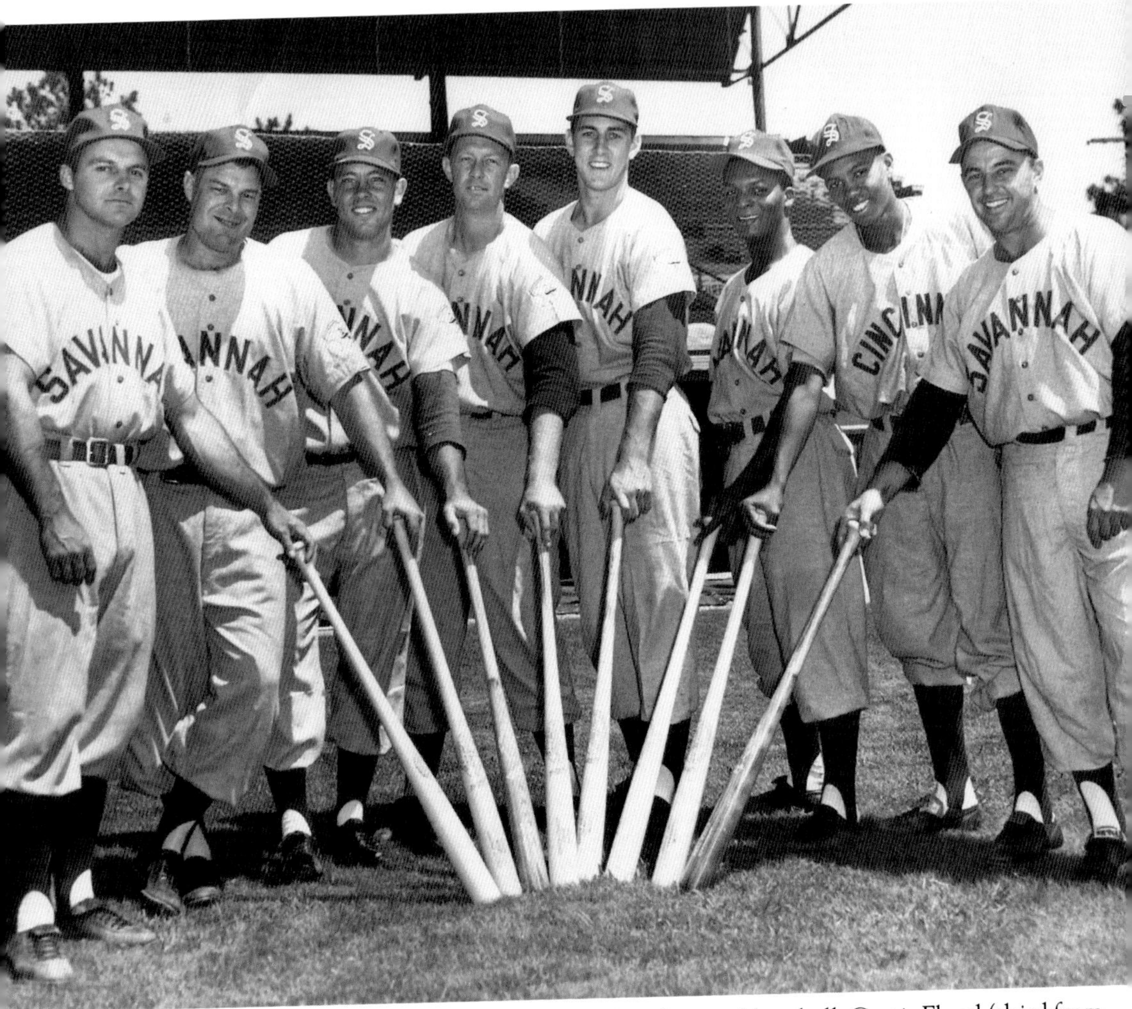


Appearing in Savannah during his second year of professional baseball, Curtis Flood (third from right) had a .299 batting average and hit 14 home runs for the Savannah Redlegs. After three seasons in the minors, Flood was called up to join the Cincinnati club full-time at the age of 20. Having a stellar career through his time for the Reds and later St. Louis Cardinals, Flood was traded to the Philadelphia Phillies in 1969. However, he refused to report to the Phillies, claiming that the reserve clause in players' contracts kept them unfairly tied to the teams that signed them for life, even after players had fulfilled the terms of their contracts. Flood's case eventually wound up in front of the Supreme Court, which ultimately ruled against him. As a result of the controversy, the Major League Baseball Players Union and team owners agreed on a compromise. Sometimes called the "Curt Flood Rule," players with 10 years of service, with the last five being with the same team, could veto any trade. After sitting out the 1970 season, Flood only played 13 games in 1971. He is often credited with the creation of free agency in sports. (Courtesy of Buddy Gilbert.)

With future stars such as Chico Cardenas and Curt Flood on the 1957 Redlegs, it was Tom St. John who led the Savannah squad at the plate. His league leading .326 average and 169 hits helped propel the Redlegs to a third place finish in the Sally League and 81-72 record. St. John only played four seasons of minor league ball, three of them in Savannah.

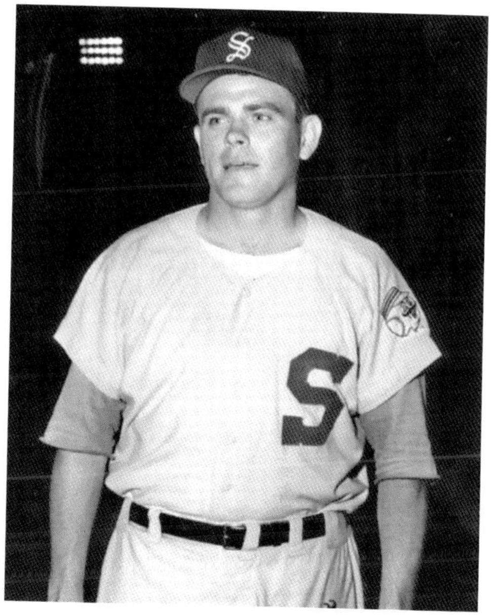

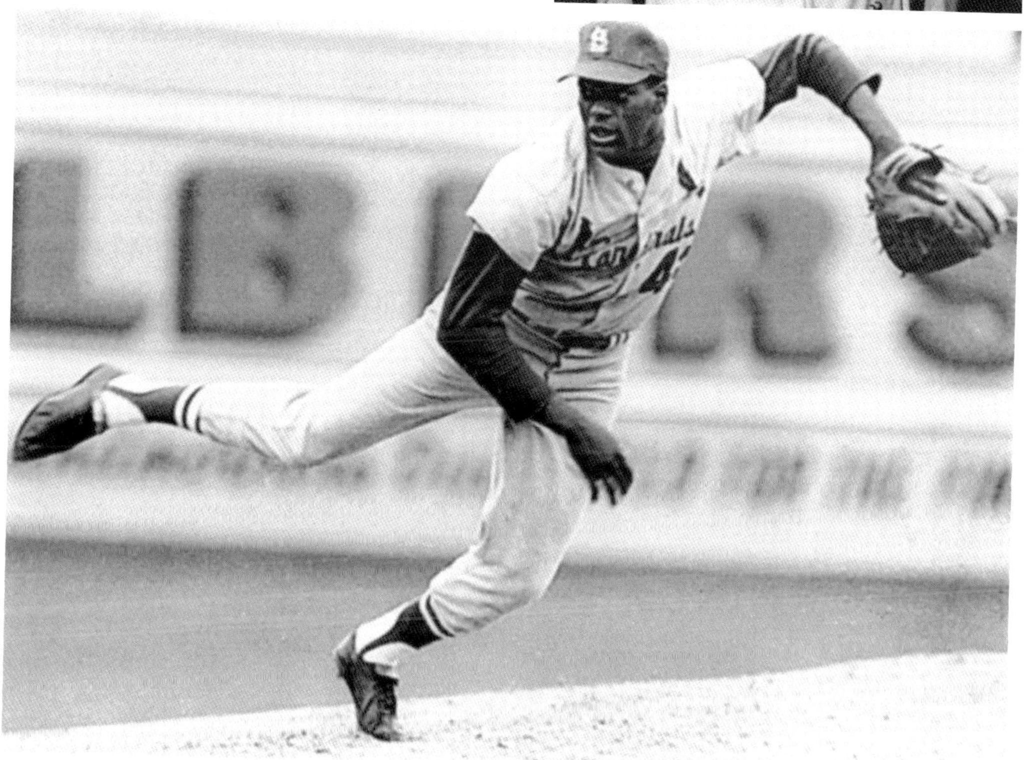

Tom St. John and the rest of the 1957 Redlegs would have had to bat against a 21-year-old pitcher for the Columbus Foxes named Bob Gibson. After spending four seasons in the minors, Gibson joined the St. Louis Cardinals in 1959. Through his 17-year career, Gibson won 251 games, two Cy Young awards, and two world championships, and was voted to the National League All-Star team nine times. He was elected to the Baseball Hall of Fame in 1981.

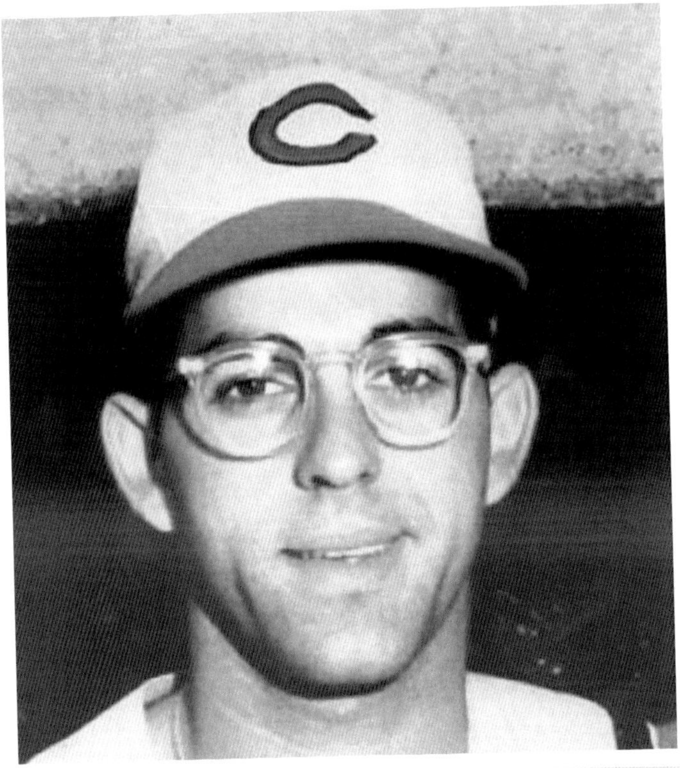

More than 68,400 fans came out to watch the 1958 Savannah Redlegs throughout the 1958 season. One of the players cheered the most was second baseman Octavio Victor Rojas. "Cookie," as he was affectionately known, hit .254 with 24 doubles over the course of the season. Following his call up to the majors in 1962, Rojas spent the next 16 seasons in the majors and made five all-star teams.

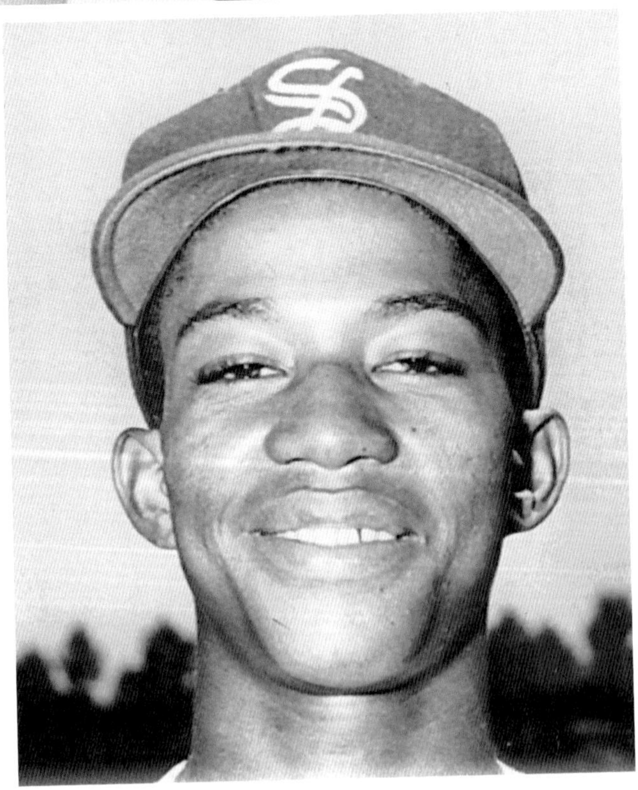

While Cookie Rojas went on to become an all-star in the major leagues, his teammate John Ivory Smith spent his professional career in obscurity in the minors. Through eight seasons of professional baseball, Smith's best season was in 1955 for the Daytona Beach Islanders, winning 19 games. During his year in Savannah in 1958, he appeared in 13 games and posted a 1-6 record. The 1958 Redlegs finished with 61 wins and in sixth place.

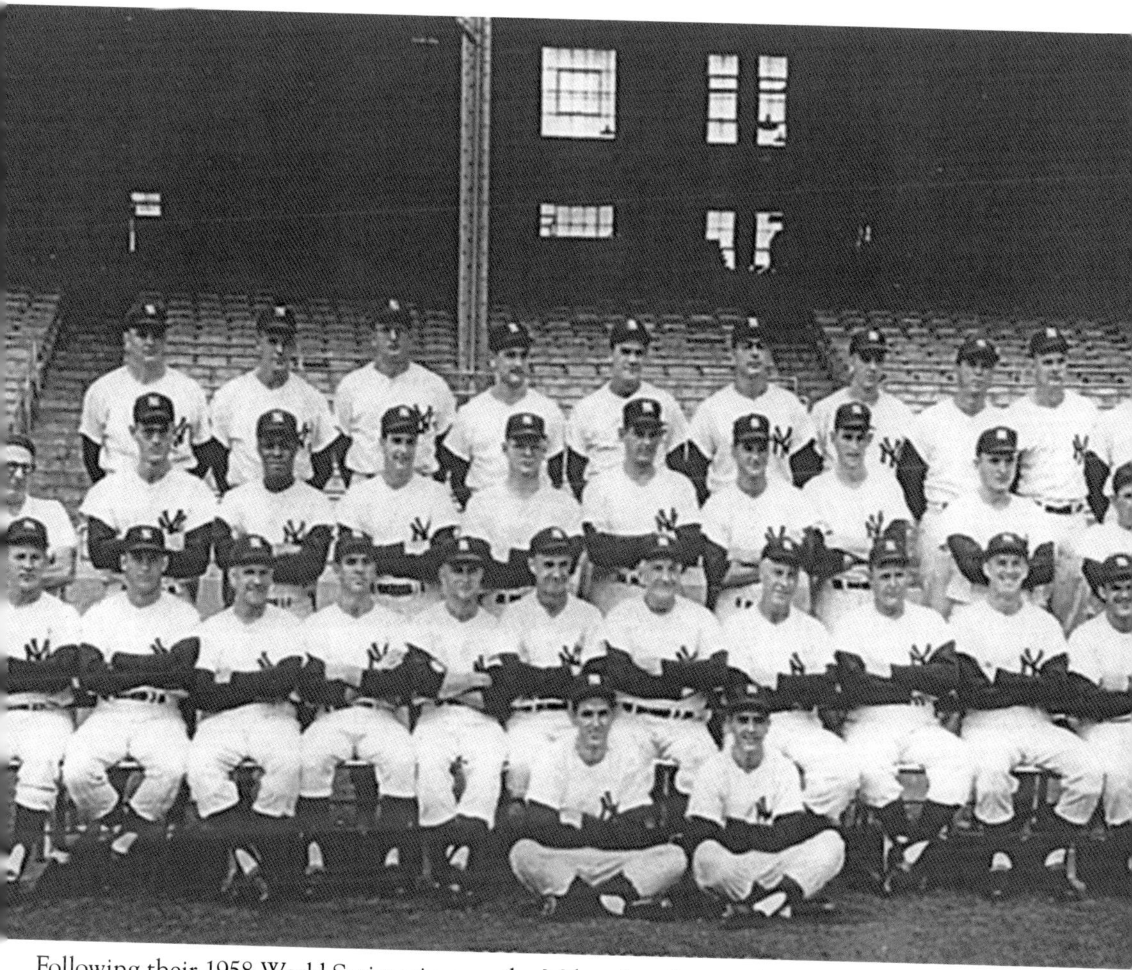

Following their 1958 World Series win over the Milwaukee Braves, the 1959 New York Yankees looked to claim their seventh championship of the decade. Stopping in Savannah as they played their way north to begin the season, the Yanks brought basically the same squad of stars back to Grayson to play the Cincinnati Reds in an exhibition in front of a crowd of more than 8,500. The *Savannah Morning News* again covered the game in great detail, describing how the Reds won on a dramatic Gus Bell home run in the bottom of the 10th inning, thrilling the Savannah fans. The Yanks left Savannah disappointed but confident that their success in the American League would continue during the 1959 season. The end result was not up to the normal Yankee standards. They finished in third place, 15 games behind the Chicago White Sox.

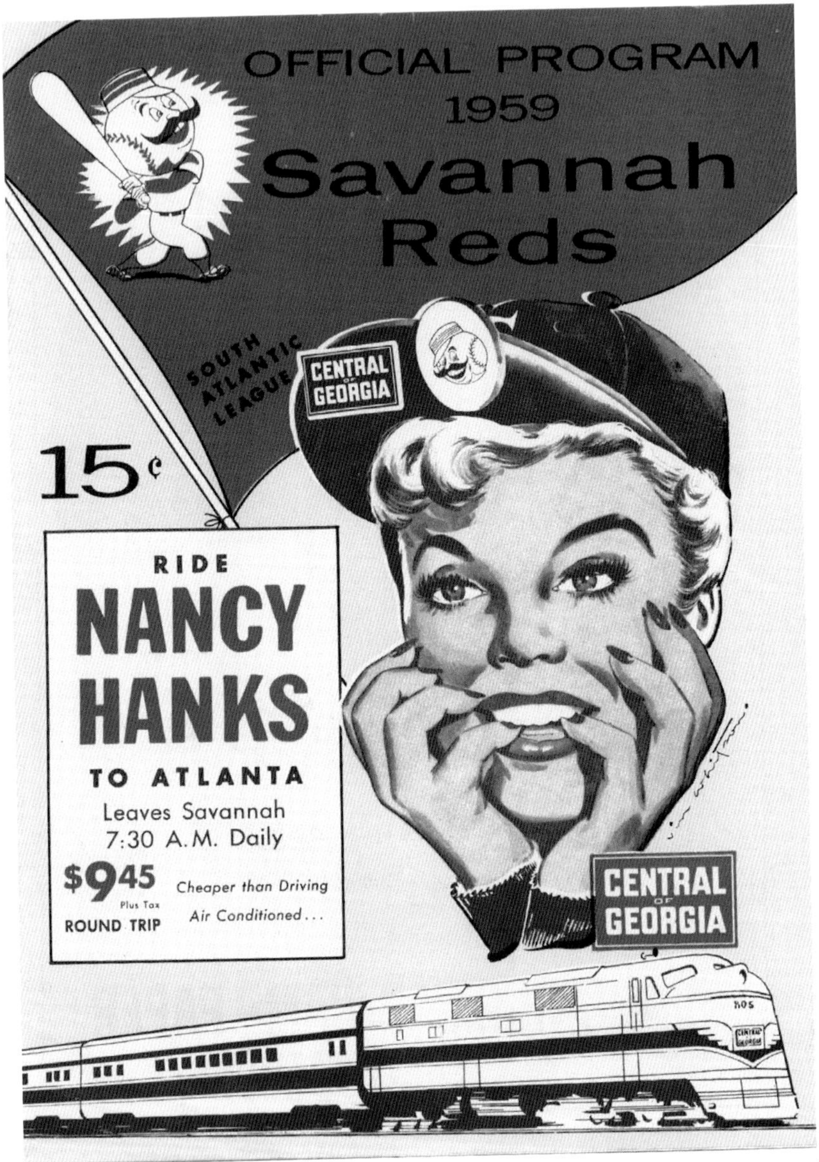


The concerned look of the logo for the Nancy Hanks locomotive on the cover of the 1959 Savannah Reds program provided some unintentional foreshadowing for the upcoming season. The 1959 Savannah Reds drew a crowd of only 54,212 throughout the season, and finished the year in sixth place with a record of 67-73. Starring for the Reds that year was third baseman Cliff Cook. Cook led the South Atlantic League with 32 home runs and 100 RBIs. Despite his success, Cook and the 10 other Reds with major league talent could not draw enough of a crowd to sustain the franchise. The lack of attendance and other economic issues forced the Cincinnati Reds to threaten to pack up the team and take the Central of Georgia Rail Line to another town. After giving the city a list of demands to keep the team in Savannah, the Reds moved the Savannah franchise to Columbia. (Courtesy of the Lew Newman Collection of Baseball Memorabilia, National Museum of American History, and Smithsonian Institution.)

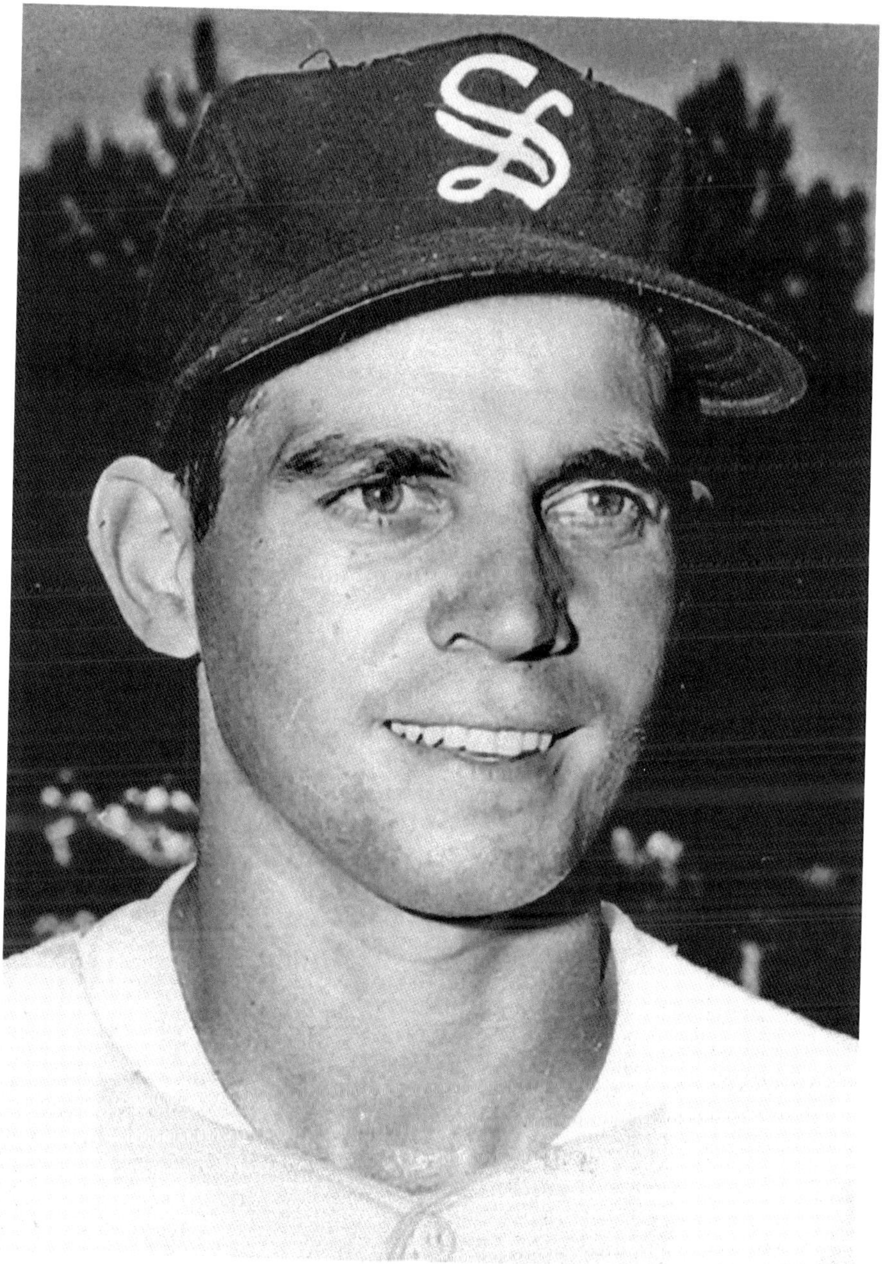

Pitching for the 1959 Savannah Redlegs was 27 year old Ken Hommel. He began his professional baseball career in 1954 with the Ogden Reds of the Pioneer League. His first season was his best as a professional. His 17 wins tied for most in the league that year. Moving up to Columbia in 1955, Hommel played in Savannah in 1956. He made his second stop in Savannah in 1957, pitching six games and notching a 4-2 win-loss record. After finishing the 1957 and 1958 seasons in Nashville, Hommel returned to Savannah once again. The 1960 season proved to be his last as a professional. At 28 years old, he split the season between Asheville and Columbia. Through seven seasons of minor league ball, Hommel could never duplicate the success of his first year.

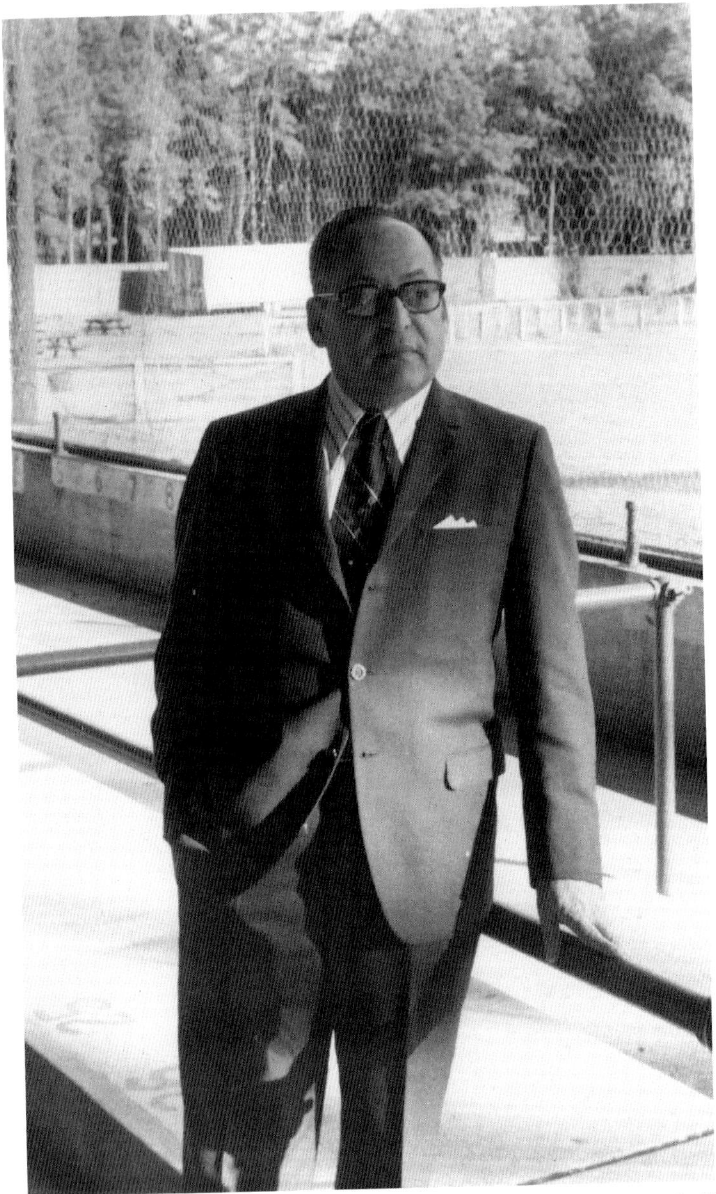

Following the 1959 season, Judge Julius S. Fine, known for years as "Mr. Baseball" in Savannah, spearheaded the effort in 1960 to keep baseball in town. Long before 1960, Fine traveled to Philadelphia in the late 1930s to pitch the idea of a farm team in Savannah to Philadelphia A's owner Connie Mack. This was the first of many times Fine went to bat in an effort to keep baseball in Savannah. Fine went on to serve the Savannah baseball community for more than 50 years. After the Reds organization moved their "A" farm team to Columbia, Fine led a group of local civic leaders in raising money and selling tickets to convince the owners of the Gastonia Pirates to relocate to Savannah. Spending his own money many times, Fine later claimed that he spent a fortune trying to keep baseball in Savannah while never being paid a nickel for his services. (Courtesy of Miles Wolff.)

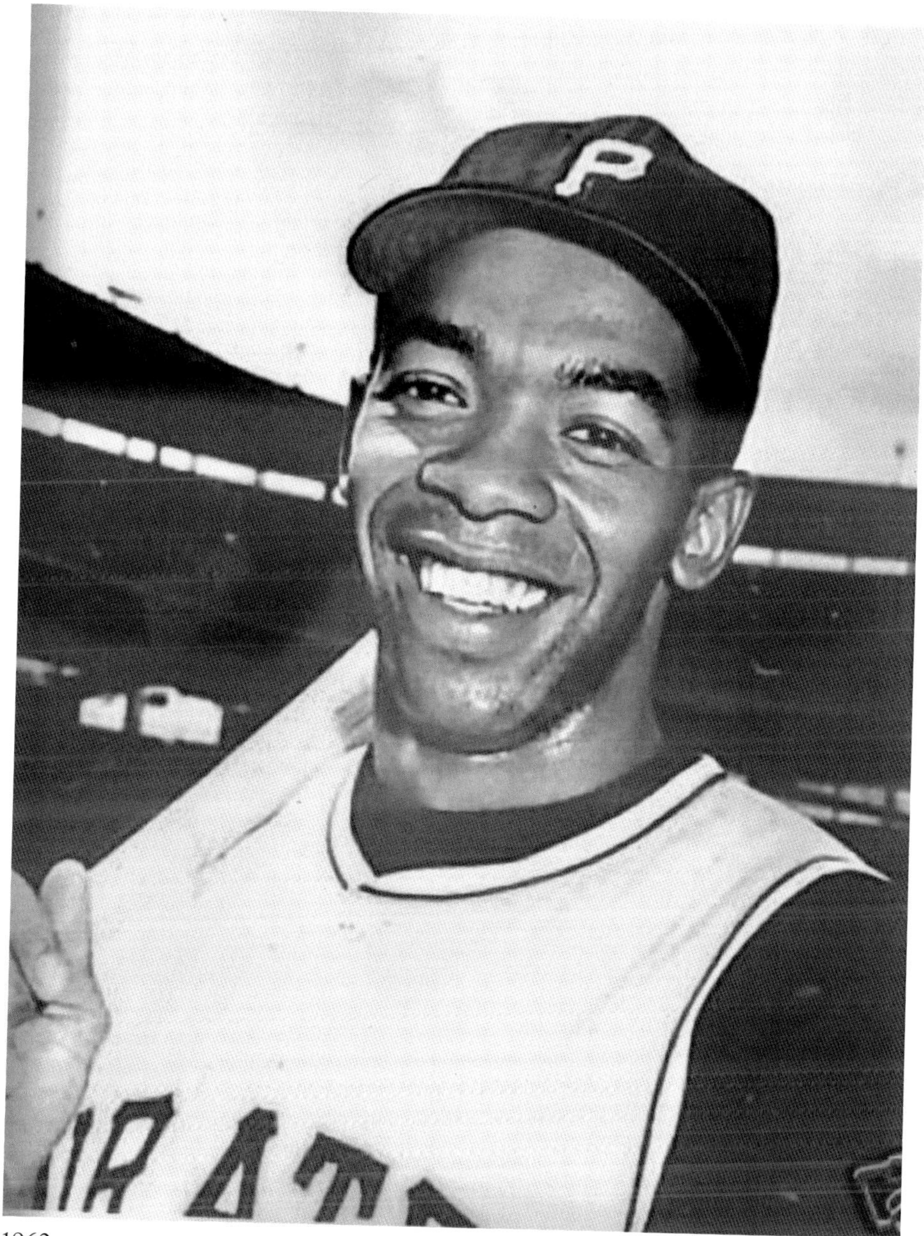


The 1960 season saw a new look for the Savannah team with the affiliation of the Pittsburgh Pirates. Finishing the year with 78 wins and a third place standing, the Savannah Pirates advanced to the Sally League playoffs and won the seventh championship for the city. Starring for the Pirates was 24-year-old first baseman Don Clendenon, who was in his fourth year of professional baseball. Leading the 1960 South Atlantic League with 28 homers, Clendenon was called up by the big league Pirates in 1961. Through his solid 12-year big league career, Clendenon played eight seasons for the Pittsburgh Pirates, one year for the Montreal Expos, and three seasons for the New York Mets. He was awarded the 1969 World Series MVP. Clendenon retired at the age of 36 following the 1972 season with the St. Louis Cardinals.

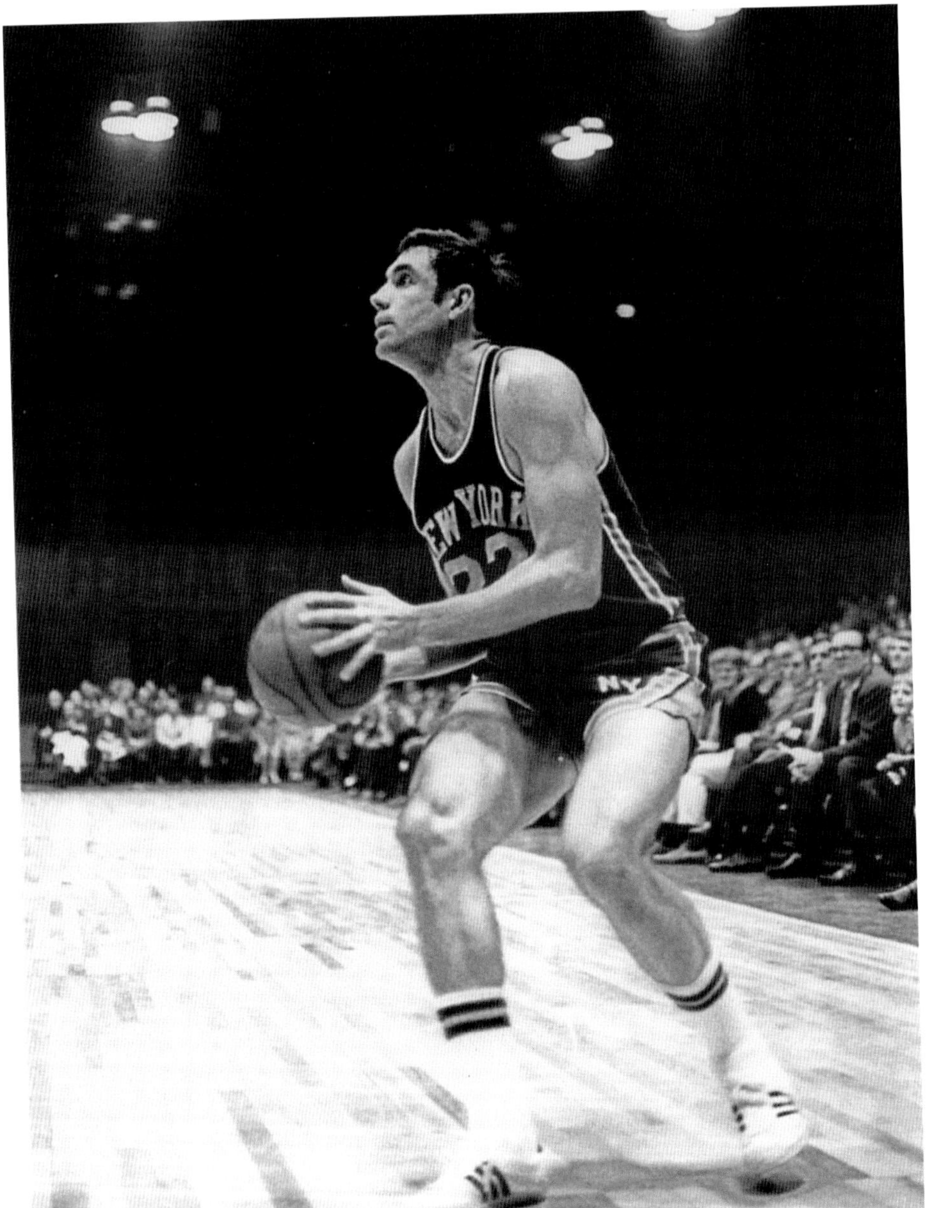

With the Pirates keeping their farm team in Savannah for one year, Savannah was without baseball in 1961. In 1962, the Chicago White Sox decided to place a team in Savannah. A young pitcher named Dave DeBusschere starred for the Savannah club with a record of 10-1. Signing the same year as an amateur free agent, DeBusshere began his first professional baseball season showing enough talent and promise to be called up to Chicago late in the year. He appeared in 12 games with the big league White Sox. In 1963, he appeared in 23 games with the White Sox. The 1964 and 1965 seasons were spent at AAA Indianapolis. Despite his potential, basketball was where his true talents lay. Winning two NBA titles and voted to eight all-star teams, he became a member of the Basketball Hall of Fame in 1983.

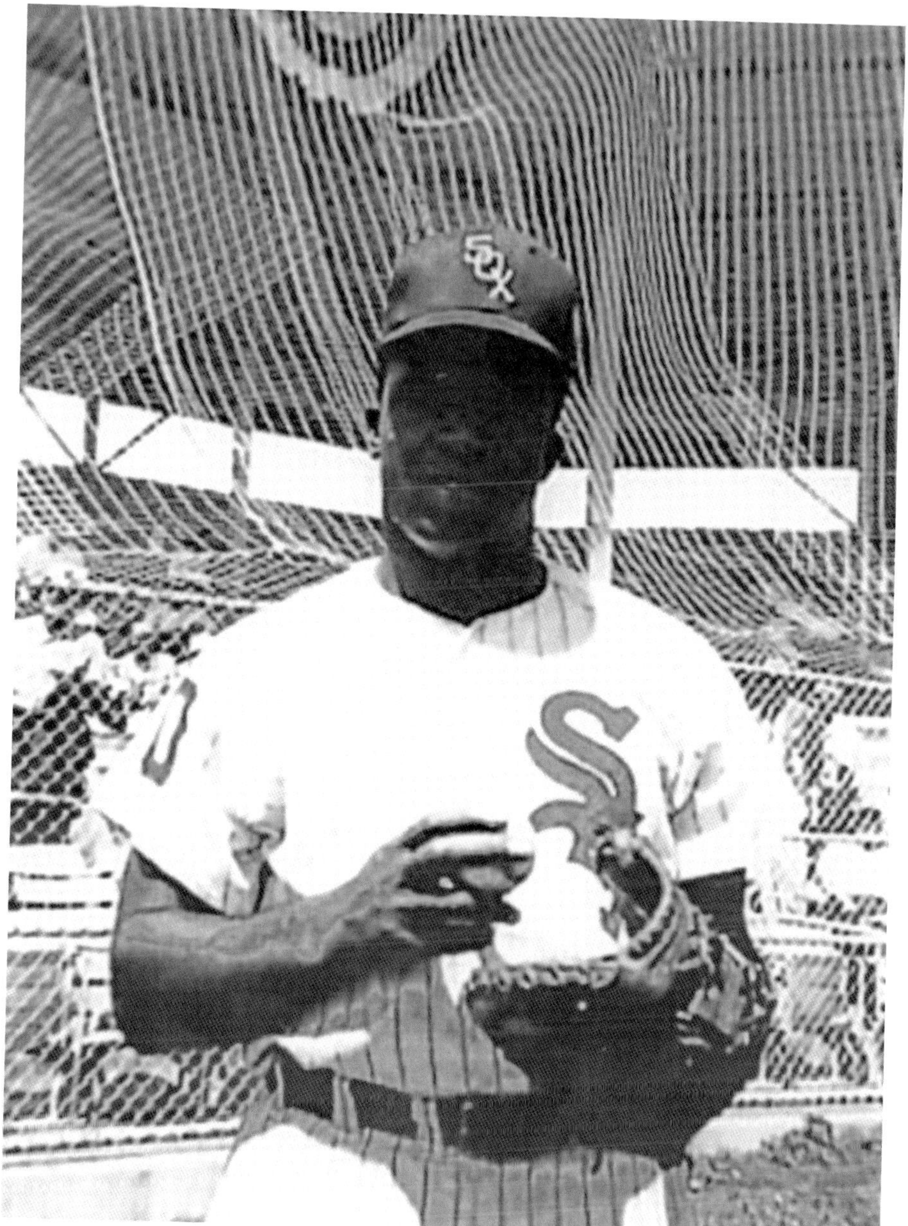

Deacon Jones hit 26 homers, collected 101 RBIs, and led the league with a .319 batting average with the 1962 Savannah White Sox. Even with his success, however, Jones found life in the Sally League difficult. Originally from White Plains, New York, Jones confronted racism directly in the deep south. He had a gun pulled on him at a rest stop lunch counter while traveling through the South Atlantic League. His wife, moved by the Civil Rights movement, was involved with protests at Grayson Stadium. She and another player's wife decided to sit behind home plate during a game instead of in the segregated section. Jones expected to receive retaliation against himself and his family as a result of her protest. During 1962, there were several instances of the local NAACP chapter protesting the segregated seating at Grayson Stadium.

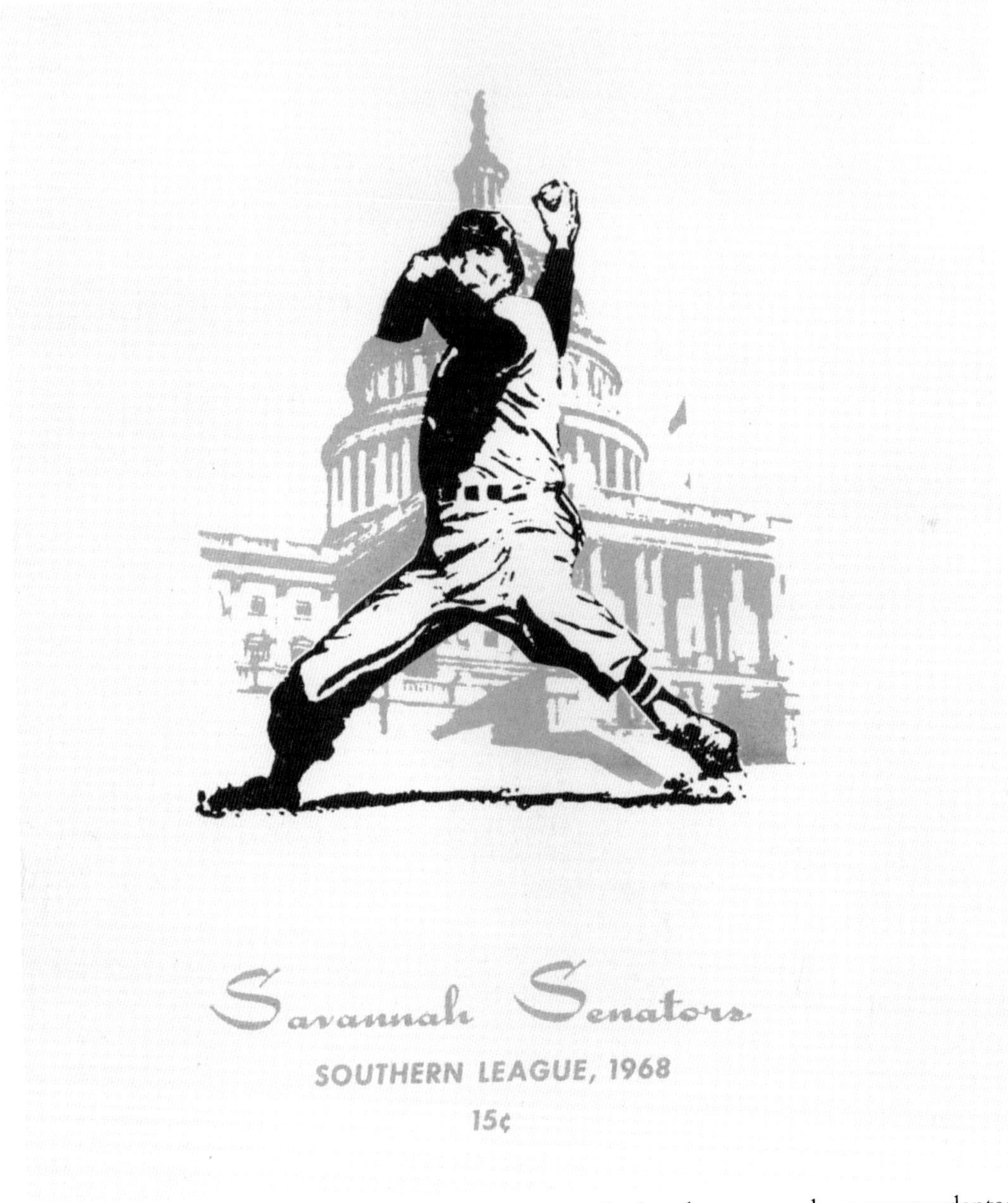


As racial tensions mounted, attendance fell so dramatically that the team made an unprecedented move to Lynchburg, Virginia, with eight games left in the season. Even with the 1962 Savannah/Lynchburg White Sox compiling 92 wins and advancing to the playoffs, it was a disappointing end to a wonderful season. The team featured 14 future major leaguers and is considered one of the best to take the field in Savannah. After the departure of the White Sox and a five-year hiatus, 3,306 fans packed into Grayson Stadium to welcome the return of professional baseball to Savannah on April 17, 1968. Playing in the "AA" Southern League, the Savannah Senators operated as a farm team for the Washington club. Finishing the year with a 57-79 record, the Senators ended the year in fifth place. (Courtesy of Skip Jennings.)

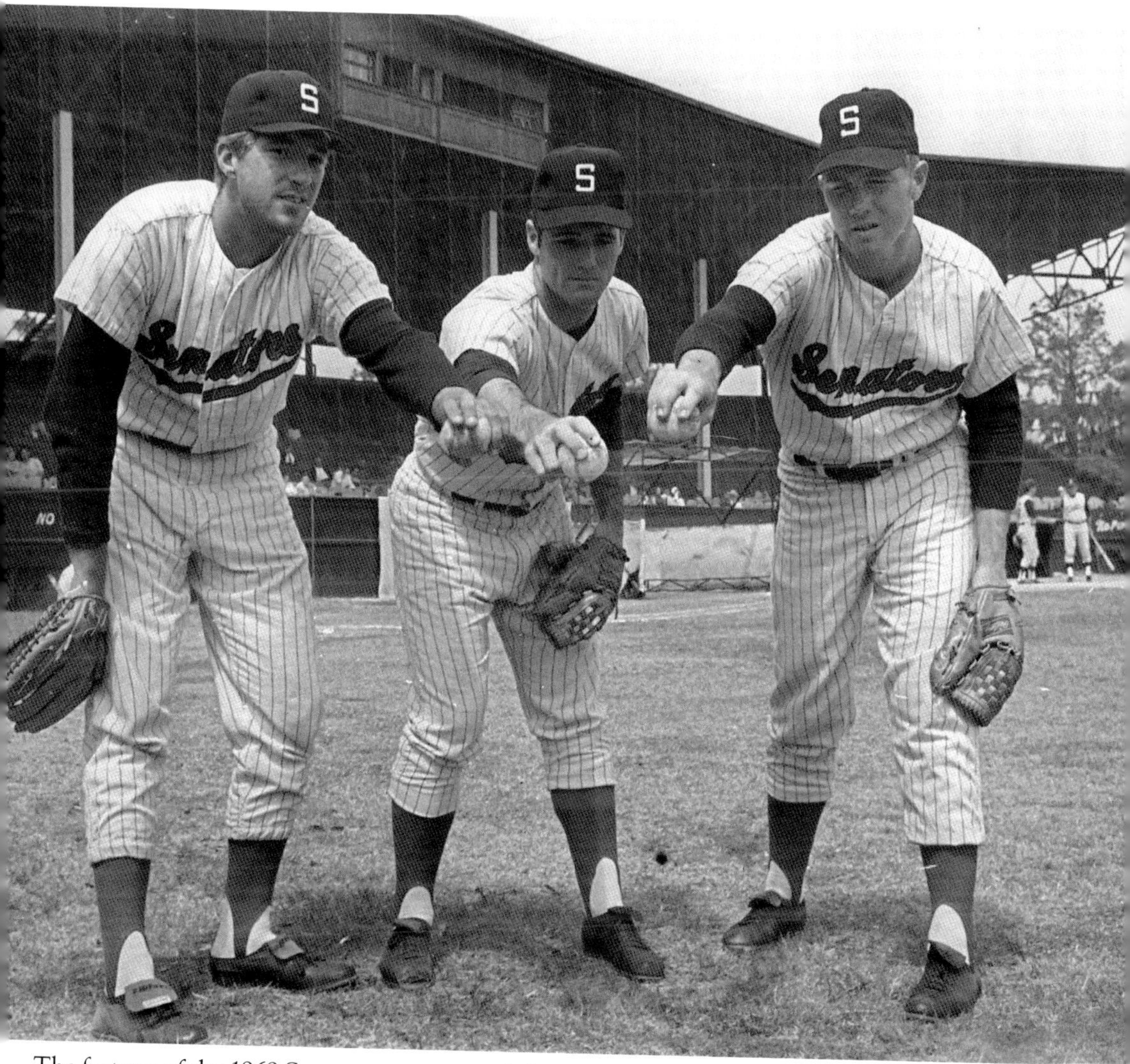

The fortune of the 1969 Senators was not much better than the previous year's team. Attendance at Grayson Stadium dropped to 31,910, the lowest total in years. Also falling was the Senators' place in the Southern League standings, slipping to sixth place. Managed by Hubert Kittle, the 1969 Senators featured 19 players with major league talent. This talent, combined with Kittle's 21 years of experience in professional baseball, should have provided a recipe for success for the Senators. For some reason though, they did not gel enough to form a winning team. Nor did the team fit in with Savannah. Following the 1969 season, Washington pulled its farm team out of Savannah. (Courtesy of the City of Savannah, Research Library, and Municipal Archives.)

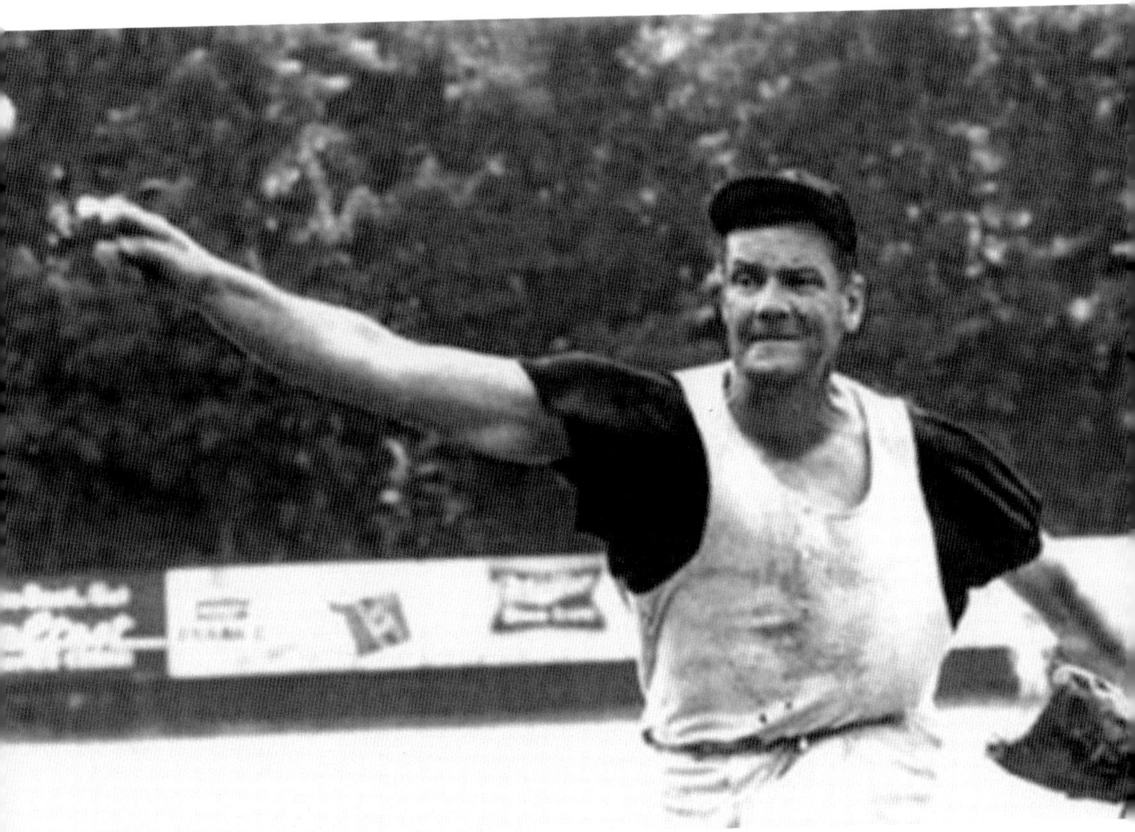

When Ray Hathaway arrived in Savannah for the 1970 season, he was close to drawing his 35-year career in professional baseball to a close. Beginning in 1939 with the Dayton Wings in the Middle Atlantic League, Hathaway spent the next five seasons of minor league ball playing in the Brooklyn Dodgers farm system. His break came in 1946, when he was called on to pitch for the big league Dodgers. His shot at the big time did not last long though, as Hathaway only played in four major league games with Brooklyn. He finished the 1946 season back in the minors and spent the next 24 playing and managing for clubs around the country. When the Cleveland Indians moved to Savannah for the 1970 season, Hathaway managed the club in his second tour of duty in Savannah. The Indians finished the year in fourth place in the Southern League. Following another year of poor attendance, with only 33,854 fans coming to Grayson Stadium, Cleveland moved the franchise to Jacksonville.

# 3

# THE MODERN ERA

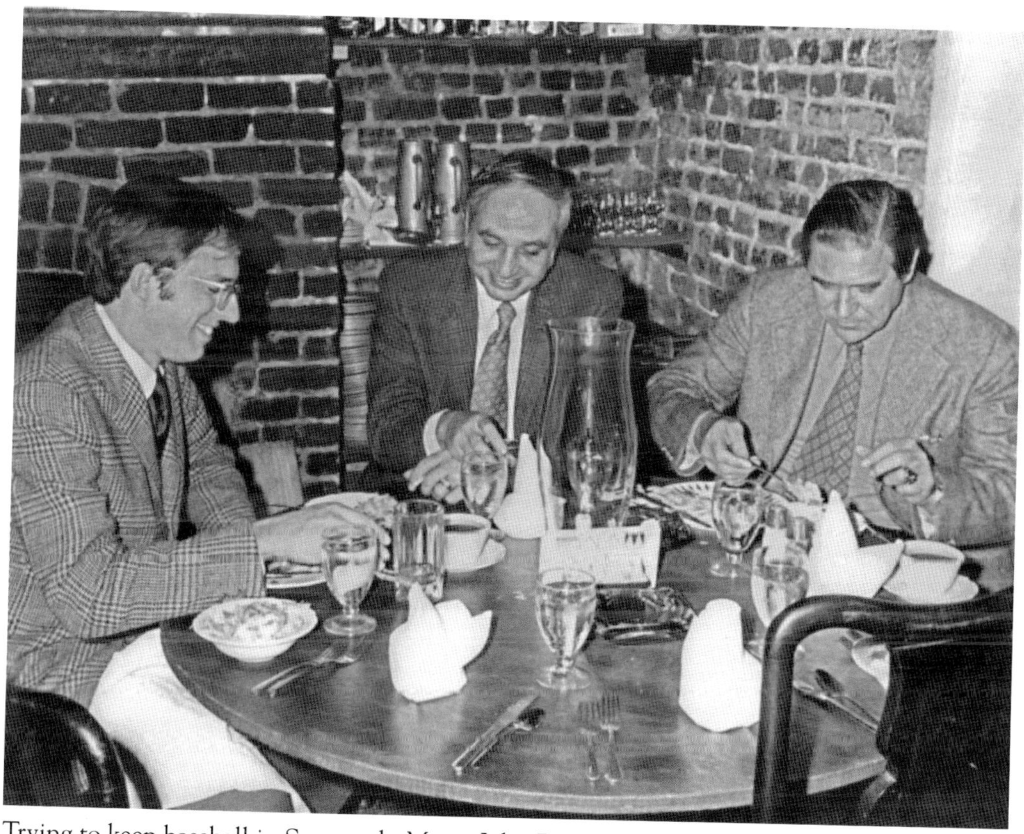

Trying to keep baseball in Savannah, Mayor John Rousakis met with officials from the Atlanta Braves about the possibility of moving their farm team from Shreveport to Savannah. In late 1970, the Braves officially moved the team. This photograph shows Savannah Braves general manager Miles Wolff (left), Mayor John Rousakis (center), and Atlanta Braves executive Eddie Robinson celebrating the announcement. (Courtesy of Miles Wolff.)

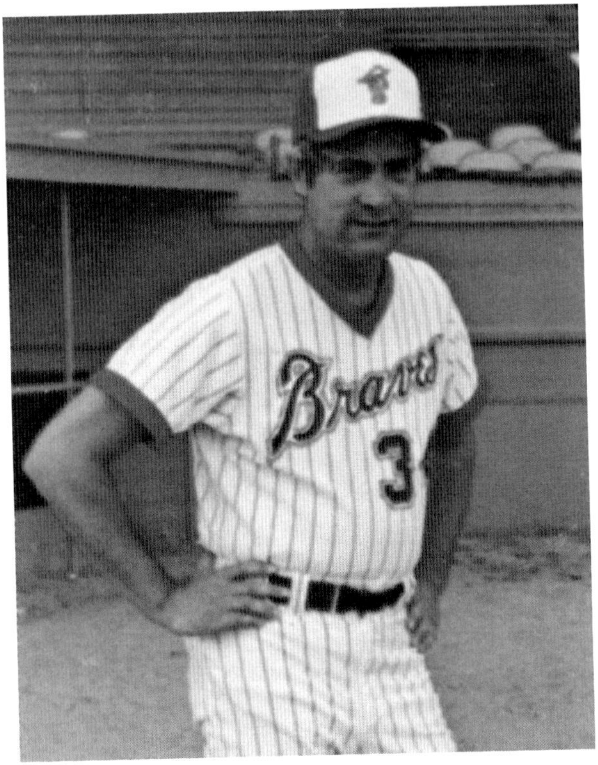

The Braves' tenure in Savannah began with more than 10,400 fans flocking to Grayson to welcome their new team. Despite the warm reception, the Braves had a long year, winning only 57 games and finishing in fifth place. Manager Eddie Haas moved on to manage the Wytheville Braves the following year. (Courtesy of Skip Jennings.)

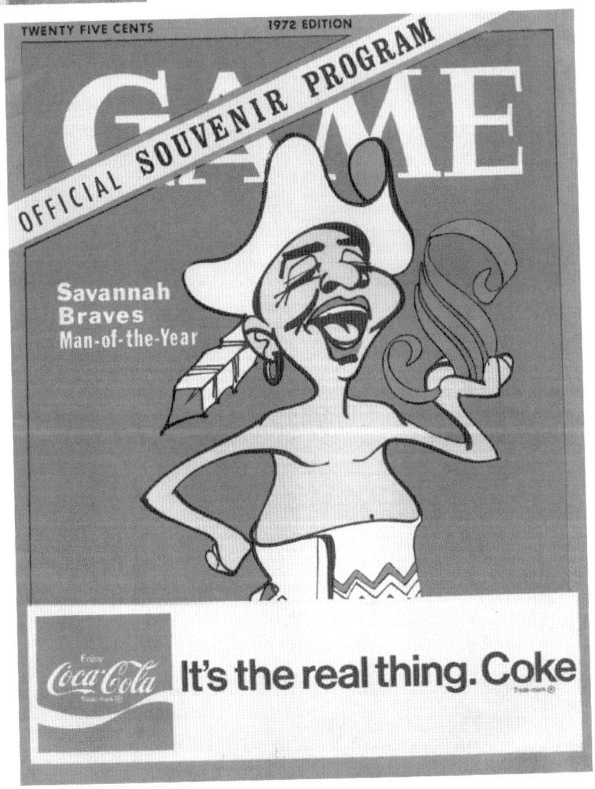


The Savannah Braves certainly were the Man of the Year in Savannah during the 1972 season. Although the big league club was stuck in mediocrity since winning the National League West in 1969, Savannah fans paid close attention to Hank Aaron's chase of Babe Ruth's home run record. With attendance increasing by almost 18,000, Savannah fans were almost certainly Atlanta Braves fans. (Courtesy of Miles Wolff.)

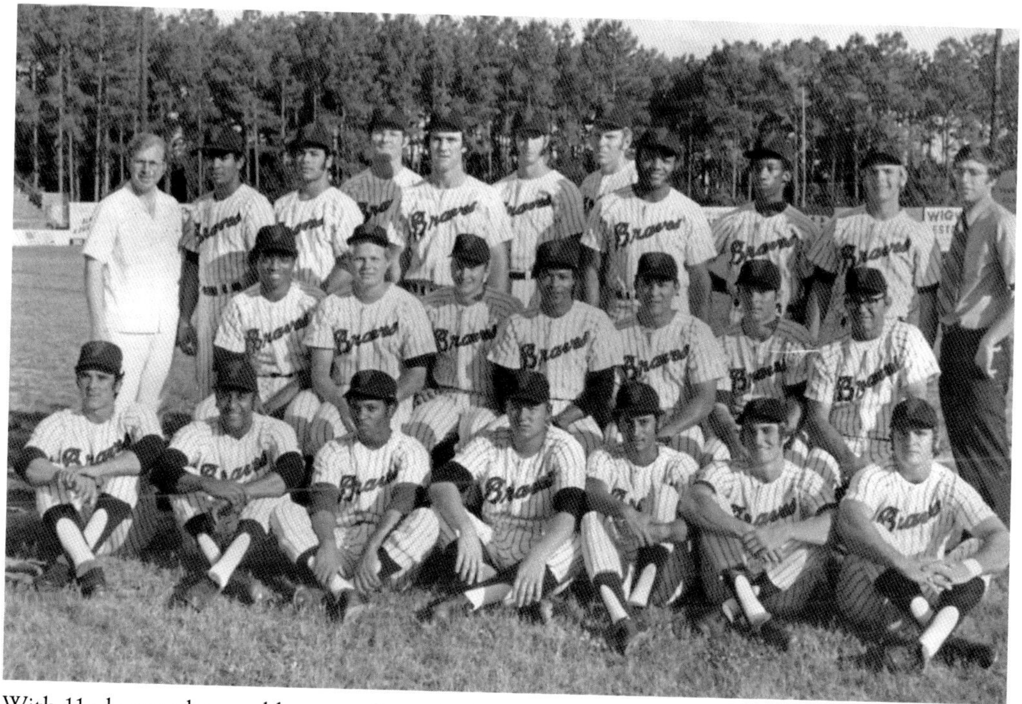

With 11 players who would eventually make the major leagues, the 1972 Savannah Braves ended the Southern League season in second place. With the slugging of Jack Pierce and Gregory Foreman, the Braves improved their record to 81 wins and 59 losses. Larry Maxie led the way on the mound, winning 13 games. (Courtesy of Miles Wolff.)

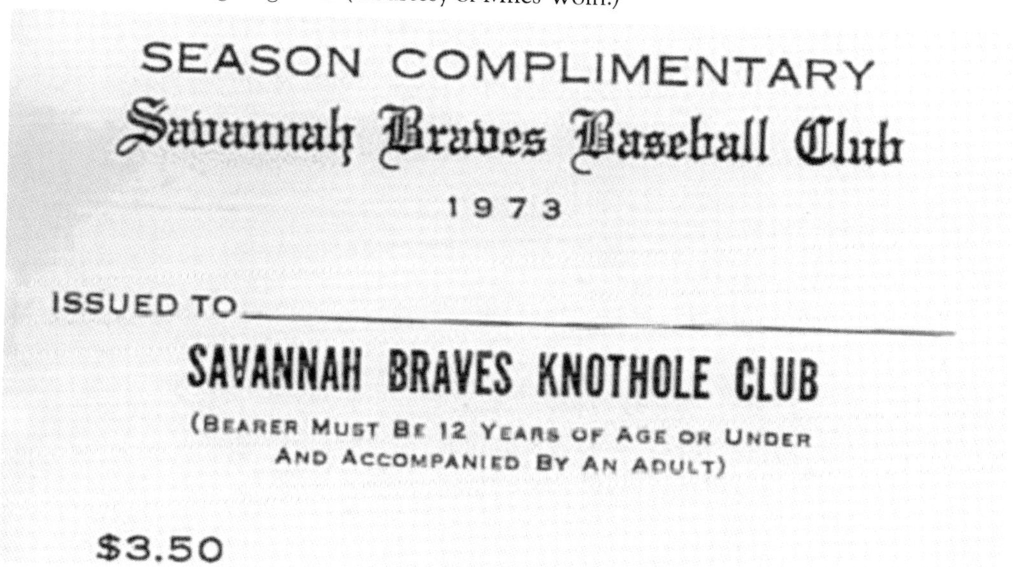

SEASON COMPLIMENTARY

Savannah Braves Baseball Club

1973

ISSUED TO ______________________________

SAVANNAH BRAVES KNOTHOLE CLUB

(BEARER MUST BE 12 YEARS OF AGE OR UNDER AND ACCOMPANIED BY AN ADULT)

$3.50

This pass enabled children 12 and younger to be admitted free of charge into all Savannah Braves home games for the 1973 season. For more than 20 years before this pass was issued, many children throughout Savannah were members of the Knothole Gang. Often sitting in the left field bleachers, many Savannah residents still have fond memories of the club.

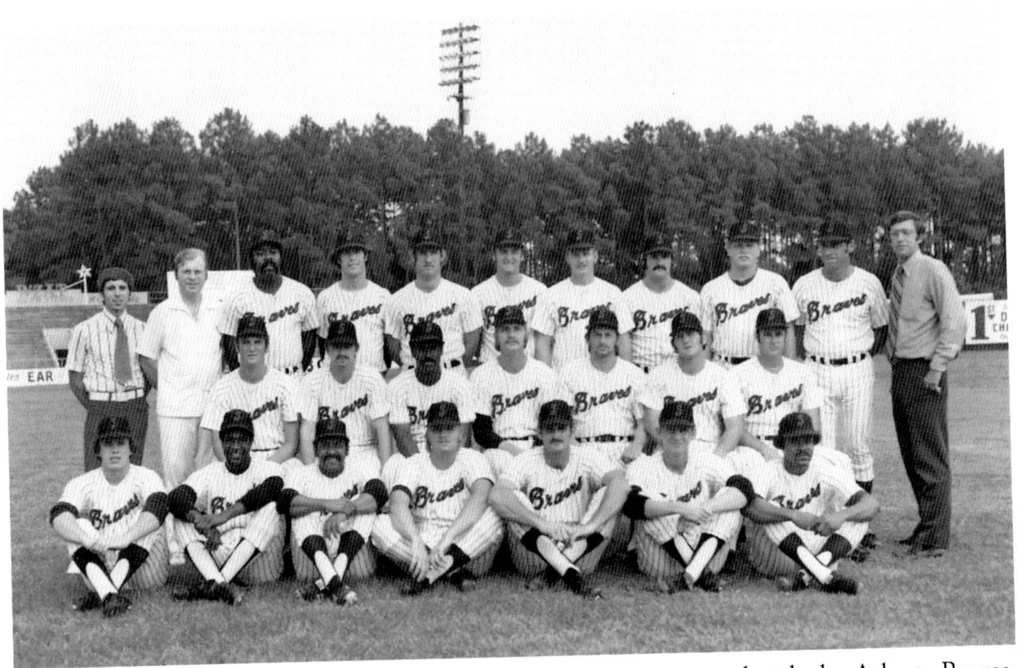

As Hank Aaron continued his chase for Babe Ruth's home run record with the Atlanta Braves, the Savannah Braves were busy developing players to play for the big league ball club one day. Playing catcher for Savannah, Biff Pocoroba batted .234 and hit 12 home runs. Despite those pedestrian numbers, Pocoroba arrived with the Atlanta Braves in 1975 and played there for the next 10 seasons. Savannah pitcher Frank LaCorte arrived in the show at Atlanta in 1975 as well and played for five seasons with the Braves. With seven players with big league talent on the 1973 roster, the Savannah franchise was doing its part to groom players for Atlanta. (Above, courtesy of Miles Wolff; below, courtesy of Skip Jennings.)

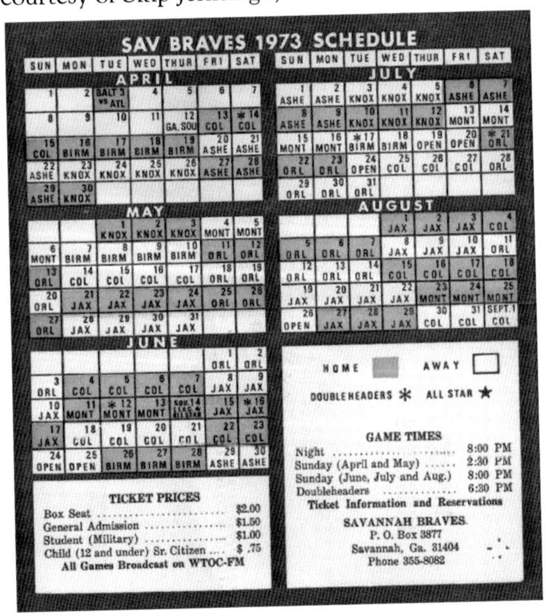

SAV BRAVES 1973 SCHEDULE

APRIL

| SUN | MON | TUE | WED | THUR | FRI | SAT |
|---|---|---|---|---|---|---|
| 1 | 2 | BALT 3 vs ATL | 4 | 5 | 6 | 7 |
| 8 | 9 | 10 | 11 | 12 GA. SOU | 13 COL | * 14 COL |
| 15 COL | 16 BIRM | 17 BIRM | 18 BIRM | 19 BIRM | 20 ASHE | 21 ASHE |
| 22 ASHE | 23 KNOX | 24 KNOX | 25 KNOX | 26 KNOX | 27 ASHE | 28 ASHE |
| 29 ASHE | 30 KNOX | | | | | |

MAY

| SUN | MON | TUE | WED | THUR | FRI | SAT |
|---|---|---|---|---|---|---|
| | | 1 KNOX | 2 KNOX | 3 KNOX | 4 MONT | 5 MONT |
| 6 MONT | 7 BIRM | 8 BIRM | 9 BIRM | 10 BIRM | 11 ORL | 12 ORL |
| 13 ORL | 14 COL | 15 COL | 16 COL | 17 COL | 18 ORL | 19 ORL |
| 20 ORL | 21 JAX | 22 JAX | 23 JAX | 24 JAX | 25 ORL | 26 ORL |
| 27 ORL | 28 JAX | 29 JAX | 30 JAX | 31 JAX | | |

JUNE

| SUN | MON | TUE | WED | THUR | FRI | SAT |
|---|---|---|---|---|---|---|
| | | | | | 1 ORL | 2 ORL |
| 3 ORL | 4 COL | 5 COL | 6 COL | 7 COL | 8 JAX | 9 JAX |
| 10 JAX | 11 MONT | * 12 MONT | 13 MONT | 14 SOU. LEAG. ALL STAR | 15 JAX | * 16 JAX |
| 17 JAX | 18 COL | 19 COL | 20 COL | 21 COL | 22 COL | 23 COL |
| 24 OPEN | 25 OPEN | 26 BIRM | 27 BIRM | 28 BIRM | 29 ASHE | 30 ASHE |

JULY

| SUN | MON | TUE | WED | THUR | FRI | SAT |
|---|---|---|---|---|---|---|
| 1 ASHE | 2 ASHE | 3 KNOX | 4 KNOX | 5 KNOX | 6 ASHE | 7 ASHE |
| 8 ASHE | 9 ASHE | 10 KNOX | 11 KNOX | 12 KNOX | 13 MONT | 14 MONT |
| 15 MONT | 16 MONT | * 17 BIRM | 18 BIRM | 19 OPEN | 20 OPEN | * 21 ORL |
| 22 ORL | 23 ORL | 24 OPEN | 25 COL | 26 COL | 27 COL | 28 ORL |
| 29 ORL | 30 ORL | 31 ORL | | | | |

AUGUST

| SUN | MON | TUE | WED | THUR | FRI | SAT |
|---|---|---|---|---|---|---|
| | | | 1 JAX | 2 JAX | 3 JAX | 4 COL |
| 5 ORL | 6 ORL | 7 ORL | 8 JAX | 9 JAX | 10 JAX | 11 ORL |
| 12 ORL | 13 ORL | 14 ORL | 15 COL | 16 COL | 17 COL | 18 COL |
| 19 JAX | 20 JAX | 21 JAX | 22 JAX | 23 MONT | 24 MONT | 25 MONT |
| 26 OPEN | 27 JAX | 28 JAX | 29 JAX | 30 COL | 31 COL | SEPT. 1 COL |

HOME ▇ AWAY ☐

DOUBLEHEADERS * ALL STAR ★

TICKET PRICES

| | |
|---|---|
| Box Seat | $2.00 |
| General Admission | $1.50 |
| Student (Military) | $1.00 |
| Child (12 and under) Sr. Citizen | $ .75 |

All Games Broadcast on WTOC-FM

GAME TIMES

| | |
|---|---|
| Night | 8:00 PM |
| Sunday (April and May) | 2:30 PM |
| Sunday (June, July and Aug.) | 8:00 PM |
| Doubleheaders | 6:30 PM |

Ticket Information and Reservations

SAVANNAH BRAVES.
P. O. Box 3877
Savannah, Ga. 31404
Phone 355-8082

Many of the 74,318 fans who attended games at Grayson Stadium during the 1973 season read this program and watched their club win 71 games. Managed by Clint Courtney, the Braves finished in second place for the second year in a row. Courtney played 11 seasons in the majors. (Courtesy of Miles Wolff.)

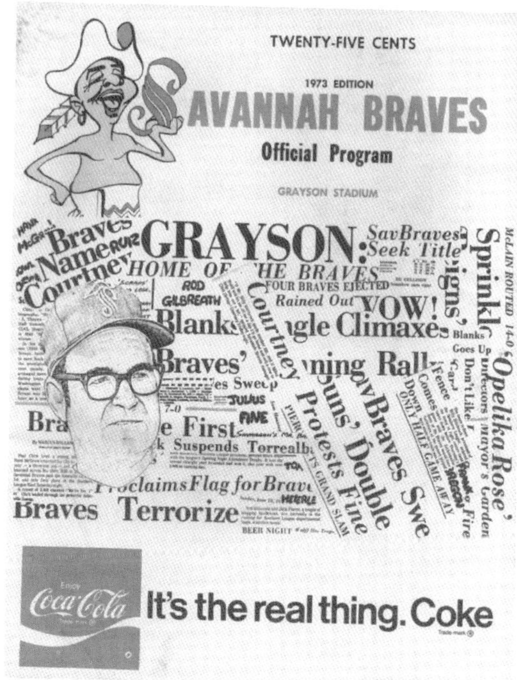


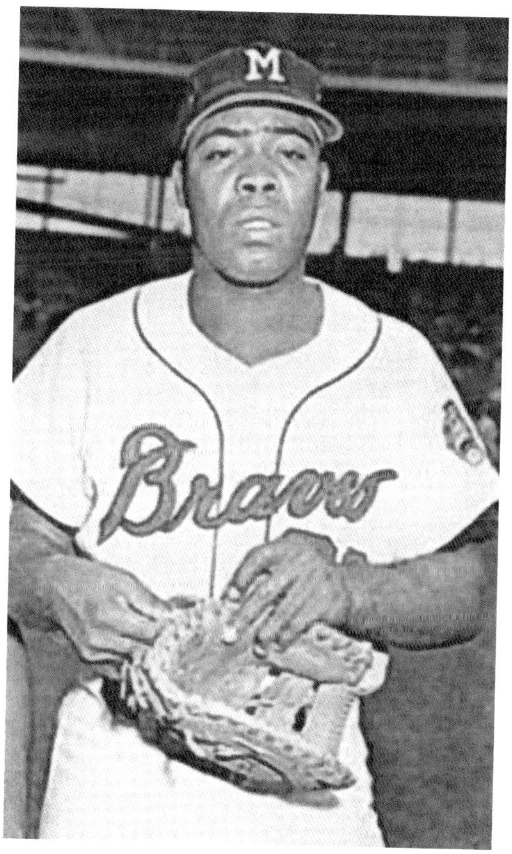


While Hank Aaron's chase of Babe Ruth enthralled local baseball fans, another player named Aaron thrilled crowds as well. Hank's brother Tommy joined the Savannah Braves at the start of the 1973 season at first base. After his playing days in the major leagues ended with the Atlanta Braves in 1971, Aaron resumed his professional career in Savannah. He took over managerial duties midway through the year and stayed at the helm through the 1976 season.

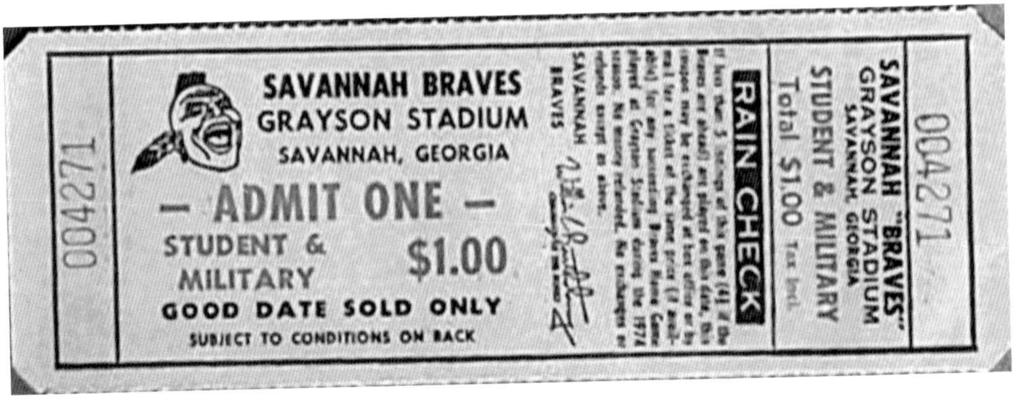


Following the 1974 season that saw the Savannah Braves win 73 games and finish in third place, the 1975 team produced nine players with big league talent. One of those was 22-year-old pitcher Rick Camp. After playing in Savannah, Camp spent nine seasons with the Atlanta Braves. Another young player, Chico Ruiz, also made it to the majors to play for the Atlanta club. Ruiz and Camp helped carry the Savannah Braves to a second place finish and a 70-win season. Despite their success, only 67,971 fans came out to Grayson Stadium to support the team.

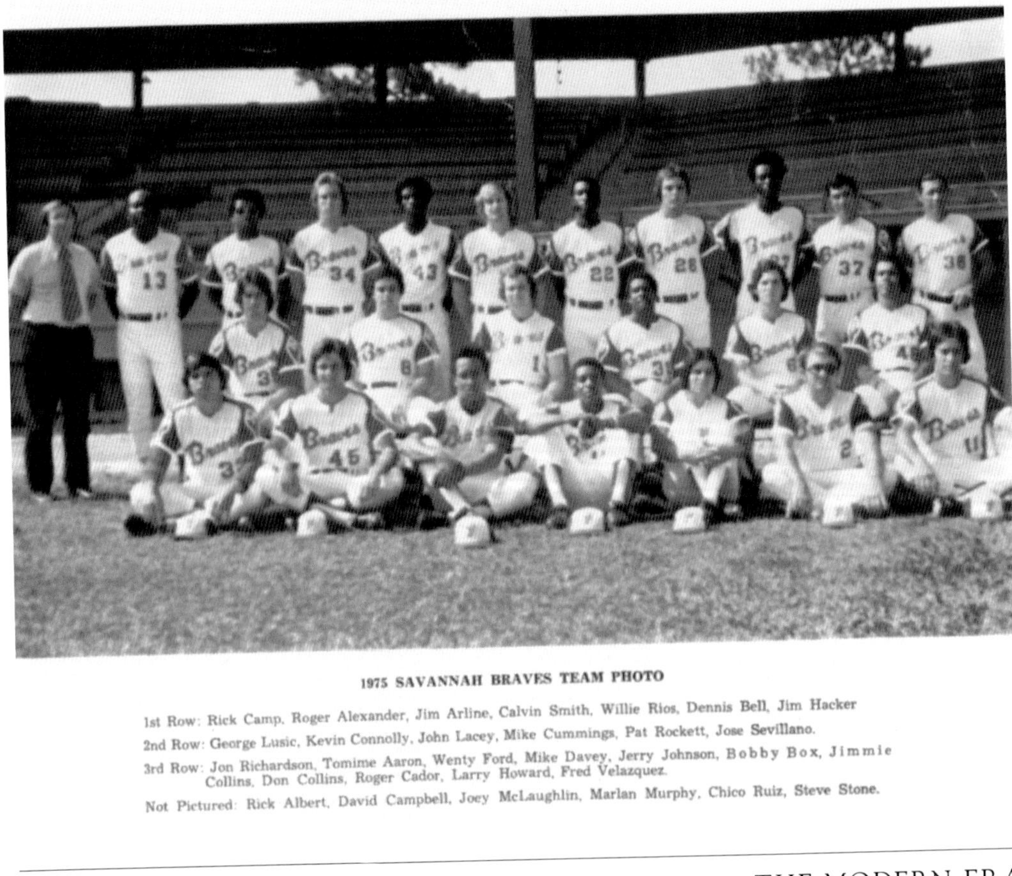

**1975 SAVANNAH BRAVES TEAM PHOTO**

1st Row: Rick Camp, Roger Alexander, Jim Arline, Calvin Smith, Willie Rios, Dennis Bell, Jim Hacker
2nd Row: George Lusic, Kevin Connolly, John Lacey, Mike Cummings, Pat Rockett, Jose Sevillano.
3rd Row: Jon Richardson, Tomime Aaron, Wenty Ford, Mike Davey, Jerry Johnson, Bobby Box, Jimmie Collins, Don Collins, Roger Cador, Larry Howard, Fred Velazquez.
Not Pictured: Rick Albert, David Campbell, Joey McLaughlin, Marlan Murphy, Chico Ruiz, Steve Stone.

Continuing the unfortunate trend in Savannah, only 58,361 fans came through the gates at Grayson to cheer on the 1976 Braves. Those who did saw the team win 69 games and finish in third place in Tommy Aaron's last year as the Braves' manager. The few fans in attendance also saw two future Atlanta Braves stars, Bruce Benedict and Dale Murphy, playing in Savannah. (Courtesy of Skip Jennings.)

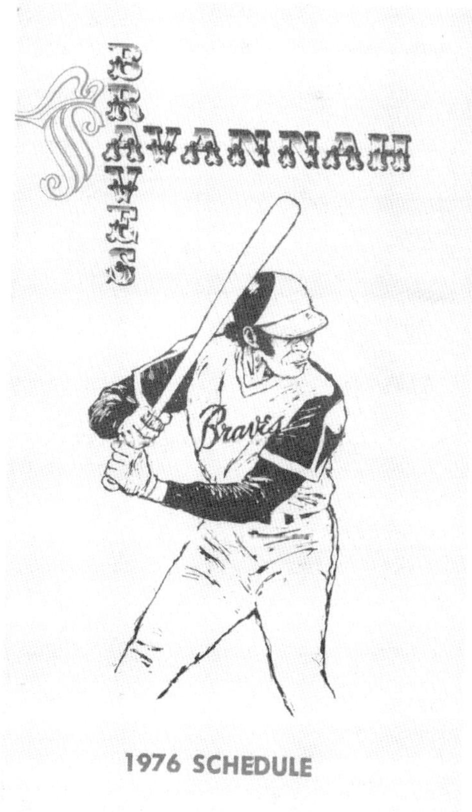


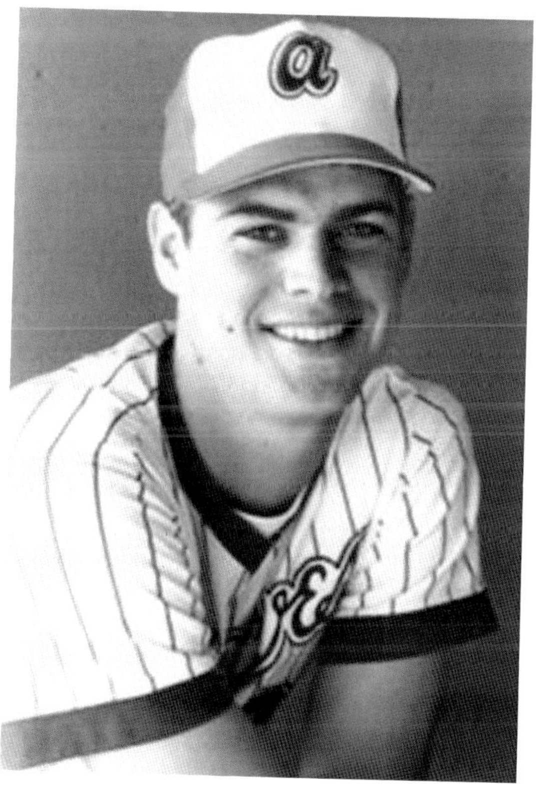

Before he was known as "The Murph" while patrolling the outfield for the Atlanta Braves, 20-year-old Dale Murphy sat behind the plate catching for the 1976 Savannah Braves. In his third year of professional baseball, Murphy played 104 games in Savannah, hitting for a .267 average and knocking 12 home runs. A seven-time all star, five-time Gold Glove winner, and two-time National League MVP, Murphy is fondly remembered as one of Savannah's favorite former players.

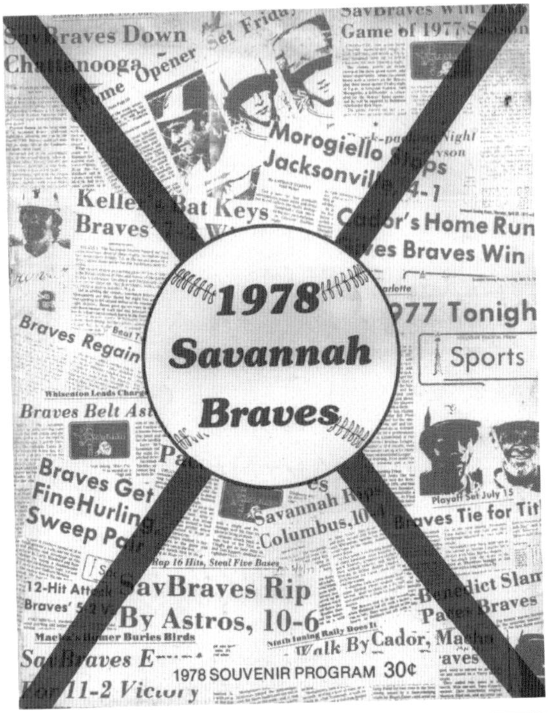


The 1977 season saw more than 80,000 fans come to Grayson Stadium to support the local Braves team. Losing in the first round of the playoffs to Jacksonville, the 1978 Savannah squad looked to advance further. Although the Braves finished the Southern League season in third place, winning 72 games and losing 72 games, they moved into the postseason once again, but lost once again to Jacksonville to conclude the 1978 season. (Courtesy of Skip Jennings.)

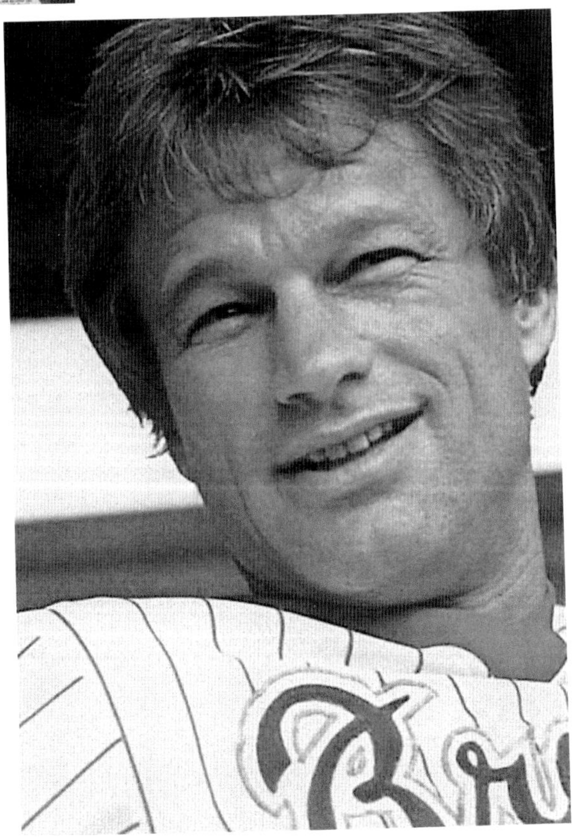

Making national headlines for the 1978 squad was former major leaguer Jim Bouton. After a nine year career with the New York Yankees, Seattle Pilots, and Houston Astros, Bouton retired from the majors. Bouton's retirement coincided with the release of his controversial memoir *Ball Four*, which described candidly an insider point of view of the clubhouses he had played in. After being shunned by the baseball community as a result, Bouton began a comeback to the majors that included a stop in Savannah, where he won 21 games. His return to the majors came late in 1978, when he appeared in five games for the Atlanta Braves.

After spending nine years pitching in the minor leagues, the Atlanta Braves hired Leo Mazzone and placed him with the 1979 Savannah Braves. Moving his way up through the organization, Mazzone was named pitching coach for the Atlanta Braves in 1990. His pitching staff led the Braves to 14 straight trips to the playoffs and won six Cy Young awards. (Courtesy of Skip Jennings.)

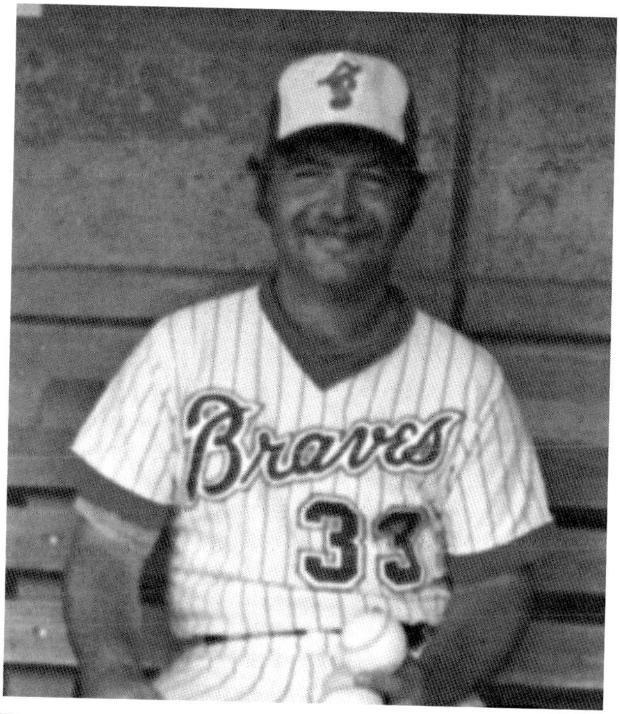


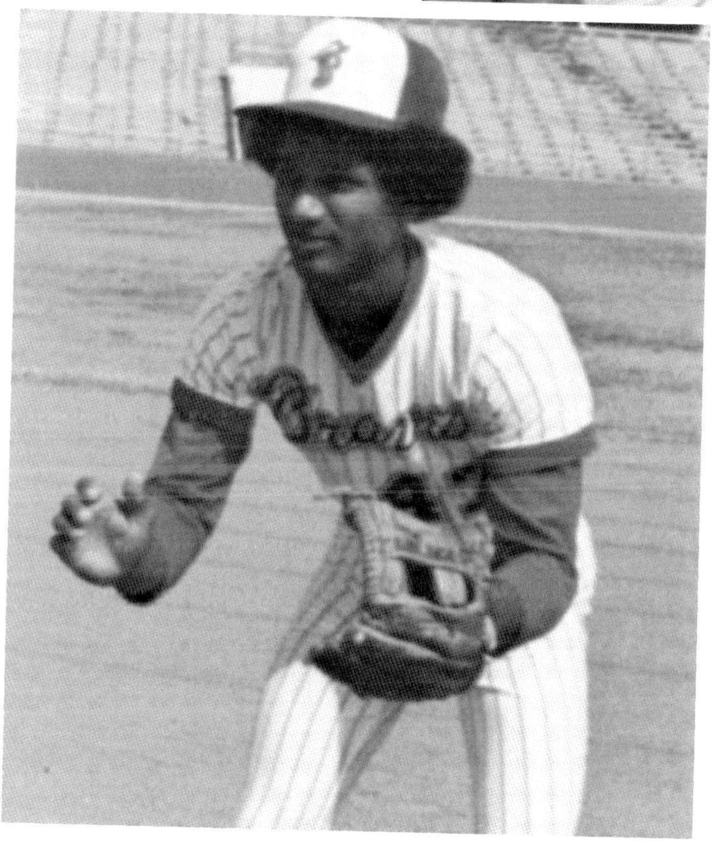

Rafael Ramirez, a 21-year-old shortstop, was one of 12 future major leaguers who played with the 1979 Savannah Braves. Despite his poor production from the plate, his talent in the field helped propel Ramirez through the minors and into the majors in 1980. After spending eight years with Atlanta, Ramirez spent his last five years with the Houston Astros. (Courtesy of Skip Jennings.)

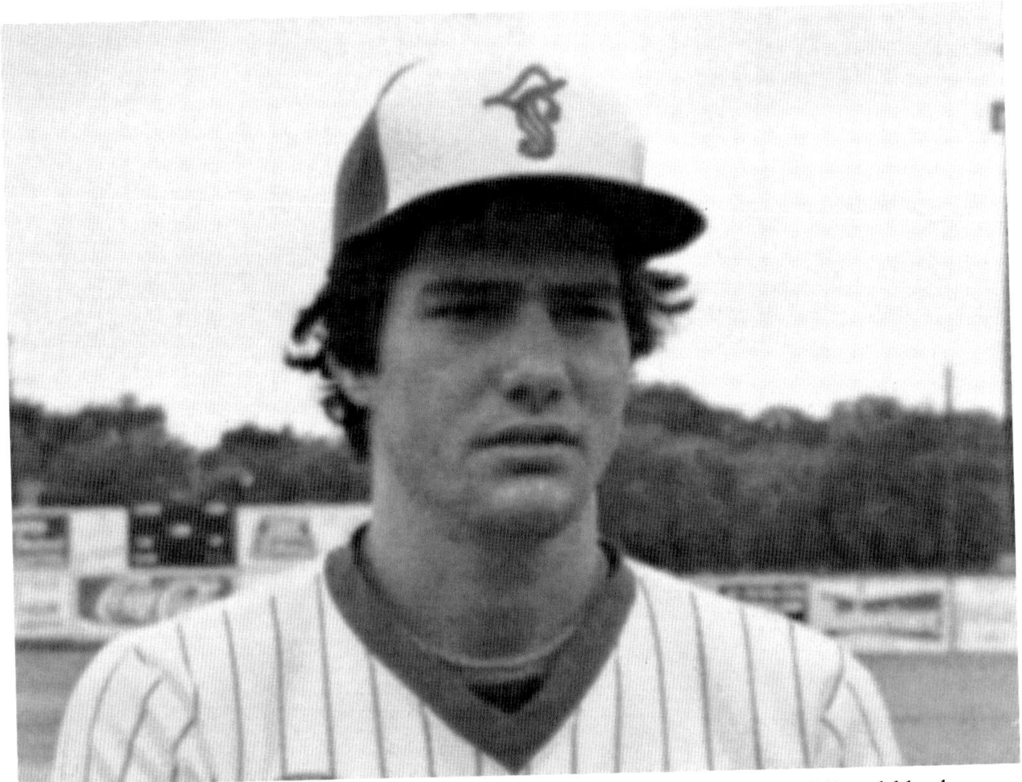

The 1979 Savannah Braves fell to fifth place in the Southern League. On that team and returning to Savannah for the 1980 season was right-hander Steve Bedrosian. Also known as "Bedrock," Bedrosian appeared in 29 games for the Savannah Braves with a record of 14 wins and 10 losses. His Savannah team finished in first place yet lost in the first round of the playoffs. (Courtesy of Skip Jennings.)

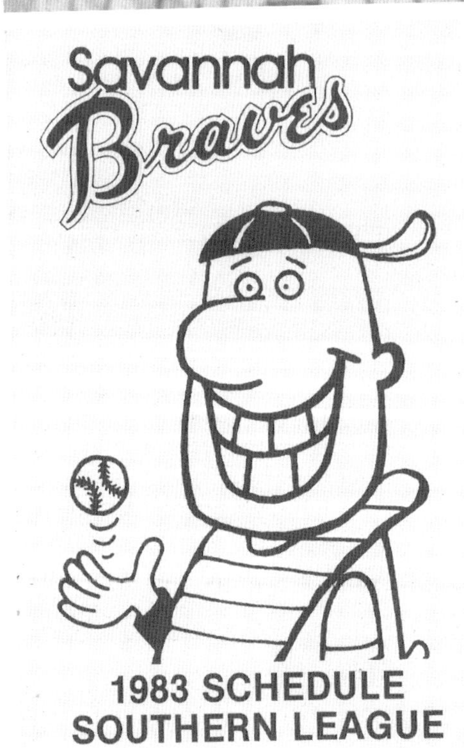


After a third place finish in 1981 and fourth place finish in 1982, the 1983 Savannah Braves provided a record of 81 wins and 64 losses. That record was good for a first place finish and return trip to the playoffs, where the Braves lost in the first round to Jacksonville. (Courtesy of Skip Jennings.)

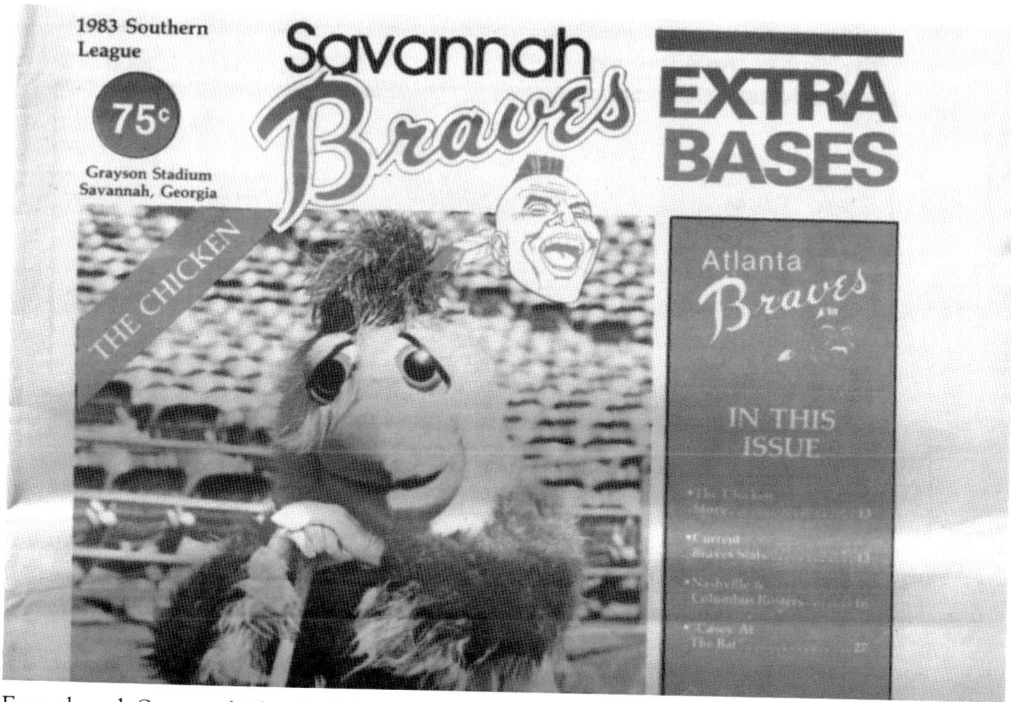


Even though Savannah's baseball fans enjoyed having the local Atlanta Braves farm team in town, the attendance and support offered was not adequate for a class "AA" city. As the Savannah Braves were wrapping up their season, it was announced that 1983 would be the least year of the Braves in Savannah. The Braves moved their farm club to Greenville, and thankfully for Savannah fans, a new team was scheduled to call Savannah home for the 1984 season.

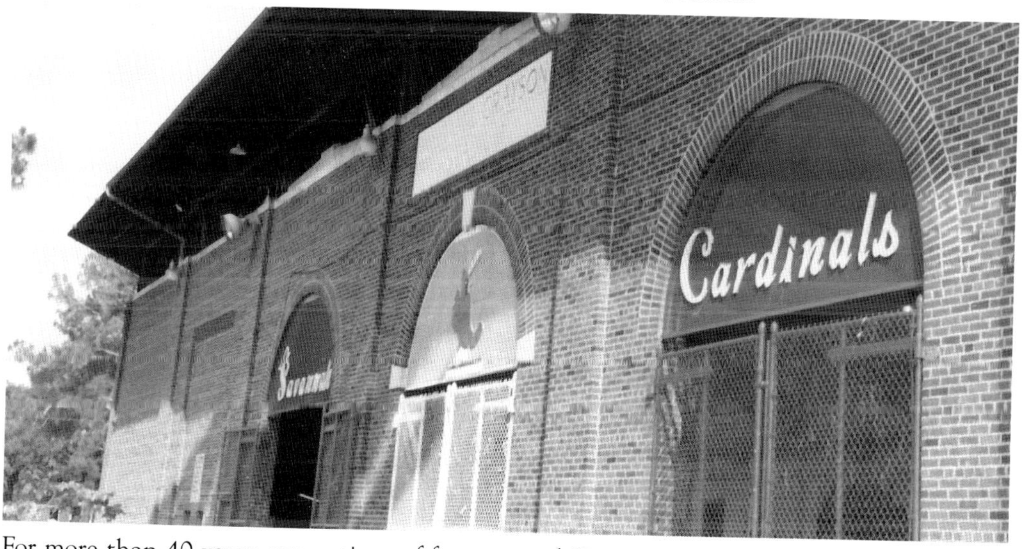


For more than 40 years, generations of fans entered Grayson Stadium through this entrance. In 1984, however, only 37,897 fans took the opportunity to notice that the entrance had a new appearance. In their return to the South Atlantic League, the Cardinals finished in second place during their first year in Savannah. (Courtesy of Skip Jennings.)

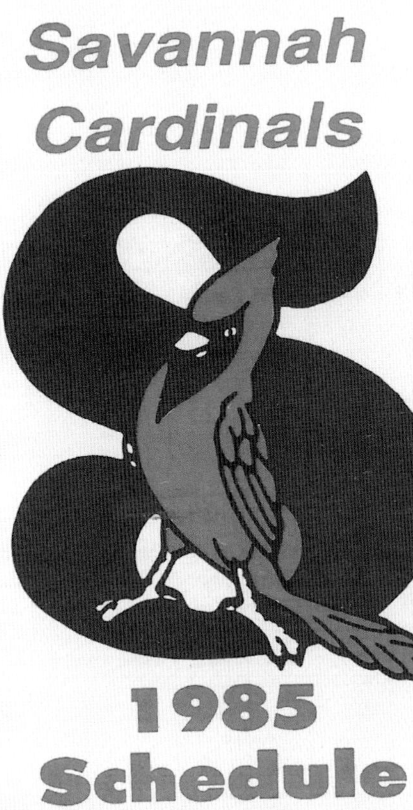


For the Savannah Cardinals, the 1985 season took a turn for the worse. Drawing just over 34,000 fans, the Cardinals dropped to fourth place. Pitcher Scott Arnold and catcher Ray Stephens were the only players from manager Gaylen Pitts's squad to play in the major leagues. (Courtesy of Skip Jennings.)

Minor league history was made once again in Savannah in 1986 when James Hutchinson and Thomas Lewis bought the Savannah Cardinals. Hutchinson and Lewis became the first African American owners of a professional baseball franchise. As this photograph shows the Cardinals warming up before a game, the Cardinals franchise was also heating up, improving their record to 75 wins and a second place finish. (Courtesy of Thomas Hagerty.)

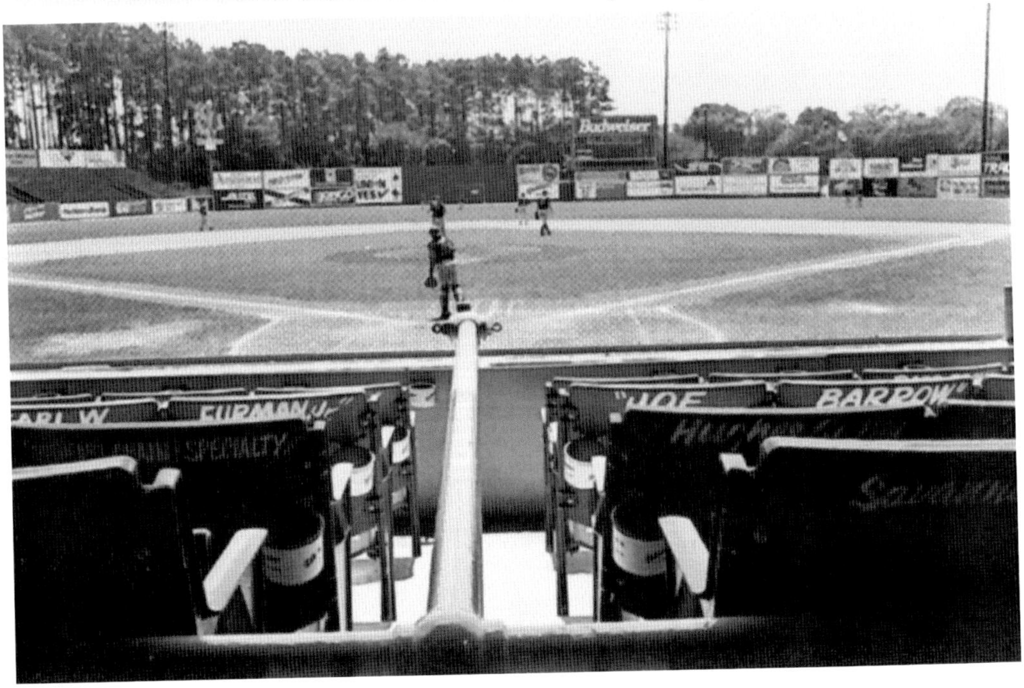

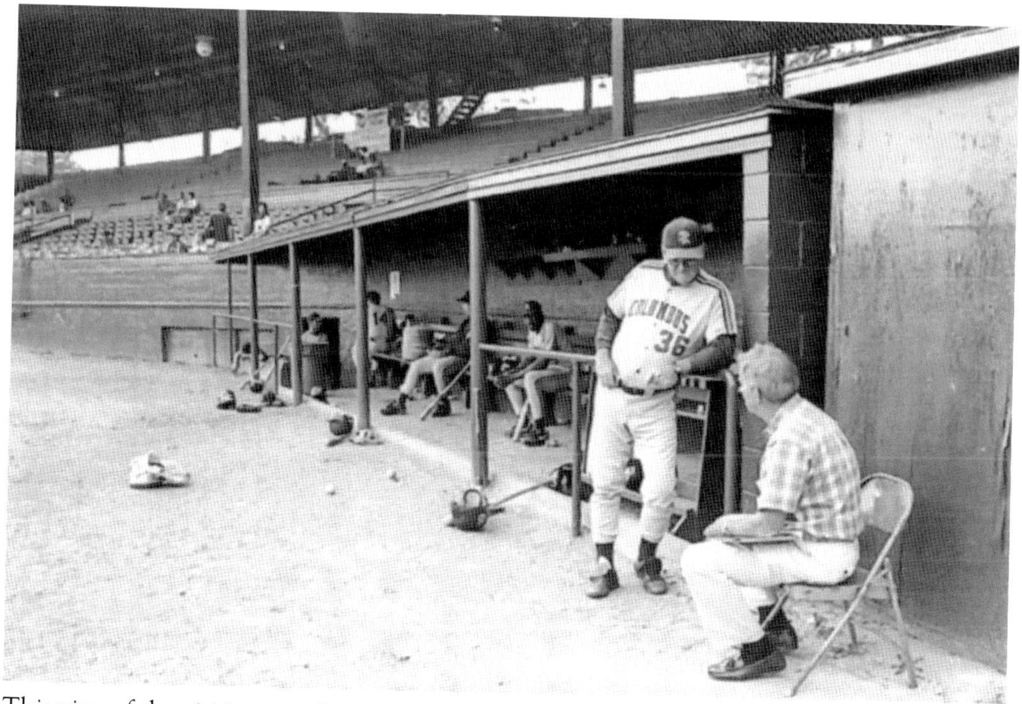

This view of the visiting team's dugout at Grayson Stadium shows a nearly empty grandstand. Only 33,363 fans turned out to Grayson Stadium to cheer on the 1987 Cardinals. Finishing with a record of 69 wins and 69 losses, the Cards finished the Sally League season in fourth place. (Courtesy of Thomas Hagerty.)

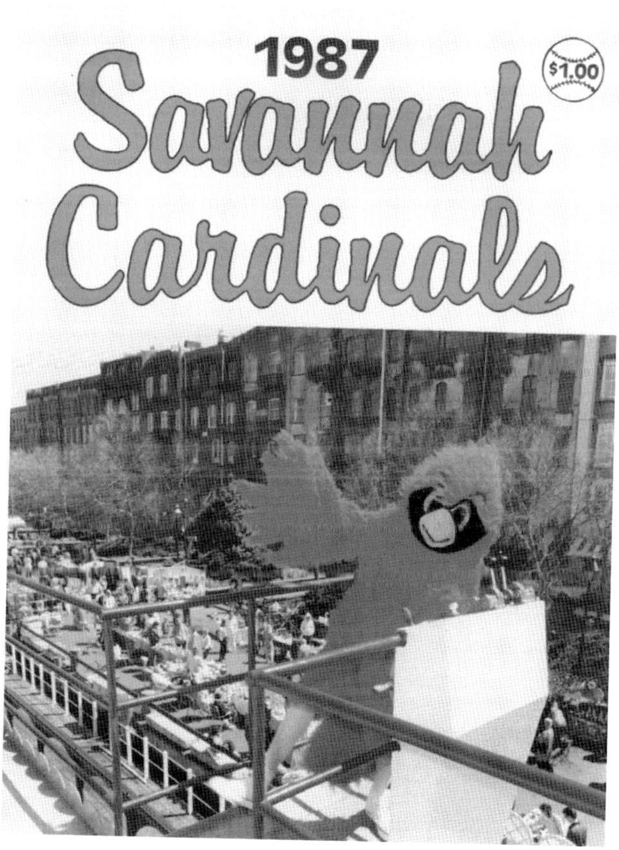


Managed by former utility infielder Mark DeJohn, the 1987 Cardinals featured 20-year-old second baseman Geronimo Pena. Pena went on to play seven seasons in the major leagues with the St. Louis Cardinals. With the Savannah Cardinals franchise struggling because of poor attendance, the St. Louis organization purchased the farm team in Savannah. (Courtesy of Skip Jennings.)

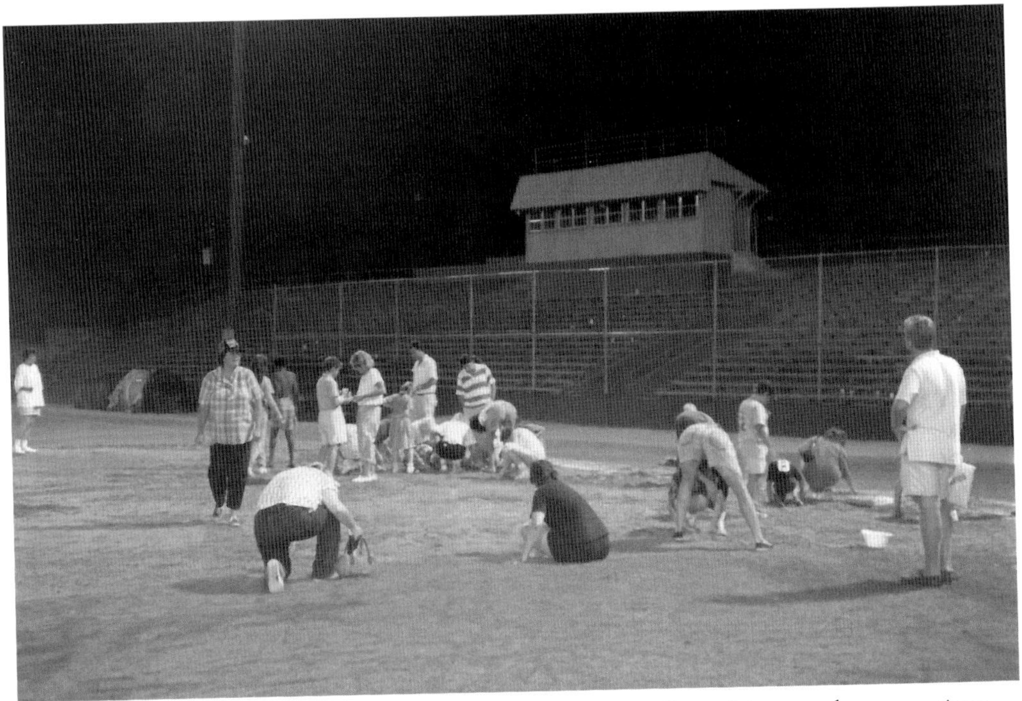

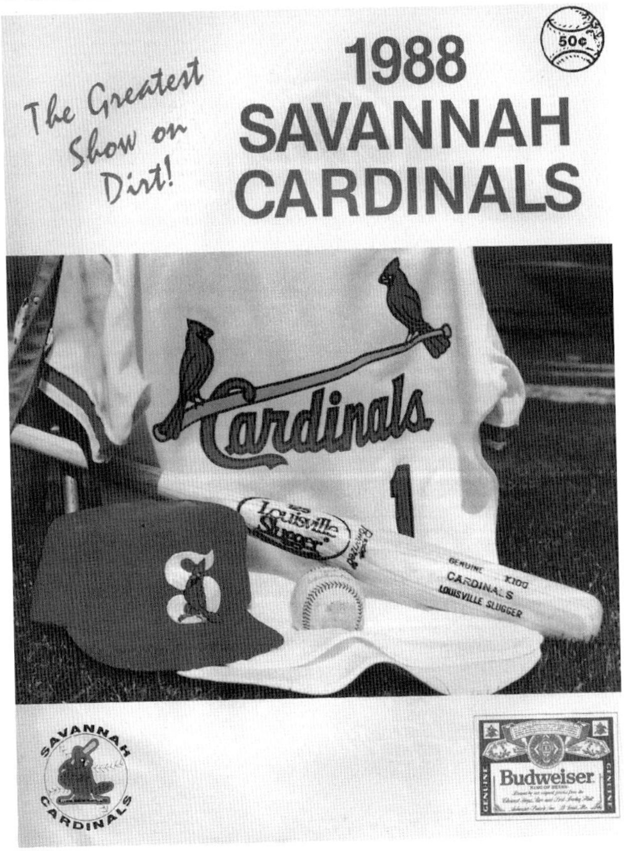


One of the popular promotions used to attract fans to Grayson Stadium was the "Digging for Diamonds" contest. After a game, fans would be invited onto the field to dig throughout the infield looking for buried diamonds, usually with a small spoon or tongue depressor. (Courtesy of Skip Jennings.)

Promotions such as Digging for Diamonds provided a boost to attendance at Grayson Stadium. The 1988 Savannah Cardinals drew almost 25,000 more fans than the year before. The increase of fans in the seats did not reflect an increase in wins, as the Cardinals finished the 1988 season in fifth place. (Courtesy of Skip Jennings.)

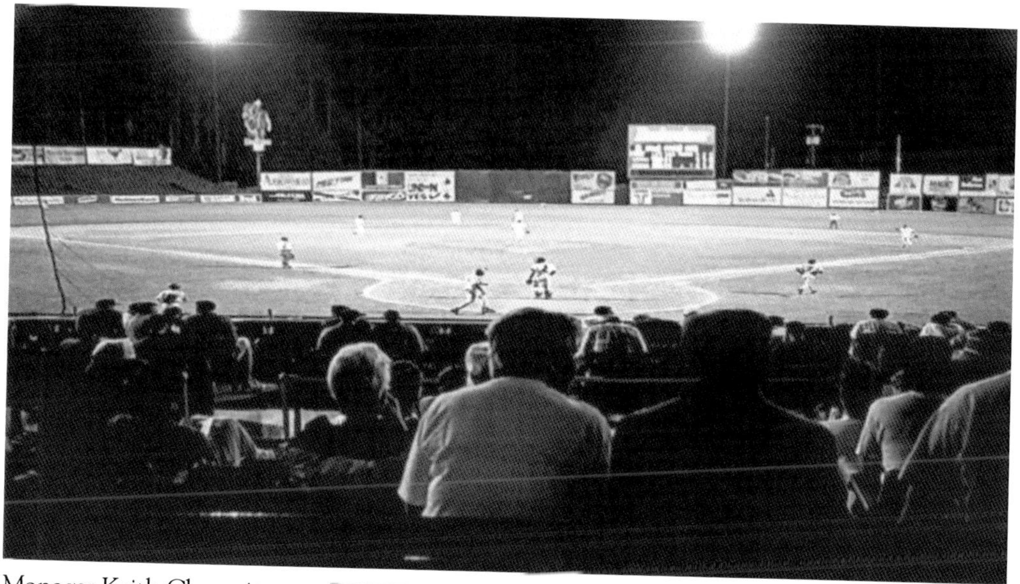

Manager Keith Champion returned in 1989 for his second season as Savannah Cardinals manager. Despite a team that would not produce any big league talent, attendance at day and night games throughout the season rose to more than 76,000. The Cardinals also improved by one spot in the Sally League standings, finishing in fourth place despite a losing record. The Cardinals also closed out the 1980s with their attendance on the rise. After several years of the lowest attendance in Savannah baseball history, the 1990s were looking to be an exciting time for baseball at Grayson Stadium. (Above, courtesy of Thomas Hagerty; right, courtesy of Skip Jennings.)

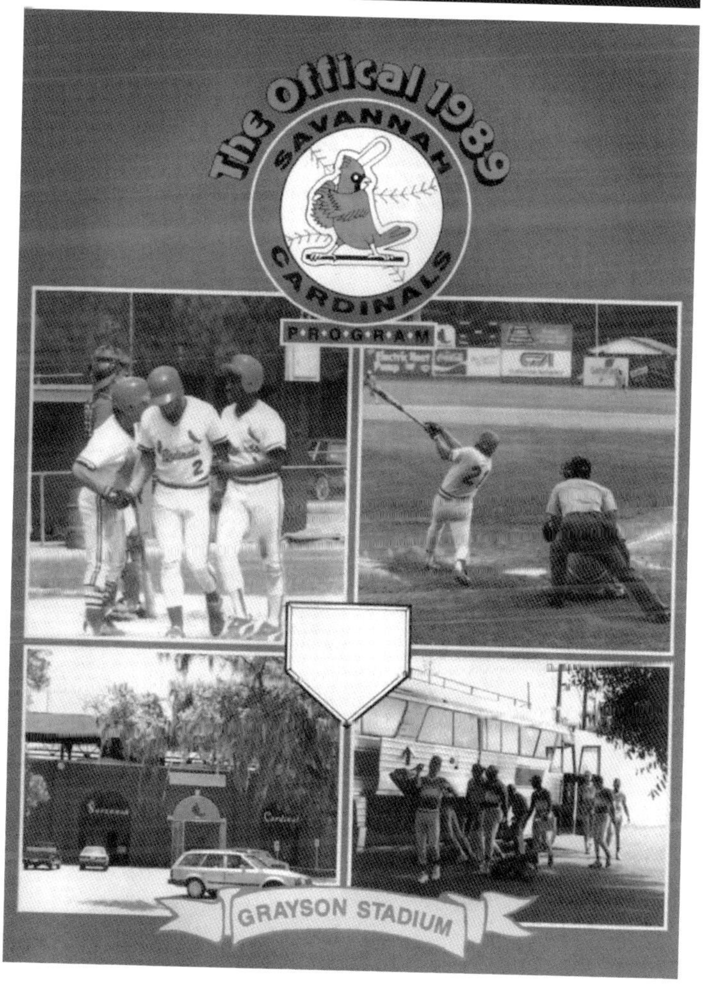

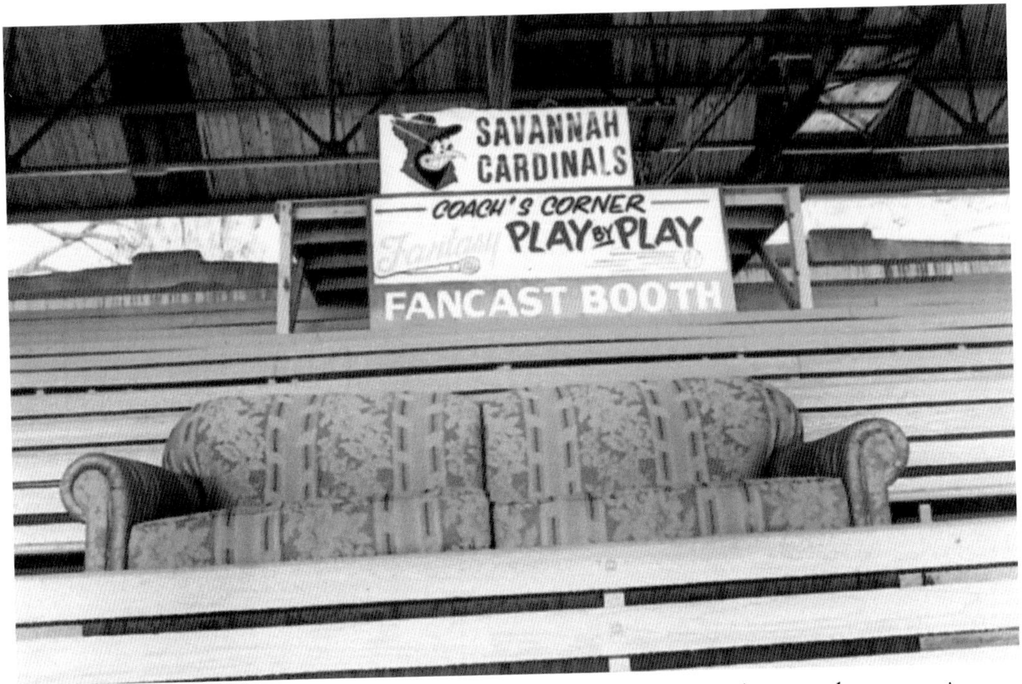


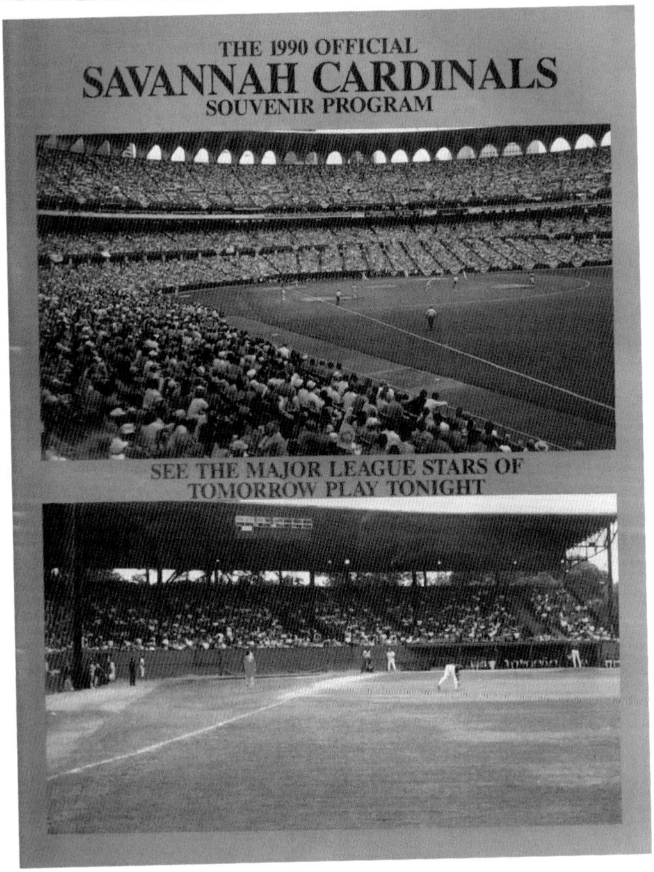


Another popular promotion at Grayson Stadium was the Fancast Booth. Lucky winners got to watch the game from the comfortable couch and receive refreshments throughout the game. The promotions were working as attendance increased for the fourth year in a row to almost 95,000 fans. Those Savannah fans sitting on the couch watched the 1990 Cardinals end the season with 76 wins and 68 losses. The 1990 Cardinals also won the second half title but got swept in the playoffs by the Charleston Wheelers in three games. (Above, courtesy of Thomas Hagerty; left, courtesy of Skip Jennings.)

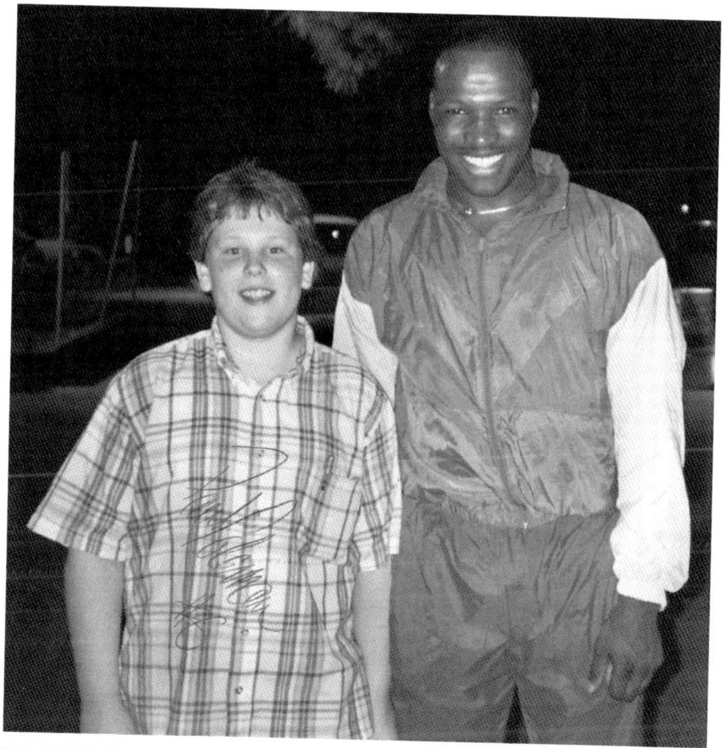

Fans of all ages wanted a chance to meet the St. Louis Cardinals' sixth overall pick in the 1989 draft. Playing for the 1990 Savannah Cardinals, Paul Coleman failed to live up to expectations. He hit .209 with six home runs and 35 RBIs. Coleman finished his tenure in the Cardinals farm system in 1993.

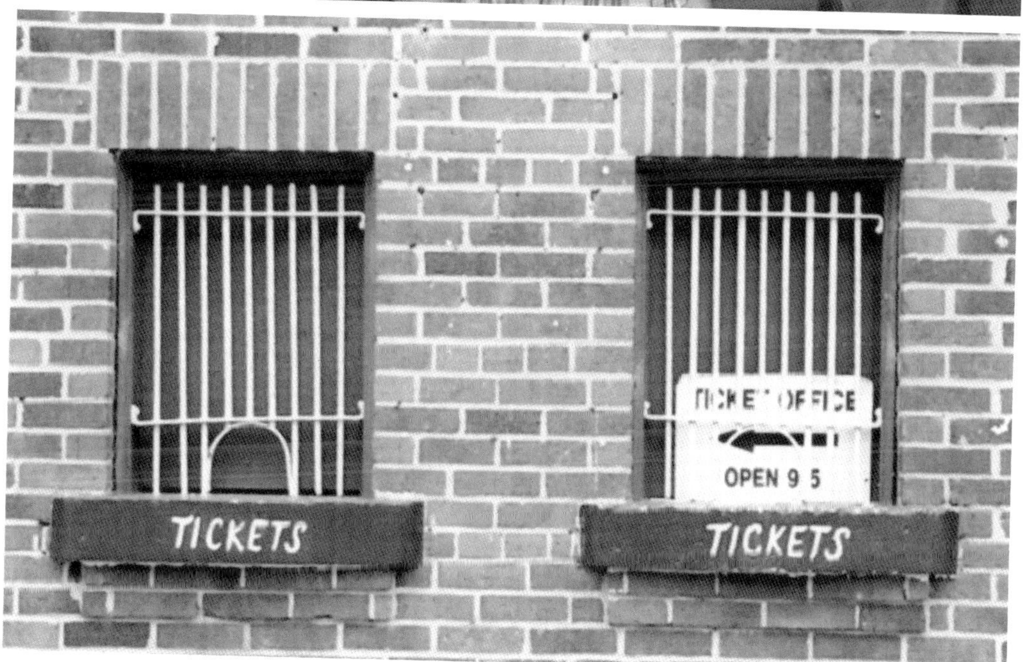


The 1991 season marked the 50th anniversary of baseball at Grayson Stadium. Many fans during those five decades purchased their tickets from these ticket windows. Although no longer in use, they serve as a reminder of the many years that Grayson hosted baseball in Savannah. (Courtesy of John R. Bennett.)

## 32nd Annual South Atlantic League 1991 All-Star Team

| | Southern Division | | Northern Division | |
|---|---|---|---|---|
| Mgr. | Tim Blackwell | Columbia | Trey Hillman | Greensboro |
| Coach | Roy Majtyka | Macon | Dave Miley | Ch'ston, WV |
| Coach | Bruce Tanner | Ch'ston, SC | Mark Shiftlett | Greensboro |
| Pitchers | Jose Martinez | Columbia | Rafael Quirico | Greensboro |
| | John Kelly | Savannah | Steve Dreyer | Gastonia |
| | Rick Steed | M. Beach | Richard Hines | Greensboro |
| | Juan Castillo | Columbia | Wm. Martinez | Sumter |
| | Joe Ganote | M. Beach | John Roper | Ch'ston, WV |
| | Joe Waldron | Ch'ston, SC | Jim Daughtery | Asheville |
| Catchers | Carlos Delgado | M. Beach | Kiki Hernandez | Greensboro |
| | Tyler Houston | Macon | Mike Lieberthal | Spartanburg |
| 1B | Bill Ostermeyer | Ch'ston, SC | Tom Raffo | Ch'ston, WV |
| 2B | Jose Olmeda | Macon | Corey Thomas | Spartanburg |
| SS | Chipper Jones | Macon | Tom Nevers | Asheville |
| 3B | Butch Huskey | Columbia | Bobby Perna | Ch'ston, WV |
| Utility | Ernesto Rodriguez | M. Beach | David Lowery | Gastonia |
| | Howard Battle | M. Beach | Kelly O'Neal | Fayetteville |
| R-F | Terry Bradshaw | Savannah | Steve Gilbralter | Ch'ston, WV |
| C-F | Kyle Washington | Columbus | Carl Everett | Greensboro |
| L-F | Edward Fully | Columbia | Marty Posey | Gastonia |
| Utility | Gerrod Davis | Columbia | Todd Samples | Sumter |
| | Scott Bullett | Augusta | Michael Farmer | Spartanburg |
| D-H | Rod McCall | Columbus | Brian Saltzgaber | Fayetteville |
| Trainer | Bob Burton | Columbia | Greg Spratt | Greensboro |
| Umpires | Steve Graley | | Robert Hefner | |
| | Chris Laettner | | Jeff Sharpstene | |
| | Brad Geaslin | | Michael Landsman | |

## 32nd Annual South Atlantic League All-Star Game

Monday, June 24, 1991

MONDAY, JUNE 24, 1991 7:15 PM
(RAINDATE JUNE 25, 7:15 PM)
HISTORIC GRAYSON STADIUM
SAVANNAH, GA
NO REFUNDS – NO EXCHANGES
ADMIT ONE
GOOD FOR 1991
SAL ALL-STAR GAME

| SEC/BOX | ROW | SEAT |
|---|---|---|
| H | 3 | 20 |

FIELD BOX SEAT
$5.50

In January 1991, the St. Louis Cardinals organization sold their franchise to the Savannah Professional Baseball Club, headed by Ken Silver. Silver and company watched their new club finish the year with a losing record and in sixth place. The highlight of the year, however, was the South Atlantic League All Star Game that was played at the Historic Grayson Stadium. Savannah fans packed the park to see many players who eventually played in the major leagues. Among the all-stars that night were Chipper Jones, Carlos Delgado, and Mike Lieberthal. (Courtesy of Skip Jennings.)

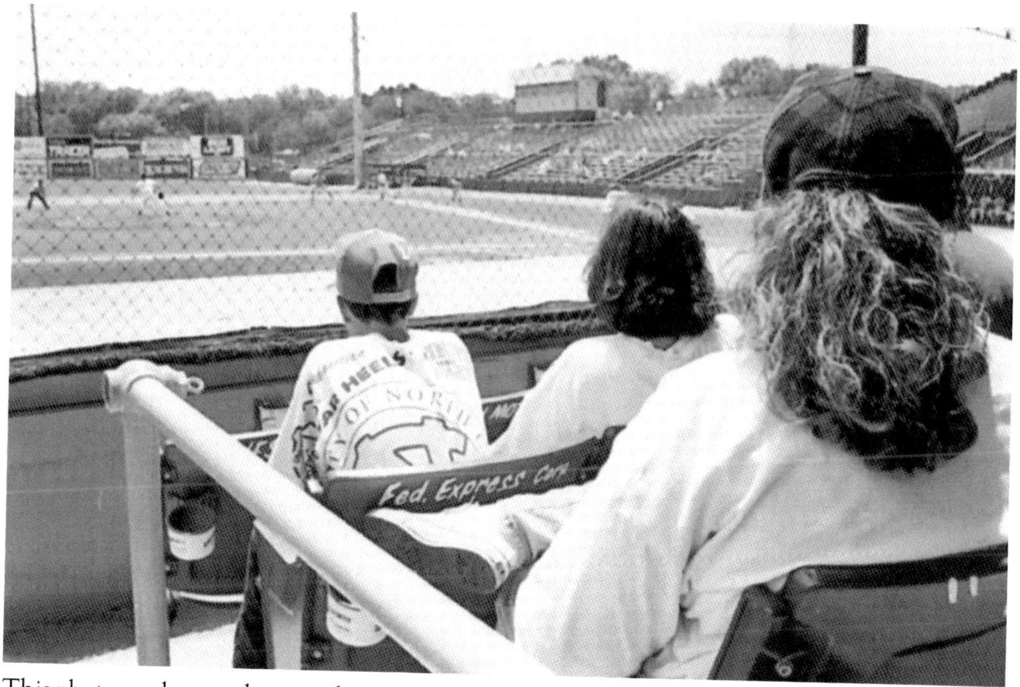


This photograph was taken at a day game during the 1992 Cardinals season. Featuring four players who eventually got a chance to play in the majors, the Cards finished that year with a losing record for the second year in a row. Winning only 62 games, the team finished in fifth place. (Courtesy of Thomas Hagerty.)

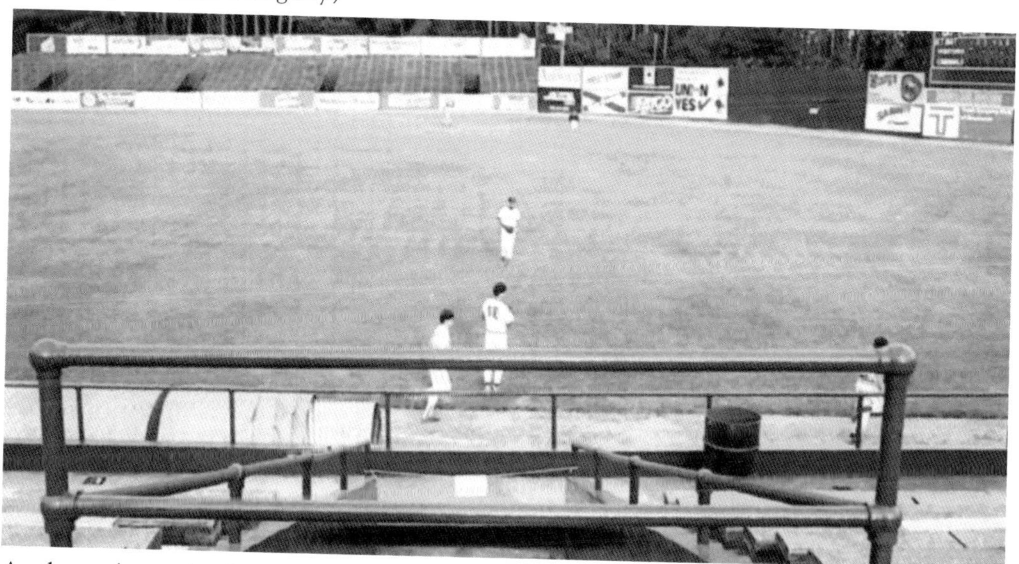

As these players for the 1993 Cardinals were warming up before a game, the team as a whole began to heat up as the season wore on. Led by manager Chris Maloney, the Cards featured two players who eventually played for the parent club. Pitcher Mike Busby spent four years in St. Louis while catcher Joe McEwing played in the majors through the 2008 season. (Courtesy of Thomas Hagerty.)

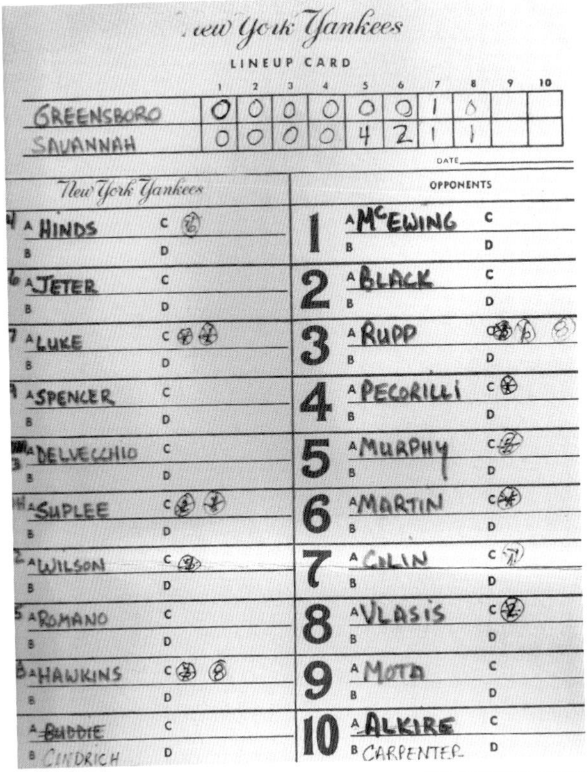


The 1993 Savannah Cardinals finished in first place for the first time in 10 years. Winning 94 games with only 48 losses in front of more than 106,000 fans, the Cardinals and Grayson Stadium were primed for a successful playoff run. Playing the Greensboro Hornets in the finals for the Sally League pennant, the Cards had their hands full. Led by future New York Yankees Derek Jeter, Shane Spencer, and Mariano Rivera, the Hornets led the league in batting. The Cardinals, however, were able to overcome the hot hitting Hornets and won the pennant in the fifth game of the playoffs. Capturing the eighth championship for Savannah, the 1993 Cardinals provided a new generation of Savannah baseball fans with memories of a pennant. (Courtesy of Skip Jennings.)

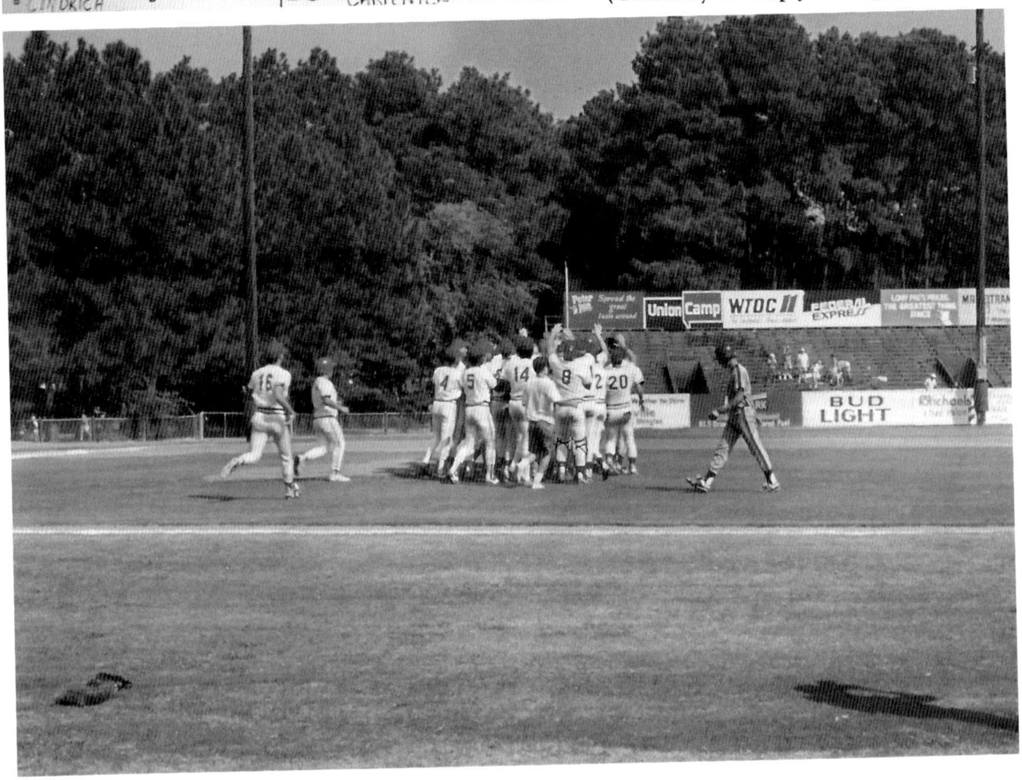

The 1993 Cardinals program celebrated the franchise's 10th anniversary in Savannah. Tying the 1940 Savannah Indians for the most wins in a season, the Cardinals ended the year winning the first pennant the city had seen in 33 years. The 1994 program celebrated that championship. Seven other Savannah baseball teams came up short when trying to win two titles in a row. The 1994 Cardinals were the first to do so. Despite their third place finish, the Cardinals advanced to the playoffs yet again and defeated the Hagerstown Suns three games to none, winning the ninth championship in Savannah's history. (Courtesy of Skip Jennings.)

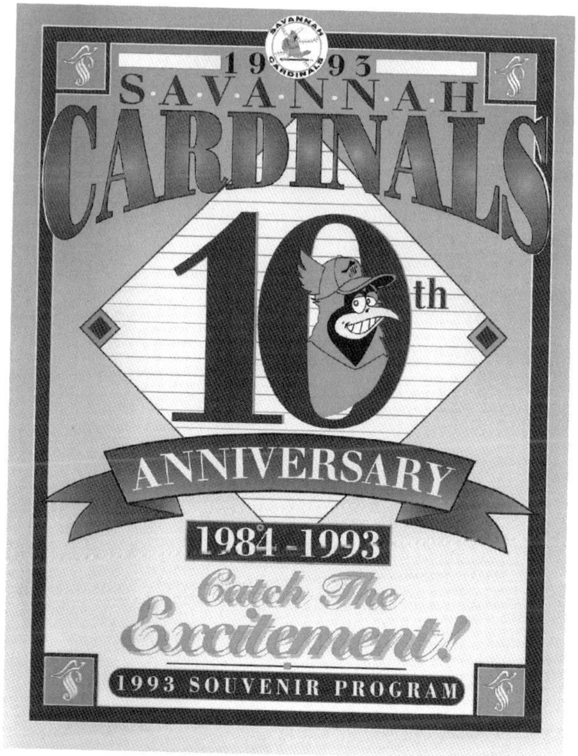


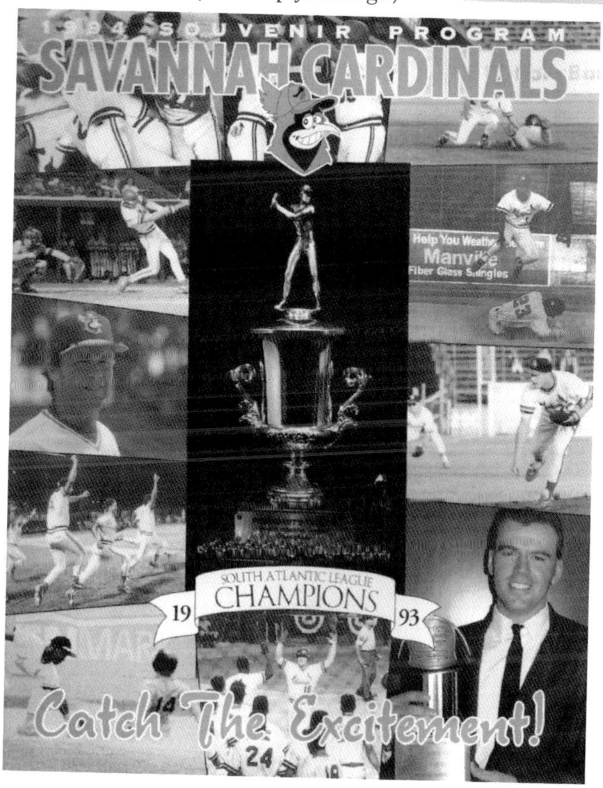

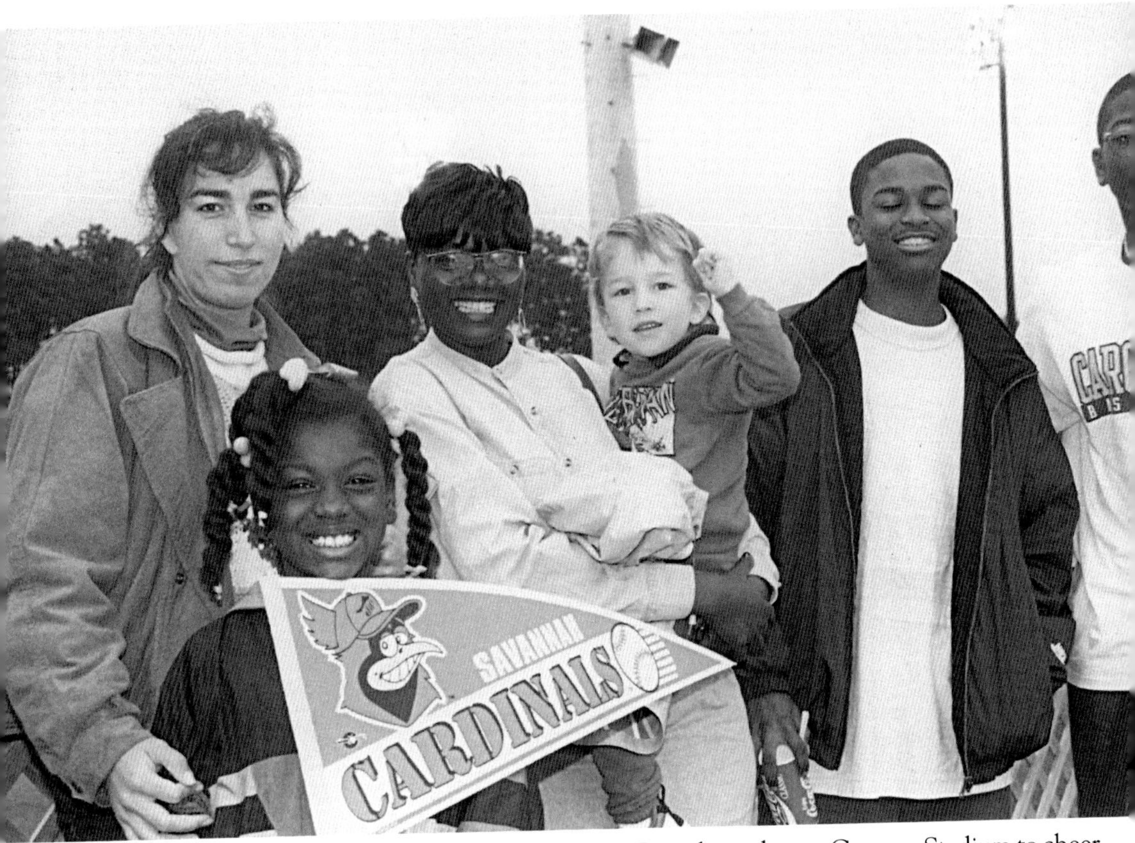


This photograph was taken on opening day in 1995. Fans showed up to Grayson Stadium to cheer on the Savannah Cardinals as they began their quest for a third straight South Atlantic League championship. Savannah's luck on the diamond, however, had run its course. The 1995 Cardinals ended the year winning 56 games while losing 83. As a team, the Cardinals finished last in the South Atlantic League in batting, hitting only .215 collectively. The Cardinals finished 12th out of the 14 teams in the Sally League. The last year of the Savannah Cardinals was 1995. In December, it was announced that the Los Angeles Dodgers would be placing their franchise in Savannah. (Courtesy of the City of Savannah, Research Library, and Municipal Archives.)

The 1996 baseball season began with the Savannah franchise becoming a farm team of the Los Angeles Dodgers after 12 years with the St. Louis Cardinals. After a contest open to the public to name the new team, the votes were tallied and the winner was the Sand Gnats. Named for the pesky bugs that torment Savannah through the year, the name was truly unique. Ending the regular season in seventh place, the Gnats advanced to the playoffs and beat the Delmarva Shorebirds to win the 10th South Atlantic League pennant for Savannah. The Dodgers' relationship with Savannah only lasted one year when the Texas Rangers chose Savannah as one of its farm teams in 1997. With attendance growing to 125,729 fans, the Gnats finished the year in third place. (Right, courtesy of Skip Jennings; below, courtesy of the Georgia Sports Hall of Fame.)

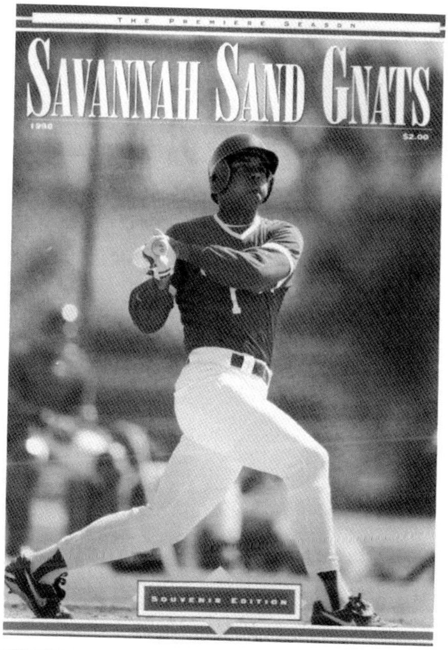


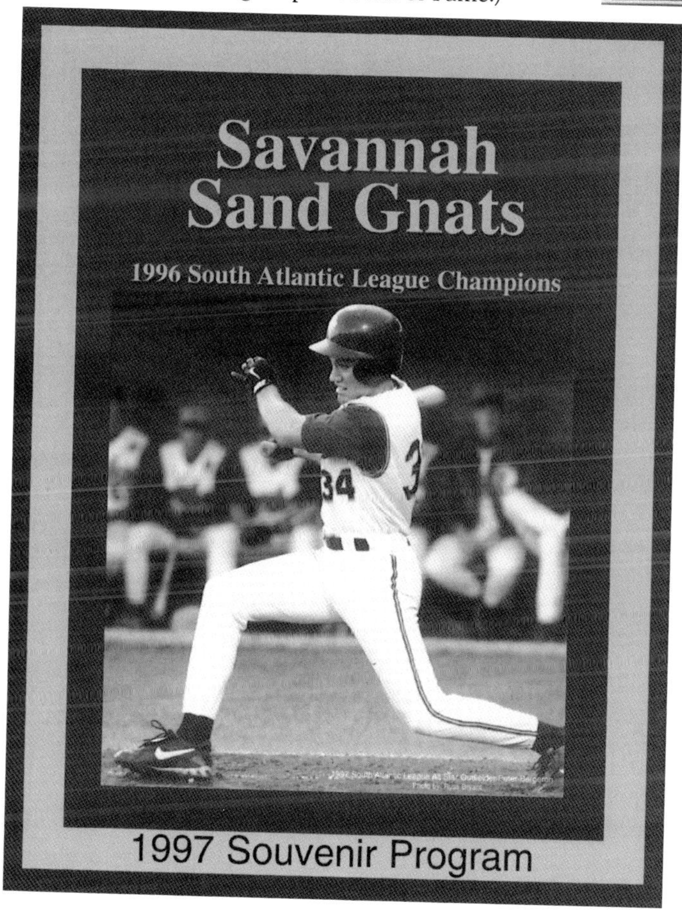

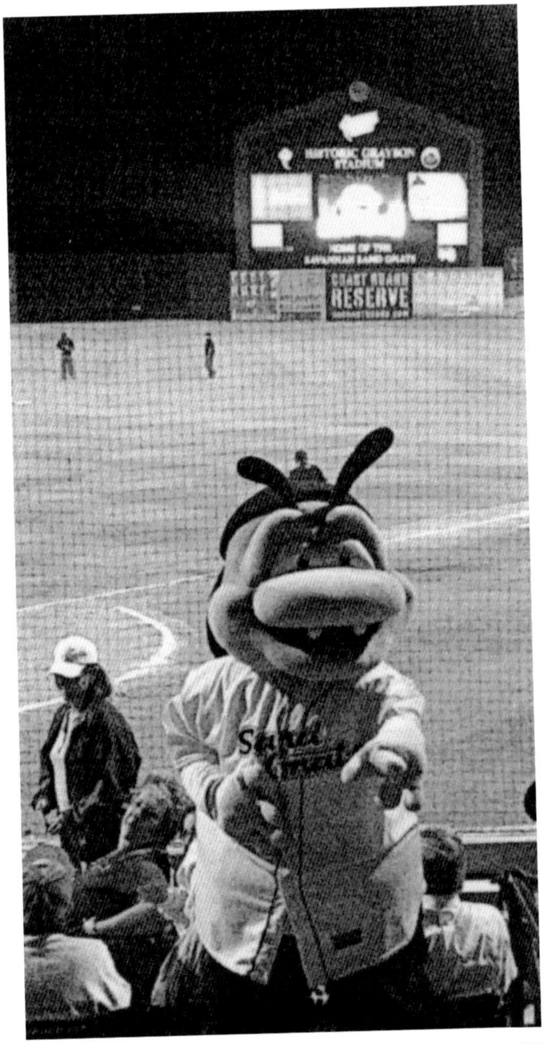


After seven years of mediocre play and an affiliation change to the Montreal Expos/Washington Nationals, the Sand Gnats made another change to begin the 2005 season. Hoping to change the fortune of the Gnats, Gnate the Gnat was brought on to serve as the mascot, replacing his brother Gnic. Success for Gnate and the Gnats would have to wait though, as the 2005 and 2006 Sand Gnats finished near the bottom of the Sally League.

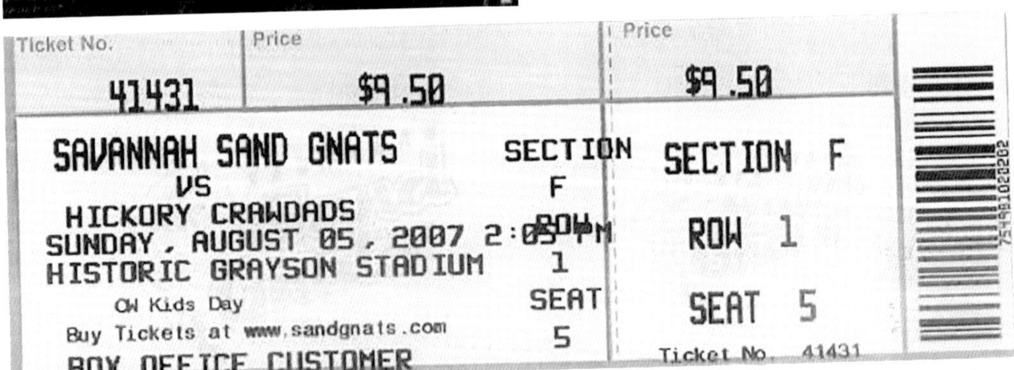


The 2007 season of the Savannah Sand Gnats saw the local club slip from mediocre to last place in the South Atlantic League. Despite having World Series champion and 11-year major league veteran Tim Teufel as skipper of the Gnats, the 2007 team only won 41 games and lost 94. The Gnats affiliation with the New York Mets organization began in 2007.

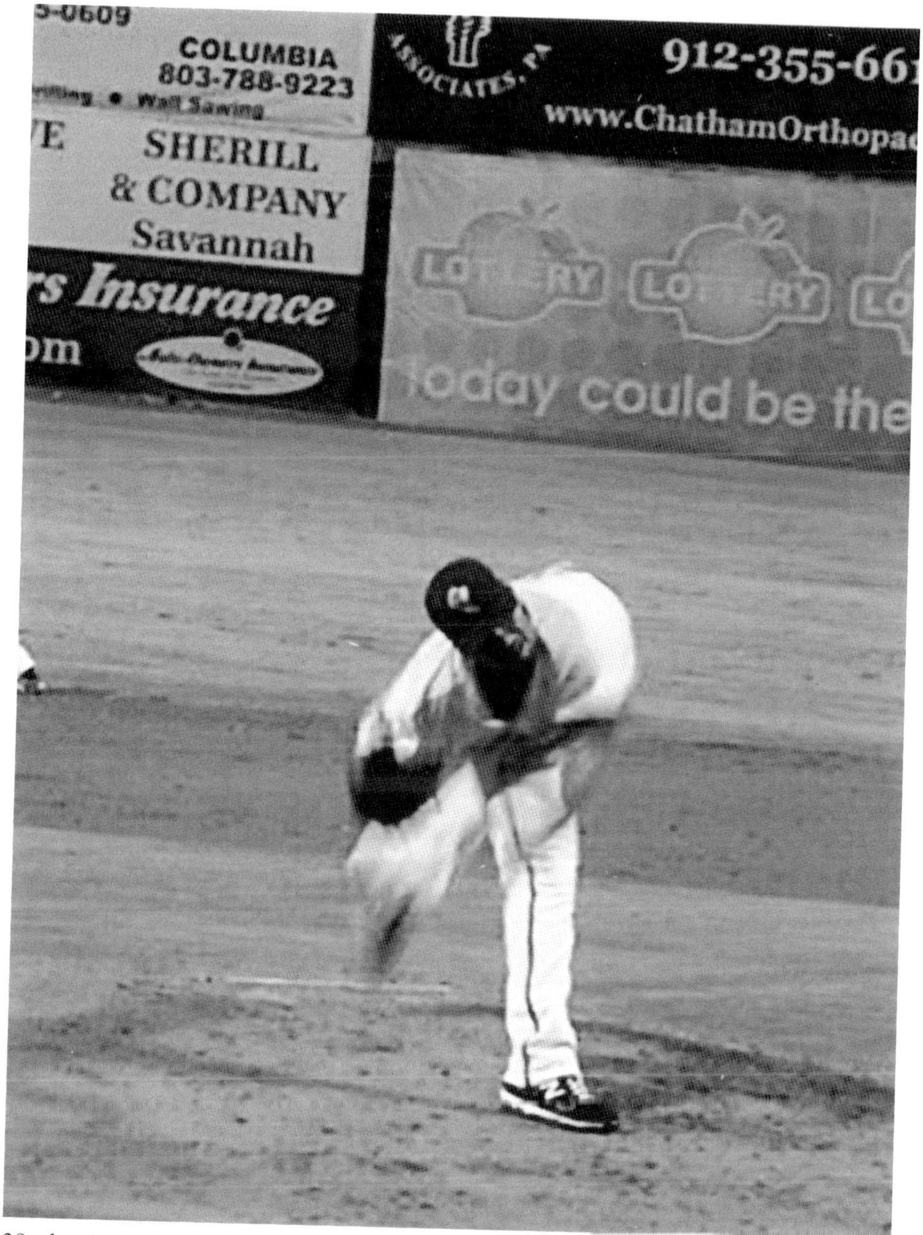


In 2008, the Gnats ended the year with a 61-76 win-loss record and 2009 was similar with a 65 and 72 record. In 2010, success came back to Grayson Stadium. The 2010 Gnats won the first half division and qualified for the playoffs for the first time in 14 years. The 2011 Gnats accomplished the same, advancing to the playoffs for the second time in two years. Helping them along the way was two-time Cy Young award winner and New York Met Johann Santana, making a rehab start during the playoffs. Advancing past the Augusta Green Jackets by winning two of the three games in the series, Savannah faced the Greensboro Grasshoppers in the finals. With the series advancing to the fifth and final game, Savannah fell to Greensboro by a score of 3-1. (Courtesy of Skip Jennings.)

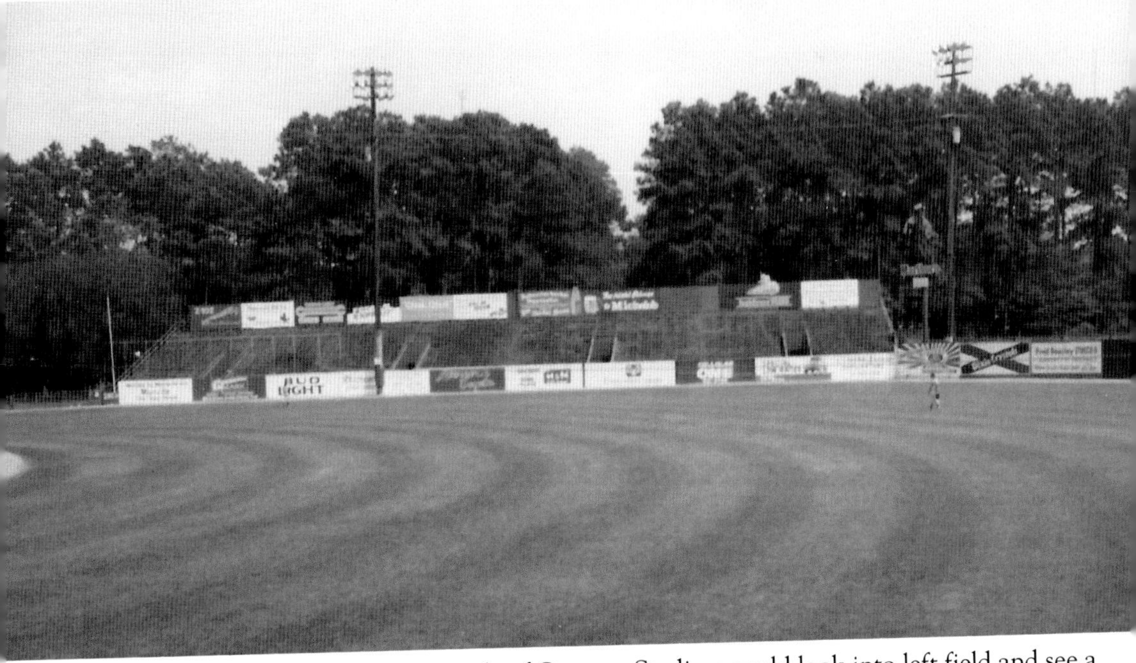

For more than 50 years, patrons inside of Grayson Stadium could look into left field and see a relic from Savannah's baseball past. The concrete bleachers were the only remnant from the original Municipal Stadium that was not destroyed by the 1940 hurricane or removed to make room for Grayson Stadium. In 2007, the bleachers were demolished as part of a $5 million renovation project. This allowed the short left field fence to be moved back from a distance of 290 feet to a more formidable distance of 320 feet. In addition to these improvements, the playing surface of Grayson received an upgrade in drainage and irrigation systems. The improvements, among others in 2007, helped to keep Grayson Stadium as modern as possible. With the continuing debate over whether or not to build a new stadium in Savannah, these improvements and others that have been proposed should keep baseball at Grayson for the near future. (Courtesy of Skip Jennings.)

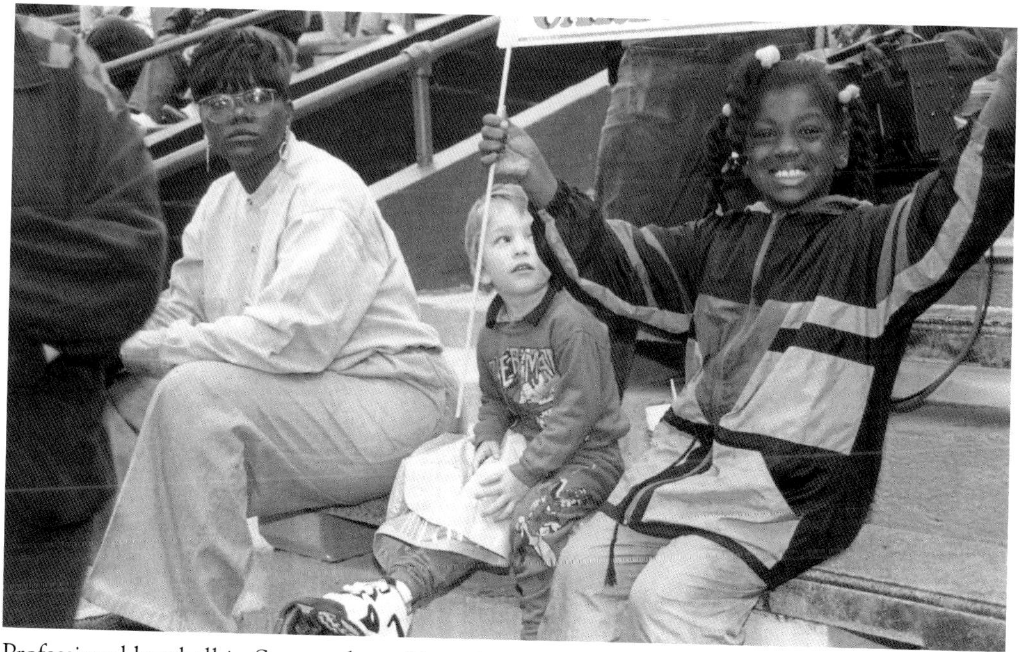

Professional baseball in Savannah could not have existed for more than 100 years if it were not for the support of the local fans. While attendance numbers for some years were not impressive, Savannah's baseball teams have always had loyal fans coming to cheer them on. Generations of supporters have filled the stands for more than a century and will continue to do so. (Courtesy of the City of Savannah, Research Library, and Municipal Archives.)

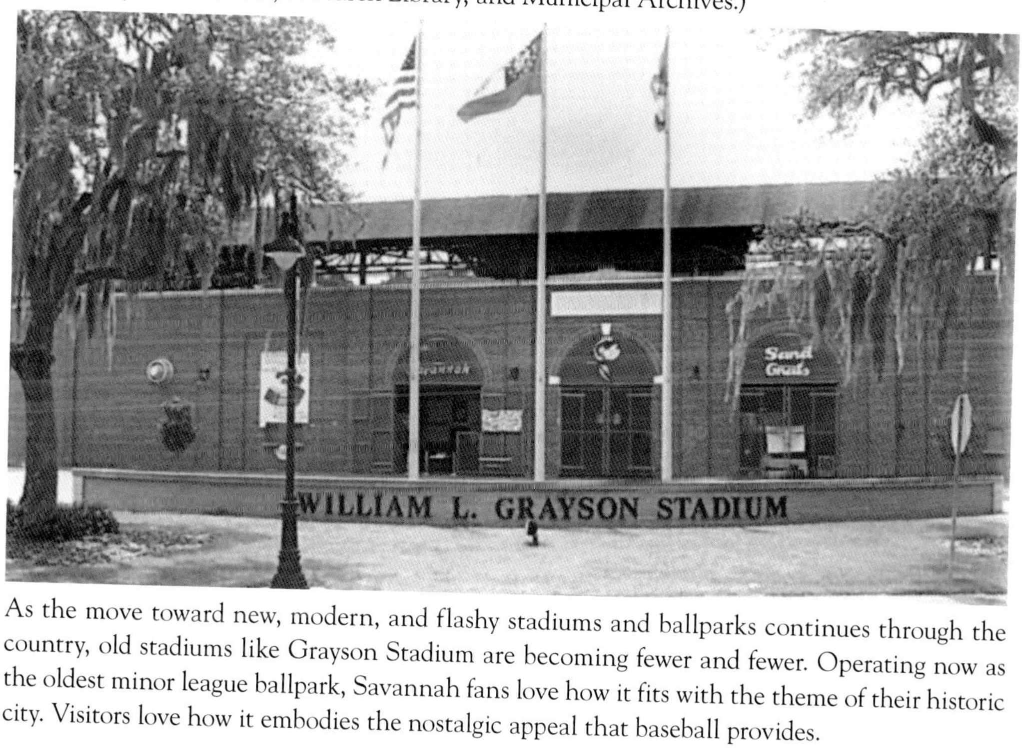


As the move toward new, modern, and flashy stadiums and ballparks continues through the country, old stadiums like Grayson Stadium are becoming fewer and fewer. Operating now as the oldest minor league ballpark, Savannah fans love how it fits with the theme of their historic city. Visitors love how it embodies the nostalgic appeal that baseball provides.

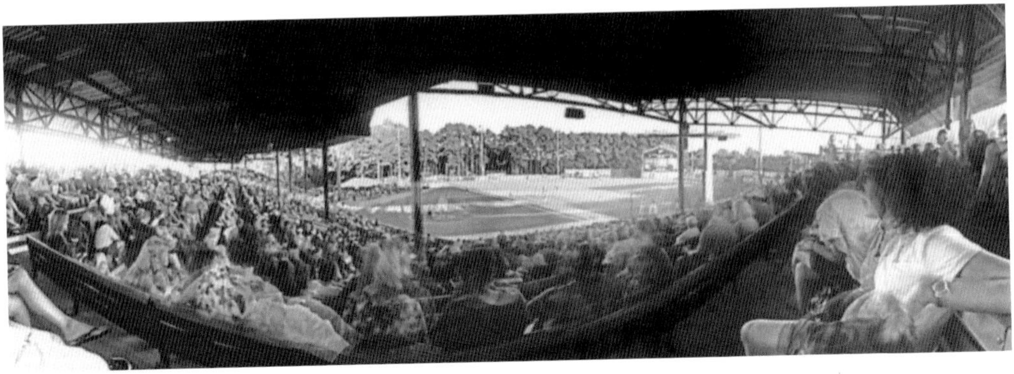

Since 1941, crowds sitting under the grandstand at Grayson Stadium have looked out to the field and watched some of the best players the sport has produced. In addition to the players who are well remembered, there are far more who played at Grayson who have faded from memory. These players in the field have in turn looked back at this classic ballpark. Ballparks like Grayson Stadium are now relics of a treasured past in the baseball community. All of these players, the famous and the forgotten, helped create the countless memories in this historic stadium. The story of baseball in Savannah is truly a treasured part of this city's treasured past. (Above, courtesy of Joseph Trotz; below, courtesy of Skip Jennings.)

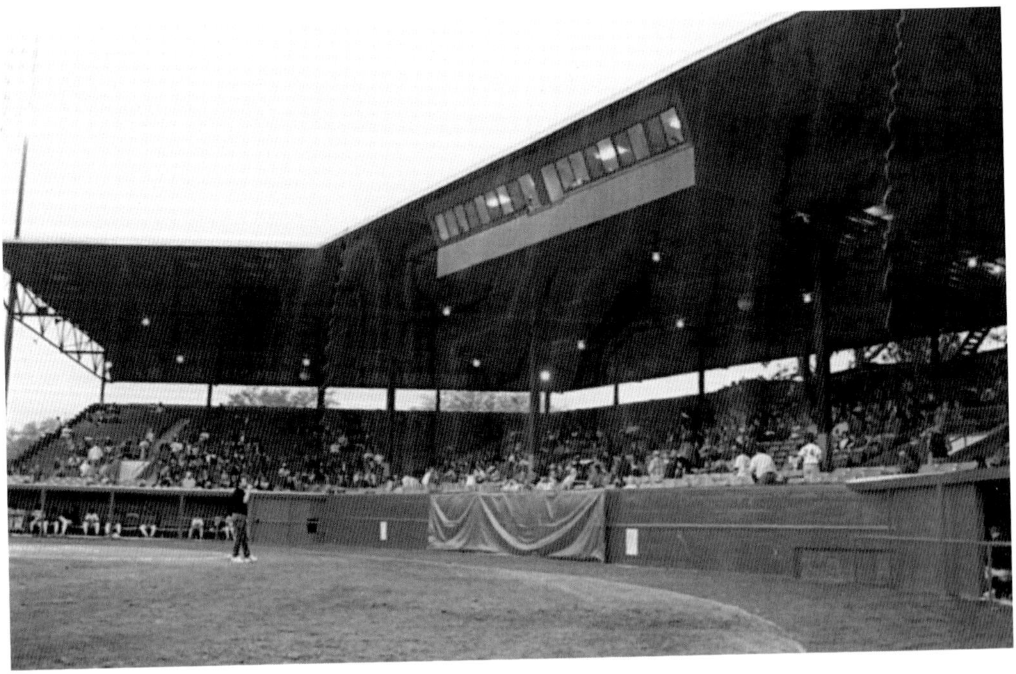

# INDEX